PASTORAL LEADERSHIP FOR
MANHOOD AND WOMANHOOD

FOUNDATIONS FOR THE FAMILY SERIES

PASTORAL LEADERSHIP
for
MANHOOD
and
WOMANHOOD

WAYNE GRUDEM AND DENNIS RAINEY,

EDITORS

CROSSWAY BOOKS

A DIVISION OF
GOOD NEWS PUBLISHERS
WHEATON, ILLINOIS

Crossway's publication of *Pastoral Leadership for Manhood and Womanhood* is in cooperation with FamilyLife and the Council on Biblical Manhood and Womanhood.

Cover design: Josh Dennis

Cover photo: Getty Images

First printing, 2002

Printed in the United States of America

Library of Congress Cataloging-in-Publication Data
Pastoral leadership for manhood and womanhood / Wayne Grudem and Dennis Rainey, editors.
    p. cm. — (Foundations for the family series)
    ISBN 1-58134-419-8 (tpb. : alk. paper)
    1.Pastoral counseling—Congresses. 2. Marriage counseling—Congresses. 3. Single people—Pastoral counseling of—Congresses. 4. Christian gays—Pastoral counseling of—Congresses. 5. Single. I. Grudem, Wayne A. II. Rainey, Dennis, 1948-   . III.Series.
BV4012.27 .P37   2002
259'.1—dc21   2002015619
                                                CIP

DP		13	12	11	10	09	08	07	06	05	04	03	02
15	14	13	12	11	10	9	8	7	6	5	4	3	2	1

We dedicate this book to our pastors and their wives:

*Darryl and Holly DelHousaye of Scottsdale Bible Church,
Scottsdale, Arizona
Steve and Robin Farish of Crossroads Church,
Libertyville, Illinois
and
Robert and Sherard Lewis, Bill and Ann Parkinson, and
Bill and Carolyn Wellons of Fellowship Bible Church,
Little Rock, Arkansas,
who in their teaching and in their daily lives
have given us excellent examples of
biblical manhood and womanhood
lived in obedience to God*

CONTENTS

III. THE CHALLENGES TODAY

THE CONTRIBUTORS

Danny Akin earned his B.A. in Biblical Studies from Criswell College (1980), his M.Div. from Southwestern Baptist Theological Seminary (1983), and his Ph.D. in Humanities from University of Texas at Arlington (1989). He is currently serving as the Vice President for Academic Administration, Dean, School of Theology, and Professor of Christian Preaching at The Southern Baptist Theological Seminary. Daniel has been married to his wife, Charlotte Tammy, for twenty-four years and is the father of four sons.

Timothy B. Bayly is a teaching elder of the Presbyterian Church in America serving as the Senior Pastor of the Church of the Good Shepherd in Bloomington, Indiana. Bayly took his B.A. in history at University of Wisconsin (Madison) and his M.Div. at Gordon-Conwell Theological Seminary. Married for twenty-seven years to Mary Lee (Taylor), the Baylys have three daughters, two sons, one son-in-law, and one grandson.

Bob Davies is an administrative assistant in the Worship & Music department at University Presbyterian Church, Seattle. He is a graduate of Prairie Bible College, Three Hills, Alberta. He and his wife, Pam, have been married since 1985. From 1985-2001, Bob was North American Director of Exodus International, a worldwide Christian outreach to men and women seeking freedom from homosexuality.

Wayne Grudem received his B.A. from Harvard, M. Div. from Westminster Theological Seminary, and Ph.D. in New Testament from Cambridge University. He is currently Research Professor of Bible and Theology at Phoenix Seminary. He has published several books, including *Recovering Biblical Manhood and Womanhood* (coedited with John Piper) and *Systematic Theology.* He and his wife, Margaret, have been married for thirty-three years and have three adult children.

R. Kent Hughes has been in the pastoral ministry for forty years, the last twenty-five years as pastor of College Church in Wheaton (Illinois). He is a graduate of both Talbot Seminary and Trinity Evangelical Divinity School. Dr. Hughes is also the author of twenty-five books, among them the best-selling *Disciplines of a Godly Man.* He is also editor of the ongoing fifty-volume Preaching the Word series, to which he has made numerous contributions. He and his wife Barbara have been married for forty years and have four children and eighteen grand children.

Bob Lepine is co-host of the nationally syndicated radio program "FamilyLife Today." He speaks internationally on subjects related to marriage and family. He and his wife, Mary Ann, have been married for twenty-three years, and they are the parents of five children. They live in Little Rock, Arkansas.

H. B. London earned his D.D. from Nazarene Theological Seminary, Point Loma Nazarene University. He is currently serving as the Vice President of Ministry Outreach/Pastoral Ministries at Focus on the Family. He has been married to his wife, Beverley, for forty-five years, and together they have raised two children and currently have four grandchildren.

C. J. Mahaney is the Senior Pastor of Covenant Life Church, located in the northern suburbs of Washington, D.C. He is one of the founding pastors and has served the church since 1977. He also leads Sovereign Grace Ministries, which is involved in planting and supporting local churches in the U.S., Mexico, Canada, and the U.K. He is the executive publisher of Sovereign Grace Media's *Sovereign Grace* magazine and serves on the board of the Christian Counseling and Educational Foundation (CCEF) and on the Council on Biblical Manhood and Womanhood (CBMW). He has edited or coauthored four books in Sovereign Grace Media's Pursuit of Godliness book series: *Why Small Groups?, This Great Salvation, How Can I Change?,* and *Disciplined for Life.* C. J. and his wife, Carolyn, have been married for twenty-seven years and have three daughters and one son, as well as a grandson. They make their home in Gaithersburg, Maryland.

Paige Patterson is President and Distinguished Professor of Theology at Southeastern Baptist Theological Seminary in Wake Forest, North Carolina. He previously served as President of The Criswell College and was twice elected President of the Southern Baptist Convention. His passions are missions, evangelism, and bringing scholarship to the life of the church. He has been married to his wife, Dorothy, for forty years, and together they have raised two children.

David Powlison received his A.B. in Social Relations from Harvard College, M. Div. from Westminster Theological Seminary, M.A. and Ph.D. from the University of Pennsylvania. He edits the *Journal of Biblical Counseling*, teaches at the Christian Counseling and Educational Foundation (CCEF), Westminster Theological Seminary, and counsels at CCEF. He is the author of *Power Encounters: Reclaiming Spiritual Warfare* and *Competent to Counsel?: The History of a Conservative Protestant Anti-Psychiatry Movement* and edited *Counsel the Word* as well as writing numerous articles on counseling and on the relationship between faith and psychology. He has been married to his wife, Nancy, for twenty-five years, and they have three children.

Dick Purnell is an internationally known speaker and author and is the Executive Director of Single Life Resources, a division of Campus Crusade for Christ. A graduate of Wheaton College, Dick holds a Master of Divinity degree from Trinity International University, as well as an M.S. Degree in Education (specializing in counseling) from Indiana University. He has been married to Paula for twenty years, and they have two children.

Dennis Rainey received his M.A. in Theological Studies from Dallas Theological Seminary and his D.D. from Trinity Evangelical Divinity School. Dennis serves as Co-Founder and Executive Director of FamilyLife, a division of Campus Crusade for Christ. In addition, he is the daily host of the nationally syndicated radio program, "FamilyLife Today," as well as a speaker for Promise Keepers conferences. Dennis has published many books and articles specializing in marriage and family life. He has been married to his wife, Barbara, for thirty years, and they have six children.

Ken Sande is an attorney who has served as the president of Peacemaker® Ministries for twenty years. His early education in engineering and law fueled his desire to dedicate his life to biblical peacemaking. Ken and his wife, Corlette, have been married for seventeen years. They have a son and a daughter.

Paul David Tripp received his B.A. from Columbia International University, his M.Div. from Philadelphia Theological Seminary, and his D.Min. from Westminster Theological Seminary. He currently serves as the Director of Changing Lives Ministries, for Christian Counseling & Educational Foundation. He is also the Lecturer in Practical Theology (Counseling) at Westminster Theological Seminary and a Counselor with CCEF. He and his wife, Luella, have been married for thirty-one years, and together they have four children.

Edward T. Welch received his B.A. from the University of Delaware, his M.Div. from Biblical Theological Seminary in Hatfield, Pennsylvania, and his PhD.-Counseling Psychology (Neuropsychology) from the University of Utah. He is the author of numerous books including *When People Are Big and God Is Small*. Dr. Welch currently is the Director of Counseling as well as a Counselor for Christian Counseling & Educational Foundation. Additionally he serves as the Professor of Practical Theology at Westminster Theological Seminary and as adjunct faculty at Biblical Theological Seminary. He has been married to his wife, Sharon, for twenty-two years, and together they have two children.

PREFACE

In March 2000 several hundred Christian leaders gathered in Dallas, Texas, for a conference called "Building Strong Families in Your Church." The conference was jointly sponsored by FamilyLife and the Council on Biblical Manhood and Womanhood.

Over fifty seminars addressed controversial questions about the Bible's teachings regarding the roles of men and women in the family. All of the speakers represented a "complementarian" position—that is, that men and women are created by God to be equal in value but different in roles. This book is one of four being issued by Crossway Books to make the conference content available to a wider Christian audience.[1]

For pastors, the more popular seminars at the conference covered many of the difficult practical situations they face in ministering God's Word faithfully regarding manhood and womanhood issues. This book contains material from those seminars, which included these topics: the pastor's own marriage; encouraging romance in the congregation; watching out for the little things that build or destroy marriages; using small groups, marriage ceremonies, and even church discipline to protect marriages; developing a ministry that attracts men to the church; ministering to single adults and to a generation hungry to know their fathers; encouraging husbands to lead and wives to follow; and ministering to situations involving domestic violence, homosexuality, and other types of moral failure.

These are hard topics! But the authors bring decades of biblical knowledge and experience to bear in their approach to them. The result is a book packed with godly wisdom.

We issue this book with the expectation that pastors and others involved in Christian ministry will find these chapters wise, helpful, practical, and tremendously encouraging. Taken together, they show how faithfulness to Scripture regarding manhood and womanhood results in a ministry that does not run from but faces and resolves the tough problems that confront people in their lives as men and women today.

It was a privilege to have the assistance of others whose faithful work made a significant contribution to this book. We wish to thank Sharon Sullivan and Tracey Miller for excellent secretarial help with some of the chapters, Travis Buchanan for careful editing and other help with numerous administrative details including preparing the indices, Steve Eriksson for help wih proofreading, Sovereign Grace Ministries for additional administrative assistance in this project, and Bruce Nygren for his professional editorial skills that contributed to the clarity, accuracy, and readability of the book.

Wayne Grudem and Dennis Rainey

1.   The other three books are *Building Strong Families,* edited by Dennis Rainey, *Biblical Womanhood in the Home,* edited by Nancy Leigh DeMoss, and *Biblical Foundations for Manhood and Womanhood,* edied by Wayne Grudem.

FOREWORD

MANDATES FOR THE CHURCH IN THE NEW MILLENNIUM

Dennis Rainey

⸺∽∾∽⸻

Today our nation suffers from a sickness of the soul because our families are weak: weak in their knowledge of God, weak in their convictions about God, weak in their experiences of God, and weak in their understanding of how to love one another.

This is not how God intended it. He designed the family as the birthplace and residence of Christianity. It's the place where the knowledge, fear, and love of the Lord are to be taught by parents and learned by children.

With the prophet Jeremiah we cry out for America, "O land, land, land, hear the word of the LORD!" (Jer. 22:29, NASB). If the soul of America is to be restored, it will be done one home, one family at a time. In the church we will assist that by proclaiming God's truth for the family.

I offer these mandates in the spirit of a servant, someone who eagerly desires a more spiritually healthy environment for ministry to families. My goal is not to add more weight to a load of responsibility for pastors and other church leaders that is already heavy. I sincerely think that these challenges to change local church ministry to the family will drastically improve effectiveness and bring needed spiritual renewal.

FOUR MANDATES FOR THE CHURCH IN THE NEW MILLENNIUM

Mandate One: Take Care of the First Family First

In our ministry at FamilyLife we often spend time interviewing pastors. As we have probed to learn their most compelling needs related to family ministry, one issue has risen above all others: "my marriage and family."

I now am convinced that the number one reason many pastors do not preach more on the marriage covenant, compassionately preach what the Bible says about the "act" of divorce, encourage prayer with spouse or children, or advocate family altars and devotions is that their own marriages and families have their own sets of needs. So the topics are avoided or touched only lightly. And the families in the church continue their slow slide.

Psalm 101 presents some guidelines for those of us who want to be effective leaders in ministry: "I will walk within my house in the integrity of my heart" (v. 2, NASB). Later the same Psalm advises, "He who walks in a blameless way is the one who will minister to me" (v. 6, NASB).

In other words, if we want change in the families of those we lead, we have to lead and shepherd our own.

Mandate Two: The Church Must Become a Marriage- and Family-Equipping Center

Does the following statement shock you? Equipping husbands and wives in marriage and training parents to lead their children spiritually are not just part of local church ministry; they represent the greatest opportunity for the local church to spread the Gospel, build spiritual maturity, and advance the Kingdom of God in this generation!

I make this bold claim because the needs in the family dwarf all other personal felt needs in western civilization. In America what other issue, as people wake up and begin their day, causes them as much anxiety and pain? We have a generation coming of age that is screaming, "How do you do marriage and family?" Such people are coming from broken homes. Their parents' marriages didn't work. They are skeptical and afraid. And guess who could provide the answers—the local church! Our God created the family. Ministry to families is not a strategy, a goal, or a program. Ministry to families must permeate all the church does, because faith formation begins at home (see Deut. 6:1-9). If we ignore this reality, the church's job is made much more difficult.

If I were the Devil, I would want to get all the church staffs in America totally on the defensive, spending hours each week untangling the relational mayhem surrounding marriages and families. What would happen if we could reduce that commitment of staff resources by 50 percent? Just think what we could accomplish with all of that fresh energy for the advancement of the Gospel?

So how might we see change?

We need to become intentional about equipping marriages and families to be distinctively Christian. Ephesians 4:11 says that Christ gave "pastors and teachers." Why? "For the equipping of the saints for the work of service, to the building up of the body of Christ" (v. 12, NASB). Where does the work of service start? Sunday school? The sermon? Wednesday night prayer meeting? No, it begins at home. We need to resurrect and dust off a little saying from the fifties: "The family that prays together stays together."

The culture is ripe for the church to step forward with spiritual initiatives that bring hope.

Mandate Three: The Church Must Become the Guardian of the Marriage Covenant

Because marriage is a covenant among a man, a woman, and Almighty God for a lifetime, no wonder God said that He hates divorce (Mal. 2:16). One reason God despises marital demise so much is that He desires godly offspring (Mal. 2:15). We are well aware of the personal, lifelong devastation experienced by many children of divorce. Novelist Pat Conroy has profoundly written that each divorce is the death of a small civilization. God hates this. It is not the model He intended.

In our society we have dumbed down the marriage promise so that in perceived seriousness it's about one notch above financing a car. In most states you can get out of marriage easier than you can ditch an auto loan!

It's time for the church to step forward and become the guardian, protector, and enforcer of the marriage covenant. It is time for the Christian community to say no to easy divorce and yes to a marriage covenant that lasts a lifetime. This is not a time for religious business as usual. It is time for radical action.

Upholding the marriage covenant begins with the care and nurture of your own covenant. Also, as your children grow up and marry, etch on their souls the sacredness of their marriage vows and covenant.

Finally, those of us in church leadership need to call others to fulfill their marriage covenant. Abraham Lincoln said, "To sin by silence when one should protest makes cowards of men." Let's not be empty-chested in challenging people to honor their marriage vows or in protesting vigorously when they seek to abandon them.

The nation is desperate for the church to lead in protecting the institution of marriage. Let's just "do it."

Mandate Four: Challenge Laypeople to Become Marriage and Family Mentors

Dietrich Bonhoeffer wrote, "The righteous man is the one who lives for the next generation." Are we losing our generational vision, our responsibility to sow the seeds of truth and holiness that will bear fruit in our children and grandchildren? It is imperative that laymen and laywomen rediscover the vision of having God use them to reach down to a younger generation and pull them up to maturity. This won't just happen. Such mentors will need to be recruited to such a vision and mission.

A way to build a mentor corps is to set a three-year goal to recruit five mentor couples for every one hundred people in a local church.

Mentors need to be made available first to couples in the first five years of their marriage. Statistically that is when the divorce rate is at its peak. Of the five couples per hundred, I would assign one to pre-marrieds and a second to newly married couples. I would find two couples who are parenting mentors—one for young children (preschool through elementary) and one for parents of adolescents. You also need crisis mentors—a couple whose marriage was rescued from the pit who can come with encouragement to help other couples whose marriages are in trouble.

If you establish these mentor couples and present them to your church on a given Sunday, members of your congregation will respond enthusiastically to this mentoring initiative. The problem is not finding the people who want to be mentored, but challenging the right people to be mentors. You and I as leaders in the local church and parachurch ministry need to call on laymen to step out of their comfort zone, to step out of the bleachers, to step onto the battlefield to win the war for the soul of the family.

Those are my mandates for the church of the new millennium. The chapters that follow will explain in detail how they can be put into practice. The task is substantial and may require more than a generation to complete, if the Lord tarries. But I believe it is a battle our generation must fight.

I urge you to lead the charge in your congregation.

I

THE PASTOR'S PERSONAL LIFE

1

THE PASTOR'S MARRIAGE

R. Kent Hughes

—∞∞—

I was born in March 1942 in Los Angeles—the same month that a Japanese submarine shelled the oil fields of Santa Barbara. That was about two hundred years ago; at least that is how I feel whenever I look through my March 1942 copy of *Life Magazine* and see the way people dressed and the military technology of another age. I have vivid memories of the 1940s: my father's death when I was four years old, the 1948 Rose Parade, the 1949 Billy Graham Crusade in a huge tent on the corner of Washington and Hill Streets in Los Angeles. The images of the young, slender evangelist lit by the spotlights and the cowboy Stuart Hamblin singing "Just a Closer Walk with Thee" are fixed forever in my memory.

I was in high school in the 1950s, but I didn't find "my thrill on Blueberry Hill" like many of my suntanned friends, because Christ found me in 1955 just as I was beginning high school. I was a young man, but I knew I had come to Christ; I knew I had been delivered. An event that further shaped my life took place in 1956 and made the cover of national magazines. It was the death of five missionaries in Ecuador at the hands of the primitive Auca Indians. Jim Elliot's quote, "He is no fool who gives what he cannot keep to gain what he cannot lose," became the ideal for my life. I wanted to serve the Lord. In 1958, at age sixteen, I preached my first sermon. It was on Jonah and the whale—"God Has a Whale of a Plan for Your Life"—a sermon of dubious wit and doubtful quality. But just the doing of it established my pastoral persona.

Robin Williams's famous quote about the 1960s, "If you remember the sixties you weren't there," aptly captures it for many of us graybeards, and smiling we nod our assent. But I was *there* and clearly *remember* the sixties because I was doing youth ministry instead of drugs. I also happily recall those years because I met and married my lovely wife, Barbara, in 1962, and we spent the next decade in sandals and bell-bottoms and youth ministry. Our four children came during our first seven years together. Definite church growth!

The 1970s were church-planting years. The greatest thrill of my life was establishing a new church. It was also one of the hardest times in my life. Barbara and I have chronicled it in our book *Liberating Ministry from the Success Syndrome*. I was involved in the new work for about six years, and in 1979 we moved to Chicago. Our twenty-three years of ministry at College Church in Wheaton have been times of immense change. I've changed too. My over-the-ears haircut has gone the way of my seventies bell-bottoms. My hair has faded to a Mr. Rogers gray. I need glasses to read my watch. And when I bend over to tie my shoes, I look around for other things to do since I'm already down there!

Barbara and I have been married for more than forty joyous years, with thirty-eight years devoted to ministry. I've done it all—junior high, high school, college, assistant pastor, senior pastor, and senior citizen. We've had our share of troubles and joys in ministry. I've seen it all—the ups and downs; the disappointments and triumphs. And in it all, the joy of the Lord is my strength (cf. Neh. 8:10).

Ministry has been a wild and wonderful ride. I am a happily married man. My four grown children love the Lord, and my eighteen grandchildren are in process. I have a terrific wife whom I love with all my heart. My children love me, and I love them. The bottom line is: Our marriage and family have flourished amidst ministry.

CHALLENGES TO MINISTRY MARRIAGES

Nevertheless, there are pastor-centered challenges to marriage. Ministry is consuming. It's *time-consuming*. I've always been busy with staff meetings, responding to messages, prayer meetings, business meetings, appointments, counseling, and sermon preparation, not to mention weddings and funerals. Life is busy. That can be difficult on a marriage. But not only is the ministry time-consuming, it is also *all-consuming* because it is so demanding. Whether you're in a large or small church, you must learn to go to your left like a good basketball player. You'll never make the team if you can only dribble and shoot with your right hand. Likewise in ministry, you can't say, "I only do preaching" or "My gift is administration." You must do it all—and do it well. The pastor must be a Renaissance man. This can be a great thing as you develop into a well-rounded person. But the downside is that it is so demanding.

The ministry can become a mistress. You can become married to the church. In terms of that marriage relationship, you can become a very ugly man—a preoccupied man who may sit down at the table with your children but be somewhere else. Believe me, the ministry can be seductive, especially if you're deriving your self-worth from what you do.

Early on, when I was both in ministry and seminary, my wife saw that I had become so preoccupied that I often was somewhere else, distracted, as my children sought my attention. Seeing enough she confronted me: "I don't mind you're being gone so much. I can handle that. But when you're here, I would really like you to be here." She suggested that I needed some professional help. I was insulted and angry. But after I cooled down, I realized she was right. During the second counseling session, the counselor, a minister himself, observed that I was attempting to establish my self-worth by my performance as a pastor. He assured me that given my mind-set, whatever I achieved, I would never find satisfaction. The answer, he said, was to establish my worth apart from the ministry. That was the best personal advice I've ever received. Today I define myself by my relationship with God and with my nearest and dearest—*not* ministry. Sometimes my ministry is up, and sometimes it is down. But my self-worth is not tied to my professional vicissitudes. And more importantly, I am not for the most part a distracted husband or grandfather.

Ministry can also be authenticating or de-authenticating. Ministry can be authenticating if your life matches your teaching. John Piper likes to say that by preaching he "saves" both himself and his congregation every week. How so? Listen to Paul's words to Timothy: "Watch your life and doctrine closely. Persevere in them, because if you do, you will save both yourself and your hearers" (1 Tim. 4:16, NIV). When the preacher's lifestyle and his teaching match, a deep authentication takes place. But if you're not measuring up to the things you say, you can become like the train conductor who after years of announcing "All aboard to Albany. All aboard to Chicago. All aboard to St. Louis" began to imagine that he had actually been to those places. The ministry has huge potential for dissonance, disjunction, and hypocrisy, and for turning you into an ecclesiastical buffoon if you don't appropriate the truths you preach. And this can wreak havoc on the ministerial marriage.

The pastoral ministry can be a lonely occupation. You may be a gregarious soul, but there are probably very few people in your congregation who understand what your life is like. There's a sense of loneliness in that. You carry the responsibility and burden, but it's not like that for your congregation. You're vulnerable. My outgoing wife admits that with the children grown she sometimes feels lonely when she comes to church and has to look for someone to sit with. It is possible to have a sense of isolation and alienation in a busy ministry that darkens your most intimate relationship.

Financial challenges are endemic to ministry. The March/April 2000 issue of *Your Church* reports that less than half (39 percent) of churches surveyed conduct an annual salary review for their pastors. Statistics indicate that though seven in ten pastors feel they are fairly paid, 30 percent feel underpaid. Of that 30 percent, 6 percent consider themselves severely underpaid. On average, churches with annual budgets of more than $500,000 give their senior pastors more than twice the total compensation that churches with budgets under $100,000 do. There's a huge disparity in ministerial income. The report went on to say that those who opted out of Social Security are saving less for retirement than pastors in the Social Security system.[1]

Early in my ministry I used to claim that the car wasn't mine unless you could see the road through the floorboards! It was difficult in those early years. Finances often do bring severe stress to ministerial marriages. Along with this, the ministry can be exhausting, and exhaustion often leads to depression. A telling sentence from Paul presents exhaustion at the heart of ministerial depression: "For when we came into Macedonia, this body of ours had no rest, but we were harassed at every turn—conflict on the outside, fears within" (2 Cor. 7:5, NIV). The context of Paul's admonition was pressure-induced exhaustion. The same syndrome had earlier afflicted the worn-out Elijah after his victory over the prophets of Baal (cf. 1 Kings 19:4-8). Exhaustion due to ministerial pressures can make a depressive out of anyone. Sometimes it happens to the most sanguine of us. Notwithstanding the solutions that the stories of Paul and Elijah provide, depression is endemic to our people-intensive professions. And the consequences can be very hard on ministerial marriages.

Along with pastor-centered pressures there has come a rise of spouse-centered challenges due to the intrusive values of popular culture. Of late, many pastors' wives view their husbands' ministry as separate from their lives—"It's his job. I have my own interests and goals." Others do not view the ministry as a "call" but merely as a profession like that of a lawyer or schoolteacher and thus reason "He has his profession, and I have mine. They are equally important." And, of course, there is now the culturally required obligation of a woman to pursue her complete, better self as her primary responsibility. Hardly the foundation for a strong ministerial marriage.

And, of course, there are churches that are man-eaters, ecclesiastical orcas. If the pastor is inexperienced or naive, he can be eaten alive and in the process see his most precious relationships devoured. According to a survey by the Hartford Seminary Foundation in the early nineties, one in five pastors is divorced, which nearly accords with the 24 percent average of the general population. The divorce rate was only slightly higher in liberal churches than in conservative churches.

ENHANCING MINISTRY MARRIAGES

I am fond of quoting these lines from Shakespeare both to my wife and to others—about her:

> For she is wise, if I can judge of her,
> And fair she is, if that mine eyes be true,
> And true she is, as she hath prov'd herself,
> And therefore, like herself, wise, fair, and true,
> Shall she be placed in my constant soul.
> THE MERCHANT OF VENICE, II.VI

This is reflective not only of how I feel about Barbara, but of the creational bedrock of our marriage covenant. When Adam first saw Eve he cried aloud in astonished ecstasy:

> "This is now bone of my bones
> and flesh of my flesh;
> she shall be called 'woman,'
> for she was taken out of man."
> GENESIS 2:23, NIV

Adam's joyous shout echoes down to the present day, proclaiming the joy and intimacy of marriage. There in Genesis Adam's cry subsided, and the voice of Moses concludes, "For this reason a man will leave his father and mother and be united to his wife, and they will become one flesh" (v. 24, NIV). Moses' words were divine revelation, and Jesus Himself would quote them as the very Word of God (cf. Matt. 19:5). These words, this Word of God, became the deep well for the Bible's teaching on the covenant of marriage. Here is the theological rationale for my wife being my constant soul.

Married Hearts

To place my wife in my constant soul is another way of saying that she is in my heart and I in hers—perpetually. And here I must suggest some ways to enhance this covenantal oneness.

To begin with, we must have *cherishing hearts* that publicly treasure one another increasingly with the years, as Winston Churchill did his Clementine. On one memorable occasion Churchill attended a formal banquet in London, where the dignitaries were asked the question, "If you could not be who you are, who would you like to be?" Naturally everyone was curious as to what Churchill, who was seated next to his beloved Clemmie, would say. After all, Churchill could not be expected to say Julius Caesar or Napoleon. When it finally came Churchill's turn, the old man, the last respondent to the question, rose and gave his answer. "If I could not be who I am, I would most like to be"—and here he paused to take his wife's hand—"Lady Churchill's second husband."[2]

A delightful corollary is *honoring hearts*, hearts that esteem each other. This can be seen in the unspoken beauty of a couple's glance toward each other or the gentle touch as they pass between rooms. We hear it in the respectful tone of their voices—words that caress. Honoring hearts always speak well of one another to others. There are times when my wife honors me with frank, true, needed words that she would never share with others. As her husband, and pastor of a flock, I know that I am safe in her words, and she in mine.

Healthy ministry marriages demand *interceding hearts*. The demand for mutual intercession is, of course, heightened by the commonplaces of ministry and because we are public figures who minister God's holy Word and counsel and lead the church. These realities bring unique stresses and heighten our vulnerability. We each need the other's prayers. How heartening it is for your spouse to know that she is prayed for in sensitive detail. There can be few things more elevating than the knowledge that your mate, who loves you as no other does, prays for you as for himself or herself. This kind of prayer will steel a ministry marriage against its uncommon assaults.

The ministry is a serving profession. We serve God and His people. But it is also a call to care for each other with grand *serving hearts*. Here Dr. Robertson McQuilkin, former president of Columbia International University, has set the standard for all of us who serve God. Dr. McQuilkin is an accomplished preacher, leader, theologian, and writer. But the title that defines him as a leader and husband is servant. At the height of his influence and power, McQuilkin resigned his presidency to take care of his Alzheimer's-stricken wife Muriel, as his God-given duty. And this is what he said in his letter of resignation:

> Perhaps it would help you to understand if I shared with you what I shared at the time of the announcement of my resignation in chapel. The decision was made, in a way, 42 years ago when I promised to care for Muriel "in sickness and in health . . . till death do us part." So, as I told the students and faculty, as a man of my word, integrity has something to do with it. But so does fairness. She has cared for me fully and sacrificially all these years; if I cared for her for the next 40 years I would not be out of debt. Duty, however, can be grim and stoic. But there is more; I love Muriel. She is a delight to me—her childlike dependence and confidence in me, her warm love, occasional flashes of that wit I used to relish so, her happy spirit and tough resilience in the face of her continual distressing frustration. I do not *have* to care for her, I *get* to! It is a high honor to care for so wonderful a person.[3]

Such care, such sacrifice, such nurture ought to especially be at the heart of ministry marriages, so that our lives not only sustain each other but bear witness to the church and to the world of the reality of Christ.

All husbands and wives need to talk, but this is especially essential in ministry marriages—*communicating hearts*. As longtime pastor and writer Eugene Peterson has so poignantly written, there are men who wall themselves at breakfast behind a newspaper

> rather than listen to the voice of the person who has just shared his bed, poured his coffee, fried his eggs, even though listening to that live voice promises love and hope, emotional depth and intellectual exploration far in excess of what he can gather informationally from *The New York Times*, *The Wall Street Journal*, and *The Christian Science Monitor* put together.[4]

Certainly both men and women need quiet (especially those in ministry), but if such isolation becomes expected as a right, marriage is impoverished. Enjoy the newspaper? Certainly. But we must always engage each other's souls about what's happening right now, about family, about ministry, about the Word.

Indeed this exchange of soul that Barbara and I have developed in our forty years of marriage and ministry is deeper and more exciting than anything else in our full lives. Learn to listen to each other. Talk, really talk—about everything. Communicate more than facts. Use metaphors and similes and phrases that describe what's inside. You'll find that the best parts of each day are when you get to talk to your constant soul.

Romancing hearts have a Beatitude-like effect on all, as my wife and I experienced while strolling by the Ferris wheel on Chicago's Navy Pier late one summer night with our visiting friends, Church of England Bishop Wallace Benn, his wife Lindsay, and their two high schoolers. Unknown to Lindsay, Wallace had obtained a glowing fluorescent rose from a vendor, which he then grandly presented on bended knee, with a speech to his blushing wife as he was cheered on by us and the laughter of passersby.

Such great fun! But also a gift. Wallace's romancing heart heightened my love for my own wife and instructed his children in ways beyond words. When a man cherishes his wife, all are elevated.

Romance has its grand gestures and hidden intimacies. But it's the small things that enhance or diminish it.

> 'Tis not love's going hurt my days,
> But that it went in little ways.
> EDNA ST. VINCENT MILLAY

We must never allow the frantic, other-directed pace of ministry to detract us from our most significant other in ways big or small. As the years go by, affection, loving notes, endearing compliments, praise private and public ("I would like to be Barbara's second husband"), flowers, and poetry must flow to your constant soul.

You Two!

The retrospect of four decades insures that the proverb "time flies" is hard fact. I am young, beholding my dazzling teenaged bride. I blink and I'm holding our firstborn, Holly, like a star fallen from heaven. I blink again and I'm gently holding another hot star, her firstborn, Brian. Another blink and it may well be his firstborn! One more and both Barbara and I will be with Jesus. There is no other time but now—no other time to be married and enjoy the wife of your youth. Thus I have some advice for every ministry couple that will enhance your time between the blinks.

You two—take your day off. As Barbara and I get around the country to pastors' conferences, we are appalled at how many ministers and their wives don't take a regular day off. The "we're so busy" pleas don't carry much weight with us. We've served in every size of church (with no staff and multiple staff) and have written over thirty books while doing it. We've been busy, but we've always managed a day off.

We've come to understand that those who go without a day off are not taking their work too seriously as some might imagine, but rather are taking themselves too seriously. Admittedly, the work is always there, and there is always too much to do. And true, we can often do it better than others. But we also know that workaholism is often rooted in self, be it insecurity or the need to be needed or subtle self-idolatry—"God won't work unless I'm there."

Believe us—it's your moral responsibility to God and each other to take a day off. Even more, it's your moral responsibility to forget your work—to mentally dismiss your ministerial preoccupations and not allow your professional concerns to dominate your time away.

Make your day off inviolate. What about emergencies? Of course, you must drop everything and see emergencies as graces. But you must also hedge your day off well. Your day off may be the most convenient time for others to get your counsel, but their convenience is not the dominant concern. People will make time to meet with you if it's important to them. Also refrain from making doctor's appointments on your day off. Squeeze them into your busy schedule, just as you squeeze others' appointments into yours. Of course the structure of your day off will vary in the seasons of life. But give it some weekly forethought.

You two—date. Years ago, in the Midwest, a farmer and his wife were lying in bed during a storm when the funnel of a tornado suddenly lifted the roof right off the house and sucked their bed away with them still in it. The wife began to cry, and the farmer called to her that it was no time to cry. She called back that she was so happy, she could not help it—it was the first time they had been out together in twenty years! We chuckle because funny things are regularly the flip side of the tragic. We must not let the perpetual social requirements of ministry, the endemic nights out, rob us of the couple-delights we so treasured when our romance began. Wise ministerial couples will date, as Barbara and I do to our special eateries in Chicago or to a movie at the Fine Arts Theater or to the opera or on a simple walk on Michigan Avenue, the "Magnificent Mile." What can be better than a night out with the love of your life?

In 1986 *Psychology Today* surveyed three hundred couples, asking them what keeps them together. One of the major "staying" factors was time spent together.[5] Make sure you maintain this priority. Your calendar reveals what is important to you; so write her calendar into yours. Schedule weekly times together—they do not just happen. Be creative. Surprise each other. Sometimes be extravagant.

You two—vacation. We once loaned our vacation cabin to a couple for whom I had performed the wedding ceremony twenty years earlier—and later learned from them that it was their first weekend together since having had children! Neither busyness nor lack of money can excuse this. What is lacking is domestic vision and creativity and, frankly, common sense. Those in ministry especially need time away by themselves to restore their souls and explore their God-given relationship.

One of Barbara's and my favorite serendipities came in the midst of the triple stress of seminary, ministry, and four children all under ten when, at Barbara's wise insistence, we borrowed fifty dollars and spent a night and morning at Laguna Beach. Our heads and hearts cleared, and we returned with renewed perspective. Now as gray-headed preacher and wife we still understand (and practice!) this well-worn wisdom.

You two—go to bed together! Many couples never go to bed

together—that is, go to bed at the same time—because one is an early-to-bed person and the other is a night owl. This is a substantial mistake because it effectively diminishes confidential exchanges and prayers and intimacy before sleep.

Scripture views the marriage bed as a place of divinely ordained privacy and intimacy where one's wife is a walled garden, a refreshing fountain, and a garden of choicest fruits (cf. Song of Songs 4:13-16). The sensual delights of the garden are mutually fulfilling and sanctifying. And because the ministry couple loves Christ, they will cherish the bed all through life. "For this reason a man will leave his father and mother and be united to his wife, and the two will become one flesh. This is a profound mystery—but I am talking about Christ and the church" (Ephesians 5:31-32, NIV).

Your Family

Some years ago in preparation for an interview with *Christianity Today* about pastors' families, we took our four children, then ages twenty to twenty-five, out to dinner to ask them together how they felt about being raised as PKs (pastor's kids). We really wanted to know, so we could answer our interviewers with confident integrity.

Happily, they all were positive. They loved being raised in the manse with the church at the center at their lives. The only negative was voiced by one of my sons who felt that the church had asked too much of me. Actually it wasn't the church—it was me, as I explained. He understood that.

There were times when I was over the top in my devotion to ministry. Here I must credit my dear, strong, wise wife for not letting me succumb to it, and therefore ultimately for our children's positiveness and continuing memories of the manse. Here's some family-raising wisdom (Barbara's wisdom) from the manse that is rooted in attitude and perspective toward ministry.

Barbara always spoke about our being in ministry in joyous terms. When the children were small she said, for example, "Aren't we lucky that our dad's not a truck driver like Mr. Pope? Mr. Pope has to be gone overnight on deliveries. But our dad is always here for dinner."

Significantly, this was when I was doing both seminary and ministry—a very busy time in our lives. Bottom line: Mom was positive, and therefore the kids were positive!

Barbara's wisdom still amazes me. She discerned that instead of saying "Dad's at church," it would be better to say "Dad's at work." Her reasoning? The former could build resentment toward the church. But the latter merely lumped me together with everyone else's fathers who all "worked." Very subtle. Very wise!

Similarly, we never spoke ill of the church or its people. This was particularly important because when our kids were in grades four to ten we experienced great hurt and conflict that eventuated in our resignation. But to this day our grown children only have positive memories of those years.

The other area of wisdom has to do with time—leveraging our flexible schedules to best invest in our children. Ministers work a lot. I have regularly put in about fifty hours a week plus virtually all of Sunday beginning at 4:00 A.M. But because I didn't punch a time clock or have to travel to work, we could strategically invest our time. Sometimes we got up early and cooked breakfast in the park before school. We also would gather the kids after school, don backpacks, and take a hike in the hills before dinner. Other times I called their schools and got permission to take one of them out for lunch. Few dads can do that. And, oh, did my son or daughter feel special! And over the years I rarely had to miss an after-school athletic event or a school concert or a play in which my children had a part. And more, my office was always open and well-supplied with M&Ms. My children and their friends knew that they could come any time. Sometimes their friends came without them! Best of all, I was always home for dinner—an event that Barbara always worked at making special.

Yes, the ministry does have its challenges. But as I look back over almost forty years from the sixties through the nineties and now into the new millennium, I am so grateful to have followed God's call.

1.   John C. La Rue, "Seven Findings About Pastor Pay," *Your Church*, March/April 2001, 88.

2. James Humes, *Churchill, Speaker of the Century* (Briarcliff Manor, NY: Stein and Day, Scarborough House, 1980), 291.

3. From Dr. Robertson McQuilkin's March 1990 letter of resignation as president of Columbia Bible College.

4. Eugene H. Peterson, *Working the Angles* (Grand Rapids, MI: Eerdmans, 1989), 62.

5. Jeanette Lauer and Robert Lauer, "Marriages Made to Last," *Psychology Today*, June 1985, 26.

2

THE PASTOR'S RESPONSIBILITY FOR ROMANCE IN HIS CONGREGATION AND MARRIAGE

Dennis Rainey

For centuries sailors have avoided a section of ocean located just above the equator. In this area of the ocean, winds will lie calm for days, weeks, even months. Storms will skirt the edge of this quiet expanse, and at times ships have sailed into such a patch of ocean, stalled out, and sat with sails listless for weeks.

This condition of the sea is called the doldrums. The word describes too well many married couples sitting in our churches. Relational sails that used to be full of breeze, with the power of the wind harnessed to push the boat swiftly across the marital seas, hang limp.

My charge to every pastor and others active in local church leadership is this: Do what you can to stir up the passionate winds in marriages. Without such currents, our couples become stagnant and ineffective in living out the love of Christ for each other.

An essay called "The Wall" poignantly describes the result of marital doldrums. This is not what God intends for marriage:

> Their wedding picture mocks them from the table, these two whose minds no longer touch each other. They live with such

a heavy barricade between them that neither a battering ram of words nor artilleries of touch could break it down.

Somewhere between the oldest child's first tooth and the youngest daughter's graduation they lost each other. Throughout the years each slowly unraveled that tangled ball of string called self. And as they tugged at the stubborn knots, each hid the searching from the other. Sometimes she cried at night and begged the whispering darkness to tell her who she was. He lay beside her snoring like a hibernating bear, unaware of her winter.

Once . . . he wanted to tell her how afraid he was of dying. But fearing to show his naked soul, he spoke instead about . . . [her] beauty. . . . She took a course in modern art, trying to find herself in colors splashed about on canvass, complaining to other women about men who were insensitive. He climbed into a tomb called the office, wrapped his mind in a shroud of paper figures, and buried himself in customers.

Slowly the wall between them rose, cemented by the mortar of indifference. One day, reaching out to touch each other, they found a barrier they could not penetrate. And recoiling from the coldness of the stone, each retreated from the stranger on the other side.

For when love dies, it is not in a moment of angry battle or when fiery bodies lose their heat. Instead love lies panting, exhausted, expiring at the bottom of a wall it could not scale.[1]

Barbara and I have been married for nearly thirty years. We have endured numerous moves, serious illnesses of children, Barbara's near-death experience on four different occasions, new jobs, lukewarm churches, my dad dying, our son having surgery, small paychecks, asthma, and a number of other trials. I want to promise you, we have been trapped in the doldrums with no promise of a breeze to stir our sails. That's why the subject of romance is so important to me. I know how miserable it is to be dead in the water in marriage. Boredom in a marriage is a subject church leaders have ignored too long. In addition to all the other great things we teach people about marriage, we need to encourage them to make romance a priority. And we may need to dust off that short book between Ecclesiastes and Isaiah and preach a few sermons on how God views romance, tenderness, and passion in marriage.

THE IMPORTANCE OF ROMANCE IN MARRIAGE

God made us to connect with one another emotionally, but it's interesting how something we know is important can become elusive.

Solomon writes of love, "Its flashes are flashes of fire" (Song 8:6, NASB). Love is a flame. It's intense; it's pleasurable. Song of Songs glows with marital love and passion, and its message is as God-breathed as is John 3:16 on redemption.

I do not believe that the loss of romance among Christians is *the* cause of divorce, but I do think that if husbands and wives do not experience with their spouses the "flashes of fire" spoken of in the Song of Songs, that intense fiery passion that God designed in us and said was good to experience, people begin to long for it and eventually look elsewhere or fill the void with harmful substitutes such as pornography, overeating, alcohol, rampant desires for material things, and other addictions.

Oswald Chambers said of romance and passion, "Human nature if it's healthy demands excitement. And if it does not obtain its thrilling excitement in the right way, it will seek it in the wrong. God never makes bloodless stoics. He makes passionate saints."

I like that. God doesn't make bloodless stoics. The people in our congregations and ministries are not unfeeling and dispassionate. We need joyfully to accept the passions in all of us and to encourage their appropriate expression in marriage.

Barbara and I were at Talbot Seminary a number of years ago to speak to a group of seminary wives, and afterwards one of the women present came up and said, "Mr. Rainey, I need to talk to you."

"Okay," I answered. She was young enough to be my daughter and cute as could be.

"My husband and I were driving home after youth group," she began. "He's a youth group pastor, and it was kind of dark in the car, and I decided to turn to him and say, 'Sweetheart, what would make you feel like a man of God?'"

She paused and was silent for a few moments, as though gathering her courage to continue. I had no idea where this conversation was going, so I just smiled and nodded my head.

"Mr. Rainey, do you know what he said?"

"No, I don't."

"My husband said that what would make him feel like a man of God would be to come home and find me, as I opened the door, with no clothes on." The seminary wife laughed nervously and asked, "Do you think he really means it?"

"Just try it," I said. She kind of giggled and walked away.

If men are honest, they will tell you that they want a wife to use her sexual power in an adventuresome way to affirm him like no other human being out of the six billion people on Planet Earth can affirm him. Romance encourages such passion.

I once helped present a series of talks for men at our church. The meetings were at 6 A.M. on a weekday morning, and I was overjoyed at the kickoff meeting to find five hundred men present. Several of the topics revolved around romance in marriage and how a man could go on a quest to help secure the heart of his wife. As the series continued, to my great surprise the crowd grew steadily to six hundred. Amazing! If you had told me we would finish with more men than we started with, I would not have believed you. I think this shows, though, that people are hungry to find a way to bring meaning to their marriage and to fan the flames of passion and romance.

THE IMPORTANCE OF PASSION

Sadly, today's congregations include many people making moral compromises involving adultery or "affairs of the mind"—illicit emotional attachments formed remotely via chatting on the Internet, viewing pornography, or watching lewd movies and television shows. Those of us who are shepherds and instruct the flock must back up and ask ourselves, "Why is it that Christians are being pulled into the vortex of evil?"

This is not the whole answer, but I believe that too little passion in marriage creates an environment where people are easily tempted by normal desires that later are polluted by sin. I'll use myself as an example. A huge reason why on a business trip I can go back to my hotel room exhausted, pick up the remote control, start surfing the channels, and when I come to something bad just change channels or turn the TV off is Barbara Rainey. We have experienced a lot in being married—the mountaintops, the valleys, and the plains. I love that woman! Our romance today is much better than when we were first married. Why would I want to trade a real relationship with a real person with real passion and real affirmation for minutes of false intimacy brought to me via a bloodless television screen?

It's a monumental lie, but many men believe they can find satisfying intimacy by looking at pictures on the Internet. Like all sin, that may satisfy briefly, but it's not the real thing. And in the end, instead of life it brings gnawing emptiness and, ultimately, death. We need to preach and teach the truth about intimacy because people today are hungering for it; but they are looking to be fed in the wrong places. Every man—and woman too—wants a real relationship with a real person.

What should we tell people who are missing intimacy in their marriage? Well, how is a fire built in the rain? Much creative effort and dogged persistence are required. But once a good fire is burning, it's much easier to maintain the blaze or add more fuel to make it hotter.

I know all about this. With six children and two grandchildren, Barbara and I have lives fuller than ever before. But I believe—no matter what the demands on a life from work, house, children, church, volunteer work, and so on—that it is possible to create a more romantic marriage.

The best place to start understanding romance in marriage is the Song of Songs. Because of the multiple perversions of sex evident in our society and the practice of marketers to sell everything from galoshes to prunes by appealing to sexual desire, I think it's time we heard God's words about something He made. As my seminary professor Howard Hendricks once said about sex, "We should not be ashamed to discuss that which God was not ashamed to create."

FOXES IN THE VINEYARD

Much is said in the Song of Songs about how to "do" romance. It's all good. But I want to pick up on a challenge regarding passion that concerned Solomon and his bride. We need to heed the same warning today: "Catch the foxes for us, the little foxes that are ruining the vineyards, while our vineyards are in blossom" (Song 2:15, NASB).

What is this talk about fox hunting in the midst of a book on romantic passion in marriage?

In Solomon's day rock fences surrounded vineyards. These were built as high as possible so that foxes, the predators of greatest threat to these vineyards, could not jump over them. But many times the foxes did slither through holes in the fence. The crafty critters came into the vineyard at the time of year when the flowers were budding. The little foxes loved the buds because they were so tasty. But the loss of the buds meant there would be no flowers, no grapes, no wine from the vineyard.

It's in this context that we find Solomon and his beloved Shulammite woman talking about their love and romance. They are comparing the foxes' snacking on flowers to their romance being nipped in the bud.

We need to share this awesome word picture with those we lead and teach. *Every married couple must catch the little foxes that roam about nipping romance in the bud.* Here are the five little foxes that I think do the most damage to romance in the vineyards of contemporary marriages.

Fox 1: Apathy

Marriage has robbed many a relationship of its romance! Oh, I hate to say that, but it's true. The mundaneness of daily life, if it's allowed to define how we live, leads to stifling boredom. Two people may have been married awhile and are locked into a comfortable but predictable routine. They may not notice it, but the light bulbs are slowly dimming. Excitement has left the house. Life is filled up with good tasks and pleasant interests, but the foxes are chomping down the romantic buds of passion.

Both husband and wife think the courtship is long over. The husband is like a hunter sitting in his den admiring the stuffed trophies hanging on the wall. But he's not hunting anymore! He's gotten lazy. He thinks the prize is won—forever. *Big mistake.* In the marriage relationship, for the man the hunt is never over.

I'll never forget the day when I realized that I still must compete for Barbara's affection. I wasn't competing for her with other men, but I was competing with a host of good things like kids, hobbies and interests, church work, friends—the list is endless in our complex society. And God forbid, what if I became lazy and did not work—yes, work—to connect with her soul? What if some other guy did come along who was so satisfying that she found something emotionally with him that I was not providing? That would be sin on her part, but I still must face the challenge to hang onto the beautiful relationship God gave me so many years ago.

When I realized this, I didn't wring my hands with insecurity. But I did soberly realize that I must never stop courting my wife, never stop competing for her affection, never stop pursuing her relationship with me.

For this situation a little piece of advice that God gives us about our love relationship with Him definitely applies! If you fall out of love with God, "do the deeds you did at first" (Revelation 2:5, NASB). If you have fallen out of romance with your spouse, do the things you did at first.

Fox 2: Children

This little fox is predictable. And the older the children get, the more obstacles they erect to romance. Teenagers roam the house until all hours of the night, and it seems impossible for them to believe their parents could have any interest in sexual intimacy. At least when children are little you can put them in bed and close their door. But when the little foxes grow up and become teenagers, it's a different story. They get excited and forget to knock on your door and burst in. That does not do a lot for spontaneity in your love life. A marriage must be built to outlast the children. If not, the children suddenly are gone, and a wife and husband wake up looking at a wall with a stranger on the other side. Sadly, too many people never figure out how to scale that wall.

Fox 3: A Mistress

And you thought this was a Christian book? It is.

I'm not talking about other lovers, although that can happen too, of course. I am speaking of the mistress idea—anything, even a good thing, that can enter a person's life to lead away, seduce, and destroy. This is the crafty seductress spoken of in the book of Proverbs (chapters 5 and 7) who lures with smooth words and alluring eyes. People need to understand the ways of mistresses that appear when life is out of balance related to work, children, community service, hobbies, sports, church work—the list seems endless.

Ironically, a mistress that entices those of us in "full-time" Christian service is named "ministry." We can give our heart, soul, and mind to ministry and come home nearly brain-dead and exhausted. What husband or wife receiving such treatment repeatedly could not help but conclude, *I'm just not that important to this person.* Then comes trouble. Let me say something pointed: *There is no better way for the devil to ruin a ministry, discredit Jesus Christ, and wound the church than to have a pastor or Christian leader's marriage wrecked.*

I'll never forget my own flirtation with the ministry mistress. FamilyLife was growing 40 percent a year. We'd had six children in ten years. They had needs. Barbara had needs. I had needs. We were both exhausted at the end of the day. If we had not gotten out of the marital doldrums and gotten away to focus on one another, to reconnect emotionally, romantically, passionately, I'm not sure I would be writing this chapter. Those times were like an oasis in the desert for us where we could drink deeply from one another.

The ministry mistress many times also sets up the introduction of an opposite-sex mistress. Every adulterous affair begins with an emotional attachment. Two people find a spark with each other; there's a new twinkle in the soul for another person. For people who spend a lot of time around the church or other ministry, guess what—it usually happens in those settings.

Warn your people about this. Warn yourself. Keep the mistress fox from ravaging the vineyard.

Fox 4: Unresolved Conflict

One of the things we do at our FamilyLife Weekend to Remember marriage conference is to explain, based on Ephesians 6, how the struggle as a Christian is not against flesh and blood but against the dark forces and powers of wickedness. We have the couples turn and face one another and say, "My mate is not my enemy."

Satan slips into the vineyard looking like a fox, but he's really a roaring lion. He wants to convince every husband and wife that his or her mate is the enemy. When spouses feel misunderstood, taken for granted, abused, or demeaned, the next steps down the conflict spiral are an embittered spirit, resentment, anger, isolation—and then worse.

Couples must be taught how to deal with conflict. These are learned skills that in the context of the Christian life are aided incredibly by grace, mercy, and forgiveness. I love what Ruth Bell Graham says: "Marriage is the union of two forgivers." Romance and resentment will not find harbor in the same heart; conflict can and must be resolved.

Fox 5: Differences

This is not a profound statement, but in our day it sounds like one: Men and women are different. Our magnificent Creator made us that way, so it is good. But differences ignored or misunderstood cause vineyard chaos.

I will not expand here on this idea, because many have written at length on this topic. I will say that as you teach, preach, and counsel, always keep a tight focus on this truth about people: Women and men are different. In significant ways they think, speak, listen, feel, act, and react differently. Their expectations about marriage are different. How they want to receive and give affection is different. Their patterns as lovers are different.

The key word is *different*.

MAKING ROMANCE A PRIORITY

What one thing about romance in marriage would I encourage pastors and ministry leaders to emphasize in their sphere of influence? Romance needs focus and scheduling.

A number of years ago Barbara and I slipped away with a group of couples for a retreat. We shared with the others the need that couples have today for time and focused attention, and how especially important this is to wives. I think one of the reasons romance gets short-sheeted in our marriages is that we go to bed after working hard all day and watching the late night news. Our emotional tank shows a big E—*empty*.

Knowing how true this is for so many couples, on Saturday afternoon at this particular retreat we encouraged everybody to turn out the lights early that night. And we told the couples to create some atmosphere and mood for their time alone—buy some candles, bubble bath, and body lotion.

In case they weren't getting it, we told them to take a leisurely bubble bath and use the lotion while giving each other a back rub. From 8 P.M. on they were to focus on pampering each other.

You should have seen the looks I got when I outlined this suggestion—a mixture of surprise, confusion, and terror. But mostly I saw anticipation and smug pleasure.

This occasion did provide some humor. Later that afternoon, in a small nearby town, it was fun to watch a group of high-powered forty- to forty-five-year-old executives cleaning out the local drugstores of candles, bubble bath, and lotion!

Later, at about 7:30 P.M., after a nice early-evening dinner, one of the guys at the table stretched and said, "Man, I'm really tired." He gave a little wink and headed out. That prompted kind of a lemming effect with everyone else. In minutes the restaurant was empty.

I will never forget the scene the next morning. The other men—there were four of them—came down to breakfast walking side by side, kind of puffed up, a spring in their gait, all elbowing each other. The wives followed along in a second line, giggling and blushing. I reached out and shook one guy's hand—it was unbelievably soft!

All those couples needed to make some good sparks fly was some encouragement to set aside some time to focus on one another.

Now I have a question for you: When was the last time someone told you to go to bed early? Or when was the last time you told the people you have influence over that they should go to bed early?

Romance will enhance—even save—many marriages in your church. And don't forget to preach that sermon to yourself! Here are some simple ideas to help keep the fire of love burning in your home:

• Get away for a weekend alone two or three times a year.

• Have a romantic date night at least every other week. Get a sitter, or put the kids to bed early and stay home and dine in your bedroom.

• Each of you write a list of what communicates romance to you, and then exchange lists. Start working on the list today.

• Go for walks together, and talk about something other than problems; share what God is teaching each of you.

• Write one another a love letter.

• Pick three of the most romantic times in your marriage. Talk about what made them so romantic. How can you do those same things now?

• Each year read a good book on marriage, and discuss what parts of the content could improve your relationship.

• Pray together every night.

• Surprise each other with little gifts that say, "I really love you."

---

1.   Source unknown. I regret I have been unable to determine who wrote these compelling words.

II

THE OPPORTUNITIES TODAY

3

THE LITTLE THINGS THAT BUILD OR DESTROY MARRIAGES

Danny Akin

———✏———

John Gray became a household name and an overnight millionaire with his best seller *Men Are from Mars, Women Are from Venus*.[1] He has also authored *Mars and Venus in the Bedroom: A Guide to Lasting Romance and Passion*, *Mars and Venus Together Forever: Relationship Skills for Lasting Love*, *Mars and Venus in Love: Inspiring and Heartfelt Stories of Relationships That Work*, and *What Your Mother Couldn't Tell You and Your Father Didn't Know*.[2]

In his books he struck a chord that resonates in each of us. Men and women really are different. We *think* differently; we *see* things differently; we *feel* things differently. We are different, and different by *design*. That is the way God made us and the way God intended. He did make us male and female and declared it a good thing (Gen. 1:27). However, John Gray's title is not exactly the way things really are. Men are not from Mars, and women are not from Venus. Men are from Earth, and women are from Earth, and we have to deal with that if we are going to make marriage, sex, and romance work. You see, most marriages that get in trouble do so not over the big things, but the little things. These little things are often grounded in male/female differences. We *do* sweat the small stuff.

Dorthy Rosby in an article entitled "It's Living Together That

Makes Marriage Difficult" tells the story of a woman who shot her husband because he ate her chocolate. Rosby writes: "I probably read about that incident with a Hershey bar in my hand. At the time, I may have even thought he had it coming. But now that I think about it, even I, a confirmed chocoholic, think shooting was extreme." She then adds:

> It truly is the little things that destroy relationships. Margarine, chocolate, nylons on the towel rack, hair in the sink. I once heard about a couple who fought for more than four hours— over a rubber band. He had it, and she wanted it. . . . It's the little things that happen when you're living together. . . Part of the problem is that God made opposites attract: savers marry spenders; neatniks pair up with slobs; and early birds team up with night owls. Opposing idiosyncrasies come together like weather fronts when couples live together.[3]

Dorthy Rosby is right. It is the little things, what Solomon describes as the "little foxes" (Song of Sol. 2:15), that can sneak into our relationship and do serious damage. Quietly, unnoticed, and yet effectively they destroy the tender fabric, the tender vines and grapes of our relationship whose health is essential for a happy and satisfying marriage. In that verse the bride says:

> *Catch the foxes for us,*
> *the little foxes*
> *that spoil the vineyards,*
> *for our vineyards are in blossom. (ESV)*

There are two particular types of little foxes that are especially dangerous that I want to warn you about. One I call "the foxes of danger," and the other I call "the foxes of differences."

BEWARE OF THE DANGERS TO YOUR MARRIAGE

The word "catch" in verse 15 is an imperative, a word of command. God issues a strong word about this danger to our relationship. The little foxes are unwelcome intruders who sneak into a marriage and who can destroy the purity of our love and the pricelessness of our relationship. A healthy and happy marriage must be protected. We must be on guard and catch anything that could harm the tender and vulnerable union we have established. A question now naturally presents itself: What do these little foxes look like? Let me quickly note seven of them, what we could call warning signs of a failing marriage.

Warning #1: A Marriage Will Get into Trouble When God's Role for the Husband and the Wife Is Reversed or Abused

(The Fox of Role Reversal)

God made men to be men, husbands, and fathers. A man should never apologize for being a man, for being a masculine human being. God made women to be women, wives, and mothers. No woman should ever apologize for being a feminine person. You see, no one is as good at being a man as a man, and no one is as good at being a woman as a woman. However, there is great confusion when it comes to gender roles in our culture, and men especially are suffering an "identity crisis." In our day men often struggle with their maleness. I believe the *South China Post* (April 25, 2000) got it right when it said, "What a real man needs is another man to talk to and reinforce his maleness and help him be a better husband . . . without such a friend, men risk reverting to a mother-child relationship with a spouse." Dr. Peter Karl states, "Men become helpless and insecure and increasingly revert to the classic overgrown kid who expects to be mothered . . . men have few positive role models. Often, they don't even have a good relationship with their fathers, much less any other man."

In preparing for marriage a wise man will look to an older, wiser, and successful husband and father for mentoring. A wise woman will look to another woman for the same kind of guidance and direction. Letting a mature, successfully married couple provide a role model will go a long way in capturing the little fox of role reversal.

Warning #2: A Marriage Will Get into Trouble When Initial, Sensual Love Fails to Develop into True Intimacy

(The Fox of Intimacy Stagnation)

Charlotte and I married when I was twenty-one and she was nineteen. Being transparently honest, let me tell you why I married her. She looked good and smelled good and was fun to hold, hug, and kiss. I discovered she was also a really good cook and housekeeper. She had a pleasant personality, and it appeared to me she would take good care of me for a long time. Now some of you might say, "Why, you sure are self-centered. I can't believe those were the things you were thinking about when you thought about getting married." Well, before you take me out to be tarred and feathered, let me ask a question: Why did you marry your mate? Let me pick on us guys for a minute. Did you, when looking for a mate, say, "I am going to marry an ugly woman. I want one who always has a partly cloudy disposition with thunderstorms on the horizon. I want one who is no fun to hug and kiss. I want one who can't cook or keep house and shows no potential for change. In short, I'm looking for a mate who will make me miserable the rest of my life"? I doubt this was the approach taken by any man. Being honest, you probably married, or are considering marriage, for pretty much the same reasons I did.

So what's the point? Am I saying that I did not love Charlotte when we married? Not at all! I did love her—as well as a twenty-one-year-old *boy* can love anything. Now, however, I am a forty-plus-year-old man (Charlotte says I'm still pretty much a boy in the way I act), and I must tell you, what I feel and know in my heart and soul for Charlotte is so much deeper and precious, it is almost illegitimate to use the word *love* again. Yes, I loved her at twenty-one. But I passionately and intimately love her now. Emotional love got us started, but a soul love has kept us going. We cannot stay where we started in our love relationship. It must grow from day one or the fox of stagnation will sneak in and do its destructive work.

Warning #3: A Marriage Will Get into Trouble When It Is Not Being Nourished by Regular and Genuine Communication

(The Fox of Silence/Stonewalling)

For a marriage to be healthy and vibrant, five areas require consistent attention: 1) *communication,* 2) *finances,* 3) *sex,* 4) *children,* and 5) *in-law relationships.* If any of the latter four get into trouble, mark it down: communication broke down. To walk together for a lifetime requires that we talk, and on a regular basis. From serious conversations to general chitchat, we must connect verbally if our marriage is going to do well. A wise person said it well: "A courtship begins when a man whispers sweet nothings, and ends when he says nothing sweet."

Warning #4: A Marriage Will Get into Trouble When Forces or Persons Outside the Marriage Encroach on the All-Important Time the Two of You Need Alone to Build and Maintain a Healthy Relationship

(The Fox of Time Ill Spent)

Love is a beautiful word. Sometimes it is best spelled t-i-m-e. A marriage is headed for hard times if our best time is given to things that promise only a small return for our investment. I'm not a hunter. I've never tried to shoot Bambi, Rocky the Squirrel, or Bugs Bunny. Now I have many friends who delight in such foolishness. To be honest, I don't think their elevator reaches the penthouse, if you know what I mean. Let's think about it for a minute. Here is a guy with two options. Option #1: He can, at 4:00 A.M., climb up into a tree in a contraption called a "deer stand" and freeze his behind off looking to shoot Bambi. Option #2: He can be back home in a nice warm bed holding his woman. This is a no-brainer as far as I can tell. Now let me be fair. I'm not against hunting, fishing, or many other good things men and women do. What I am against is giving our best time and quantity time to things that really do not matter.

There is a new fox in the woods who is doing some serious damage in this area. It is called the Internet. *USA Today* (July 6, 1999) reported, "Spouses Browse Infidelity Online" and stated, "The Internet is becoming a breeding ground for adultery, say experts who track the pattern of extramarital affairs. And even stay-at-home moms, who don't get to meet possible partners at work, can be seduced." "I predict [one] role of the Internet in the future will be as a source of affairs," says Peggy Vaughan, author of the *Monogamy Myth*. "Stay-at-home moms in chat rooms are sharing all this personal stuff they are hiding from their partners," Vaughan adds. The intensity of women's online relationships can "quickly escalate into their thinking they have found a soulmate. It is so predictable, it is like a script." Vaughan says she knows of women "who have left their marriages before they have even met" their new partners in person.

Shirley Glass has researched "extramarital attachments" since 1975. She warns of online relationships that go over the line. They can become so intense that they threaten marriages, even if there is no sex involved, she says. Such online liaisons involve the three elements of an emotional affair: *secrecy*, *intimacy*, and *sexual chemistry*. Glass cautions: "Discuss your online friendships with your spouse and show him or her your e-mail if your partner is interested. Invite your spouse to join in your correspondence so your Internet friend won't get any wrong ideas. And don't exchange sexual fantasies online."

Be careful with whom and where you spend your time. It is a sure sign of where your heart is.

Warning #5: A Marriage Will Get into Trouble When Real and Personal Needs Are Being Met More and More Outside the Marriage

(The Fox of Outside Interference)

Men and women have basic needs built into the very fabric of their being. For example, a man needs admiration and sexual fulfillment from his wife. A woman needs affection and intimate conversation from her husband. When we are not receiving these things from our mate, we can be tempted to look for them from another person. This is what opens the door for an affair. It comes about slowly, over time, almost without notice. This is one of the most lethal foxes that prey on our vineyard. If your needs are not being met by your spouse, then go to Jesus. As a Christian claim Philippians 4:13 ("I can do all things through Him who strengthens me," NASB).

Warning #6: A Marriage Will Get into Trouble If the Wedding Vows Are Considered Conditional, Marriage Is No Longer Considered a Sacred Covenant Before God, and Divorce Begins to Be Considered as a Possible Solution to an Unhappy Situation

(The Fox of Fatigue)

While we were living in North Carolina, my middle son, Paul, came home from school one day and asked me a very surprising question: "Daddy, do you think you and Mama will ever get a divorce?" I asked Paul why he asked me such a question. He told me that a friend of his who is always happy and talkative had come to school that day silent and sad. He told me that he saw tears in his eyes and that sometime during the morning, the school counselor came and got him and he went home. Paul said he found out at lunch from another friend that the night before, his daddy had left and his mother said they were getting a divorce and his dad would not be coming home anymore. The heartbrokenness of this little boy was something he could not hide, and Paul had noticed it. The thought of his own mom and dad splitting up began to run through his mind, and so he had decided to come home and ask me straight out if such a possibility was on our horizon. I quickly informed Paul that no, his mom and dad were never going to get a divorce, that when we married we meant it when we said "till death do us part."

That incident simply reinforced in my mind how important it is for a mom and a dad to stay together and to do their best to make their marriage work. Once we begin to entertain the idea that this relationship is conditional, contingent upon our happiness, and that divorce can be utilized at any point as an escape hatch, our marriage is moving into very dangerous waters. Humans are prone to take the easy way out, and divorce is an easier way than putting in the hard work necessary to maintain a healthy marriage.

Warning #7: A Marriage Will Get into Trouble If the Man and Woman Fail to Understand and Appreciate and Enjoy Just How Really Different They Are from One Another

(The Fox of Misunderstanding)

This fox leads us into our second major category of foxes, that is the "foxes of difference." Yes, men and women really are different, and they are different in some very significant ways. Let me highlight six of them.

COMMUNICATION

Listening is hard work for men. On the other hand, it brings happiness to women. You see, men are often intimidated in conversation because we are not nearly as good at it as women. On the other hand, women find conversation intimate and meaningful to their heart and soul. Men tend to report facts. Women are far more interested in sharing feelings. Men feel compelled to offer solutions. Women want affirmation and assurance. Women are quite subtle and coded in their conversation, and men unfortunately do not respond well to hints. The tone of a woman's voice, a glance of her eye, a particular form of body language may speak far louder than the words that are coming from her mouth. Any man who does not pick up on these nonverbal signals will fail at communication and will be a source of frustration to the woman in his life. We're not quite sure why this is the case, though some have suggested that it may be due to shrinking brain size! *Marriage Partnership* reported in Spring 1999, "The human brain shrinks as we age. A woman's brain shrinks 2.5% every ten years, while the typical male brain shrinks 5% in the same period." Personally, I'm not really impressed with that particular fact, and so I think we'll simply move on!

ROMANCE

Romance for men is a three-letter word: s-e-x. For women, romance can mean lots of things. It is very difficult for men to understand, but for women, romance may or may not include sex. Indeed women find some of the most interesting things romantic. For example, a woman will think it's romantic if a man will pray with her, help her wash the dishes, clean out the garage, or run a warm bubble bath and light a candle. All of these things are strange to the ears of a male, but they speak deeply to the heart of a woman. The simple fact is, men and women are wired differently when it comes to the area of romance. For men, romance is highly visual; it is what they see. For women, romance is extremely relational and personal; it is what they feel. Men indeed are creatures of sight; they are moved by what they see. Women on the other hand are creatures of the ear and of the heart; they are moved by what they hear and by what they feel. This point is so crucial it might be worth digressing for just a moment. What do men say romance is to them? A list of fifteen suggestions from Gary Chapman's wonderful book *Toward A Growing Marriage*[4] is not exhaustive, but it is helpful as a woman tries to understand where a man is coming from in this area of romance. A man would generally say to the woman of his life:

1. Be attractive at bedtime—nothing in the hair or strange on the face. Wear something besides granny gowns and pajamas.

2. Do not be ashamed to show you enjoy being with me.

3. Dress more appealingly when I am at home (no house-coats, slippers, etc.).

4. Do things to catch my attention: Remember that a man is easily excited by *sight*.

5. Communicate more openly about sex.

6. Do not make me feel guilty at night for my inconsistencies during the day (not being affectionate enough, etc.).

7. Be more aware of my needs and desires as a man.

8. Show more desire and understand that caressing and foreplay are as important to me as they are to you.

9. Do not allow yourself to remain upset over everyday events that go wrong.

10. Do not try to fake enjoyment. Be authentic in your response to me.

11. Do not try to punish me by denying me sex or by giving it grudgingly.

12. Treat me like your lover.

13. Listen to my suggestions on what you can do to improve our sexual relationship.

14. Forgive me when I fall short of what I should be.

15. Tell me what I can do to be the sexual partner you desire.

In contrast, what suggestions have wives made to their husbands as to how they can make romance and sexual relations more meaningful? Again, this list is to help us get the idea.

1. Show more affection; give attention throughout the day; come in after work and kiss me on my neck and ask me about my day (and stay around and listen!).

2. Be more sympathetic when I am really sick.

3. Accept me as I am; accept me even when you see the worst side of me.

4. Tell me that you love me at times other than when we are in bed; phone sometimes just to say, "I love you!" Do not be ashamed to tell me, "I love you" in front of others.

5. While I am bathing or showering, find soft music on the radio or dim the lights and light a candle.

6. Honor Christ as the head of our home.

7. Talk to me after our lovemaking; make caresses after our lovemaking and hold me.

8. Be sweet and loving (at least one hour) before initiating sex.

9. Show an interest in what I have to say in the morning.

10. Help me wash dinner dishes and clean the kitchen.

11. Pay romantic attention to me (hold hands, kiss) even during relatively unromantic activities (television watching, car riding, walking in the mall, etc.).

12. Help me feel that I am sexually and romantically attractive by complimenting me more often.

13. Pray with me about the problems and victories you are having; let me express my own needs to you.

14. Do not approach lovemaking as a ritualistic activity; make each time a new experience.

15. Think of something nice to say about me, and do it in front of others often.

NEEDS

When it comes to needs, women need to feel valued. Men need to feel successful. Indeed, if you talk to a man about feeling valued, he probably will not understand what you are getting at. But if you talk to him about his need to feel successful, he will immediately understand what you mean. Women need to be heard. Communication is invaluable in speaking to the heart of a woman. Men, on the other hand, like their canine companions, need to be praised. When a woman praises her man, she speaks to one of the most basic needs of his heart—his need for admiration. His soul soars at the special place he occupies in the evaluation of his spouse.

SELF-WORTH

Women value relational moments and fear neglect. Men value occupational achievements and fear failure. Women are relational creatures. Barbara A. Chester wisely asserts that women love to "make a memory." Men would not really understand what that is all about. However, men do gauge their own self-worth very often by what they do for a living. Furthermore, failure at one's occupational assignment can be absolutely devastating to a man's self-worth. I might add at this point, if and when a man loses his job, it is an especially crucial time for a woman to step in and affirm him and let him know that she still values him above all other men. We see this truth reiterated again and again in the Song of Solomon as the Shulammite woman praises Solomon in every imaginable way. A good wife will not forget how important this is to the fragile male ego. Men, on the other hand, must understand that the relationships of life are absolutely crucial to a woman. If she is neglected by the man in her life, he wounds her spirit and bruises her heart in a way that can hardly be healed.

TIME

Men do not think much about time. Women, however, value both quantity and quality of time. We baby boomers subjected ourselves willingly to a great lie. We told ourselves that though we did not give our children quantity time because of the busyness of our schedules, we more than made up for it with quality time. However, we now know that for a child, and for that matter a spouse, quality time is quantity time. Both a spouse and children want you when they want you, and if you're not there, they don't get you. Men in this context tend to go with the flow. We have to be honest—most of us are not very creative. This is a tragedy. Women are thrilled beyond words when their man shows his appreciation for them with specific and creative ideas.

How many times has a man blown it on a date night? He realizes that it has been some time since he took his wife out for a date, and so he approaches her and says, "Honey, how about a date this Friday night?" She of course passes out, and he is forced to call 911 to have emergency service come revive her! However, once she has regained consciousness she quickly responds with an enthusiastic "Yes!" She then asks the question that has been building within her soul since she heard her husband's offer: "What are we going to do?" Then tragically and shamefully there comes out of the mouth of the male perhaps some of the dumbest words that have ever been uttered by human lips: "Oh, it doesn't matter to me." When a man utters those words, he basically crushes the heart of his wife and destroys any possibility for good that could have come out of a romantic rendezvous on the coming weekend. A wise man will not only invite his wife out for a date, he will also be creative and specific in planning out the entire event (including the childcare!). The bottom line is this: Tell me where you spend your time and I will tell you what you love. Reba McIntyre, a country singer, wrote a song several years ago ("The Greatest Man I Never Knew") that could tragically be the theme of many a little boy or little girl as he or she reflects upon this issue of time as it relates to his or her daddy.

PARENTING

God designed mothers to nurture and provide the emotional support that is necessary for the healthy development of a child. Fathers provide strength and a child's sense of self-worth and security. Amazingly, even the simple presence of the man in the home can make a tremendous impact on the life of a child. That's why the death of a father is hurtful. But the loss of a father by divorce is utterly tragic. One of my favorite theologians is Erma Bombeck! In her book *Family—the Ties That Bind . . . and Gag!* she illustrates beautifully the importance that the presence of a father can make in the life of a child.

> One morning my father didn't get up and go to work. He went to the hospital and died the next day. I hadn't thought that much about him before. He was just someone who left and came home and seemed glad to see everyone at night. He opened the jar of pickles when no one else could. He was the only one in the house who wasn't afraid to go into the basement by himself. He cut himself shaving, but no one kissed it or got excited about it. It was understood when it rained, he got the car and brought it around to the door. When anyone was sick, he went to get the prescription filled. He took lots of pictures . . . but he was never in them. Whenever I played house, the mother had a lot to do. I never knew what to do with the Daddy doll, so I had him say, "I'm going off to work now" and threw him under the bed. The funeral was in our living room and a lot of people came and brought all kinds of good food and cakes. We had never had so much company before. I went to my room and felt under the bed for the Daddy doll. When I found him, I dusted him off and put him on my bed. He never did anything. I didn't know his leaving would hurt so much.

Yes, daddies are important to the well-being of their children, but so are their mothers. We live in a day when motherhood is not held in the high esteem that it once was. Unfortunately, many a woman has mistakenly sacrificed the gift of motherhood and the joy of childbearing for career and other enticements that in the long run will never deliver the joy and blessings that the rearing of children provides. Several years ago I came across an article that captures in a powerful fashion the greatness and importance of motherhood. I think every woman who reads these words will probably need a Kleenex at the end of the story.

"It Will Change Your Life"

Time is running out for my friend. While we are sitting at lunch, she casually mentions that she and her husband are thinking of "starting a family." What she means is that her biological clock has begun its countdown, and she is being forced to consider the prospect of motherhood.

"We're taking a survey," she says half joking. "Do you think I should have a baby?"

"It will change your life," I say carefully, keeping my tone neutral.

"I know," she says. "No more spontaneous vacations. . . ."

But that is not what I mean at all, and I try to decide what to tell her. I want her to know what she will never learn in childbirth classes: that the physical wounds of childbearing heal, but that becoming a mother will leave an emotional wound so raw that she will be forever vulnerable. I consider warning her that she will never read a newspaper again without asking "What if that had been my child?" That every plane crash, every fire will haunt her. That when she sees pictures of starving children, she will wonder if anything could be worse than watching your child die.

I look at her manicured nails and stylish suit and think that no matter how sophisticated she is, becoming a mother will reduce her to the primitive level of bear protecting her cub. That an urgent call of "MOM!" will cause her to drop her best crystal without a moment's hesitation.

I feel I should warn her that no matter how many years she has invested in her career, she will be professionally derailed by motherhood. Oh, she might arrange for childcare, but one day she will be going into an important business meeting, and she will think about her baby's sweet smell. She will have to use every ounce of discipline to keep from running home, just to make sure her child is all right. I want my friend to know that everyday decisions will no longer be routine. That a 5-year-old boy's desire to go to the men's restroom rather than the women's at a restaurant will become a major dilemma. That issues of independence and gender identity will be weighed against the prospect that a child molester may be lurking in that men's restroom. However decisive she may be at the office, she will second-guess herself constantly as a mother.

Looking at my attractive friend, I want to assure her that eventually she will shed the pounds of pregnancy, but she will never feel the same about herself. That her life now, so important, will be of less value to her once she has a child. That she would give it up in a moment to save her offspring, but will also hope for more years—not to accomplish her own dreams, but to watch her child accomplish his.

My friend's relationship with her husband will change, but not in the ways she thinks. I wish she could understand how much more you can love a man who is always careful to powder the baby or who never hesitates to play with his son or daughter. I think she should know that she will fall in love with her husband all over again, but for reasons she would now find very unromantic. I want to describe to my friend the exhilaration of seeing your child learn to hit a baseball. I want to capture for her the belly laugh of a baby who is touching the soft fur of a dog for the first time. I want her to taste the joy that is so real it hurts.

My friend's quizzical look makes me realize that tears have formed in my eyes. "You'll never regret it," I finally say. Then squeezing my friend's hand, I offer a prayer for her and me and all the mere mortal women who stumble their way into this holiest of callings.[5]

Several years ago I was doing a FamilyLife Conference in south Florida. I had talked about the fact that a mother really does become something of a bear protecting her cub whenever her children are in trouble. After the conference a man came up to me and said, "What you said this morning is absolutely the truth. Let me tell you what happened down here recently." He then relayed to me the story of a family that was in their backyard down in the Everglades. While they were out playing and doing things, an alligator came up out of the bush and grabbed their small child and began to run back into the bush toward the water. The father and mother both saw what was happening. The father, being the typical male, quickly looked for something that he might grab as a weapon to go and attack the alligator. The mother, however, looked for nothing. She immediately went into a sprint, leaped upon the alligator, and began to bite it, hit it, kick it, and scream at it. Finally, bruised and battered, the alligator let go of the small child and made its way quickly back into the safety of the water. The mother stood up, realized what she had just done, and immediately passed out there in the backyard! Why did she do this? Because being the woman, she began with her heart and not her head as did her husband. Indeed, whenever a child is in danger and both parents see it, it is almost always the case that the mother will react more quickly. Why? Does she love the child more? I don't think so. Men start with the head and then move to the heart. This takes a bit longer. Women on the other hand start with the heart and move to the head. This takes no time at all.

CONCLUSION

If we are to beat the little foxes, we must recognize that this is a fight that will have to take place on a day-by-day basis. The victories of yesterday will not be sufficient for the battles of tomorrow. Indeed it is absolutely essential that we grow a little bit every day in our relationship with one another. Several years ago Harry Chapin wrote a song entitled, "We Grew Up a Little Bit." Harry Chapin was a ballad singer. He did not have many answers, but he sure knew how to raise the right questions. The words of this song challenge our heart and our commitment to one another to at least grow a little bit every single day in this wonderful relationship we call marriage.

Yes, men and women are from Earth, and we have to deal with

that. If, however, we can with God's grace grow a little bit each day, we can move beyond "dealing with it" to "delighting in it." That was, after all, always God's plan.

1. John Gray, *Men Are from Mars, Women Are from Venus* (New York: HarperCollins, 1992).
2. John Gray, *Mars and Venus in the Bedroom: A Guide to Lasting Romance and Passion* (New York: HarperCollins, 1997), *Mars and Venus Together Forever: Relationship Skills for Lasting Love* (New York: HarperCollins, 1996), *Mars and Venus in Love: Inspiring and Heartfelt Stories of Relationships That Work* (New York: HarperCollins, 1996), and *What Your Mother Couldn't Tell You and Your Father Didn't Know* (New York: HarperCollins, 1994).
3. Dorthy Rosby, *First for Women*, February 23, 1998, 114.
4. Gary Chapman, *Toward A Growing Marriage* (Chicago: Moody Press, 1996).
5. Dale Hanson Bourke, "It Will Change Your Life," in *Everyday Miracles* (Nashville: Broadman & Holman, 1999), 5-8.

4

USING SMALL GROUPS:
THE KEY STRATEGY FOR
BUILDING STRONGER MARRIAGES

Bob Lepine

❧

Mike and Mary Murray had life all mapped out. They hadn't planned on the detour.

Mike and Mary are like a lot of couples that you may know. They live in Ben and Jerry's home state—Vermont. The high school sweethearts were married as soon as Mary graduated. Mike had been out of school for a few years and was already finding financial success in his young career. The newlyweds bought a house and a couple of cars, had a couple of children—they even got a dog. It was the American dream come true for Mary, with the exception of the white picket fence outside.

They also had what all couples begin to experience in marriage, unless they work to keep it from happening. Mike and Mary's relationship began to drift toward isolation. Because of ongoing disappointments, unmet expectations, and hurts, they had begun to erect a dividing wall between them to protect themselves from future disappointments and hurts. They were following what has become the traditional marital path in the twenty-first century. Mike grew more and more involved in his profession, while Mary turned her attention and affection toward her kids. Before long the Murrays amicably coexisted but lived emotionally isolated from one another.

That led Mike to a place he had never expected to find himself. He struck up an acquaintance with a young woman at work that led to a friendship, and that friendship had the combustible chemical reaction that ultimately led him to adultery.

Because of the growing loneliness and isolation in her marriage, Mary Murray couldn't help but wonder if there was another woman. She confronted Mike at one point, and he offered a partial confession. He told Mary that he had become emotionally entangled with a woman at work, but he lied about the fact that they had been sexually intimate. While Mary wondered how she and her husband were going to fix their marriage, Mike wasn't sure if he still wanted a marriage. He was torn between his wife and his girlfriend.

That's how Mike and Mary Murray ended up in a pastor's office. Mike had grown up in the church and had made a profession of faith at a young age. Mary had had very little church involvement. With their marriage in crisis, Mike called the church he'd attended as a child and asked for an appointment with the pastor. By the grace of God, the pastor they called happened to believe in the authority of Scripture and in the sanctity of marriage. He brought them in, spent some time with them, and wisely moved quickly to the real issue. He began asking Mike about his relationship with Christ. Mike was at a point in his life where he didn't have to be convinced of his need for the Savior. He expressed his repentance and his need for Christ.

The pastor then turned to Mary and started asking about her need for a relationship with Christ. Mary couldn't believe it. She hadn't done anything wrong here. Mike was the sinner. But as the pastor gently shared the Gospel with her, Mary realized her need for a Savior and surrendered her life to Christ.

One day when Mike came to work, he was confronted with startling news—the woman with whom he had been having the affair told him she was expecting a baby. He now faced the bitter fruit of what had seemed to be sweet-tasting sin. Mike kept a shotgun in the trunk of his car, and he seriously considered resolving his dilemma by ending his life.

Ultimately Mike chose instead to confess the affair to his wife. He told her he had lied about his relationship with the young woman at work. He confessed his unfaithfulness. And he told her about the baby. With the whole truth now exposed, they went back to the pastor to discuss where to go from here now that the whole truth was out.

That was the beginning of the rebuilding process for Mike and Mary. The pastor told them about an advertisement he had seen in the newspaper, of all places, for a small-group Bible study that was forming in their area on the subject of building a stronger marriage. The couple agreed to supplement the pastor's counseling by signing up to be part of that small group.

So Mike and Mary Murray found themselves in a stranger's living room one evening. As they look back on that experience today, they say that interaction with other couples around God's Word was the turning point in their marriage. Their marriage and their legacy were transformed because of God's grace and because of the ministry of the Holy Spirit through small-group interaction around what the Bible teaches about marriage. Mike broke off his relationship with the other woman (who later told him she had aborted the baby), and the Murrays began the difficult work of rebuilding hope and trust in their marriage.

Dennis Rainey has said, "If, in our culture today, divorce was a physical disease, we would declare a national emergency." The problem becomes even more obvious as we look at the state of marriage not just in our culture, but in our churches as well.

A study by the Barna Research Group says that in the culture, 24 percent of all the men and women walking around today have been involved in some kind of divorce.[1] Among those who refer to themselves as evangelicals, Barna found that the number divorced goes up: 27 percent in that group have been through divorce. And among those who refer to themselves as fundamentalists, the number jumps to 30 percent who have been through divorce. Now it may be that many of those came to the church for healing after a divorce, but that cannot account for the whole number. In some cases we need to wonder if churches are contributing significantly to the problem rather than to the solution.

At the end of the twentieth century, FamilyLife surveyed more than twelve thousand individuals in more than a hundred evangelical churches, asking them to rate their own marital health. Sixty percent of those who responded characterized their marriage as being in some form of marital distress, with 18 percent of the respondents describing the marital distress as severe. Now think back to last Sunday. If you had a hundred couples coming to your church last Sunday, that would mean eighteen of those couples went home thinking, "I don't know how to make my marriage work, and I don't know how much longer I can hold it together." At church they smiled and looked happy. They acted very nice to each other, they talked very civilly and smiled, and they seemed to be getting along fine with each another. But when they got back in the minivan at the end of the worship service and the doors were shut, that creeping isolation reemerged, the silence came back, and without anyone realizing it, an upstanding family in the church was heading back home to pain and agony.

There is a marriage problem in our churches today. The question is, why are Christians failing and frustrated as they try to hold together the primary relationship that God has given us here on earth? I think the frustration can be traced back to four sources that help explain why so many Christians today find themselves clueless about how to make a marriage work to the glory of God.

The first root cause of the problem is *unchecked selfishness*. That's just a fresh way of saying that we are dealing with a sin problem. Peel back the problems in all struggling marriages and you'll find a common denominator—two depraved people trying to live together. Now put those two depraved people into a culture where selfishness is not only endemic but encouraged and celebrated, and you have a formula for marital disharmony. Today we don't discourage selfishness—we promote it. Your happiness and your self-fulfillment are thought of as divine entitlements or Constitutional guarantees, and our sin nature can't resist the idea. Madison Avenue knows this. That's why advertising is built around what you deserve—whether it's a "break today" or having it "your way." Advertisers know that if they can appeal to our base nature, the sin nature of man, we are putty in their hands.

I heard not long ago about a husband and wife who are struggling in their marriage—his second and her first. The husband has recently committed adultery with a woman at work. In confessing to his affair, the husband mentioned that his wife has put on weight since their wedding, and as a result he is not sexually attracted to her any longer. My friends who told me about this couple asked me, "What should we tell this husband? How should he deal with the fact that his wife has put on weight? Should he encourage his wife to slim down a bit so he might be attracted to her again?"

I told my friends that the real issue here has nothing to do with weight. It's about a selfish husband—a man who is acting like a spoiled adolescent and who needs to grow up. I said, "Tell him he should go to his wife and talk to her about her weight problem once he is perfectly carrying out his responsibility to love, care for, protect, provide for, and honor his wife."

Selfishness. I'm convinced that's what lies at the root of the vast majority of marriage problems couples are facing today.

There's a second major reason why marriages are falling apart today. It can be traced back to *the homes in which we grew up*. Now, let me be very clear. I'm not suggesting that our parents are to blame for the sad state of marriages in the church. I'm suggesting that we have carried over into our marriages some of the bad habits and patterns our parents modeled for us—subtle patterns we observed in their marriages that silently became a part of how we relate to one another in our marriages. Apart from having our minds renewed by God's Word, those habits and patterns inevitably resurface.

There is a third significant contributor to our epidemic of troubled marriages. We live today in *a culture that does not honor marriage as a permanent, covenantal relationship*. A recent survey reported that well over half of the people who attend a wedding on any given Saturday don't believe that the vows they are hearing will be honored. We apparently routinely witness two people making a covenant oath to one another in the presence of God, and we smile and cry and think to ourselves, *This couple isn't going to make it.*

And it's not just the witnesses. Many of the people exchanging the vows are thinking the same thing. Paul Overstreet is a case in point. Paul is a singer/songwriter, a former Country Music Association Songwriter of the Year. He wrote Randy Travis's hit song "Forever and Ever, Amen" and many other number one songs in country music. Many of his songs celebrate commitment in marriage. But when Paul proposed to his wife Julie he told her, "We can give this a try. If it doesn't work out, we'll just get a divorce." That was his actual marriage proposal. He was surprised when his girlfriend Julie said, "No, Paul. If I'm getting married, it's for life." He said later, "I'd never thought of that."

Do you have any idea how many twenty-somethings there are in our culture today who think that marrying one person for a whole lifetime is just a romantic fantasy? Their parents' marriages didn't last, and now they're watching their friends' marriages disintegrate. So when they stand at the altar, many of them are thinking, *It may not work, but we'll give it a shot.*

The fourth thing that is working against marriages is that *no one has taught us or has modeled for us basic relationship skills.* We have a generation of young people today who don't know the basics. They don't know how to communicate effectively with one another. They don't know how to resolve conflict. Before they ever rent a tux or buy a wedding gown, most of them have been through a series of relationships that have ended in a breakup. So when times get tough in a marriage—as they inevitably will—those couples don't have any plan for making their marriage work. All they know how to do is move on to the next relationship.

I'll never forget hearing from a twenty-two-year-old who listens to the radio program "FamilyLife Today." She told me she had been married for about a year. She explained that she had first heard the program one evening when she was trying to find something to listen to on her radio. "Your conversation intrigued me," she said. "At that point in our marriage we were having a lot of problems, and we were fighting a lot, and I had been thinking about getting a divorce." She said it as casually as that—kind of like "I had been thinking about ordering a pizza when I got home."

She went on, "On the radio, they were talking about resolving conflict, and I thought to myself, 'Maybe we could do that.'" The idea that there might be some relationship skills she and her husband could use to get past their conflicts had never occurred to her. No one had ever talked to her about how to address conflict, how to lovingly confront another person, how to ask for forgiveness when you've wronged someone, or how to express forgiveness when somebody asks that of you. She hadn't seen it modeled, and no one had ever taught her how to do it. So at twenty-two she was about to end her first marriage and move on to a new relationship.

In the same way that health officials try to trace the causes of a medical epidemic, I believe we find in these four factors the cause of the divorce epidemic in our culture today. If we're going to find a cure, we have to address these root causes: the lack of basic relationship skills, the failure to model what a healthy marriage can and should look like, a culture that does not honor or support permanence in marriage, and the selfishness that is at our core.

So what is the church to do today? Most pastors I know never get a chance to put together an offensive game plan to address the issues I've outlined and to strengthen marriages in their churches. Instead pastors often wind up playing defense right from the start— working as hard as they can to help those couples whose marriages are in crisis. The solution for the epidemic is a spiritual one, and ultimately the church has the cure. Dennis Rainey has suggested that local churches need to become *marriage- and family-equipping centers* in their communities. Rather than simply addressing the needs of marriages and families that are in trouble, churches need to become aggressively proactive in addressing problems before they start.

For pastors, that's not as easy as it sounds. One pastor I know told me, "I don't like to preach on marriage; if I do, I know what is going to happen on Monday morning. The phone is going to be ringing, and I'm going to be booked with counseling appointments for the next three weeks. That doesn't happen when I preach on eschatology." But that leaves us knowing we have cancer but saying, "I'll wait until a symptom occurs before I address the problem."

Which brings us to small groups. If I had a vaccine that I could give couples in your church that would immunize many of them from serious marital distress, would you be interested? Well, let me tell you what Dr. Gary Rosberg said after doing twenty-five thousand hours of marriage and family therapy. He said, "My experience tells me that the best long-term predictor of marital harmony is for a couple to be involved in a small group with other couples, studying what the Bible has to say about marriage." He's not talking about some kind of group therapy session baptized with a few Bible verses. He's talking about normal, average, married people getting together to find out how to make their marriages work. Some of those couples would say that their satisfaction is relatively high; others would say their marriage is in trouble. But by coming together to study the Scriptures with one another, those groups provide the forum for long-term success for those marriages.

Why would Dr. Rosberg make that claim? It's because he knows that life-change and sanctification happen when God's Word is faithfully taught in the context of real community. Jesus made it clear in John 17:17 that God's Spirit uses the Word of God to transform lives. "Sanctify them in the truth," Jesus prayed. "Your Word is truth" (NASB). The sanctification process happens as the Word of God is preached, studied, memorized, and meditated on, and as we apply it in our lives. And that happens in the context of community.

C. J. Mahaney, the pastor of Covenant Life Church in Gaithersburg, Maryland, is a strong proponent of the importance of small groups in the life of a church. He says, "A church following a Biblical model will not simply have small groups, they will not merely offer small groups, they will be *built around* small groups. That's what will be at the core of the church." Small groups are the key to effective community in a church. But in order for the community to be authentic and effective, we need to narrow the focus of the groups to an examination of what the Bible teaches about key life issues. A small group needs to be less about increasing someone's Bible *knowledge* and instead be pointing people to more effective Bible *application*. A small group should be about how the sheep can learn to graciously care for each other in accordance with the Word of God.

How important is community to the process of life change? Ask yourself this question: What would happen to most new believers if, when someone became a Christian, we simply shipped him a Bible and some study helps and said, "Read this and it will fix everything"? While it is the Word of God made alive by the Spirit of God that brings about life change, it happens more quickly, more effectively, and more often in the context of community.

Four things need to happen if a small group is going to be effective for life change. First, people need to regularly be studying and interacting around God's Word. When God's Word isn't at the center of a small group, people may still enjoy their experience and build friendships, but life change isn't going to happen. The need for couples to build healthy relationships with other couples is real, and small groups will help address that need. But our goal here is to strengthen couples' marriages, and for that to happen, we must look to the power of God's Word.

The second thing that needs to happen in a small group setting is for couples to be challenged to move from knowledge to application. Dennis Rainey talks about this in his book *One Home at a Time*. Life change takes place when people know, then apply, then experience, embrace, and proclaim God's truth on marriage (see the diagram below).

FAMILY REFORMATION

WORD · GOD'S TRUTH ON MARRIAGE AND FAMILY · GODLY MARRIAGES AND FAMILIES WORLD

PROCLAIM — Repentance and Purity / Marriage Covenant / Biblical Roles / Godly Parenting — KNOW

EMBRACE — APPLY

EXPERIENCE

Most of the time when a pastor preaches a message on Sunday morning, he hopes people will have a better understanding of God's truth. He hopes that if he is persuasive enough, these people will not only have a better understanding of God's Word but will come to embrace it as a personal conviction.

But what happens for the person in the pew when what he's been taught about the Word of God collides with events in his life? It's at that point that convictions are tested. That's when a person will decide if what he has been taught about God's Word is something he embraces as a personal conviction or if it's just something the preacher preached a good sermon about one time. For knowledge to become a conviction, it must move through the process of personal application. We want what people know about God's Word to be lived out in their experience. When we have lived what we know, it becomes a settled conviction for us.

There's a third thing that needs to happen for small groups to be effective for life change, and that's for honesty and transparency to be encouraged. I've been amazed over the years at how much more honesty and transparency take place at a typical Alcoholics Anonymous meeting than in any kind of church meeting. I've wondered if we should rename our small-group ministry in our churches Sinners Anonymous. We have a critical need to be real and honest with one another in the church. The place where that is most likely to occur—and where it is perhaps most appropriate—is in a small-group environment.

If a husband and wife, meeting with other couples, can talk candidly about a recent conflict that is still unresolved, a couple of things can happen. First, they can see that they are not alone and that conflict is a normal part of marriage. Second, they can find help and hope from the Scriptures and from the lives of others in the group who have experienced the same kind of struggles. That couple can make a small course correction that can keep them out of the marital ditch (and out of the counselor's office).

That ties in with the last thing that has to be a part of a good small group—accountability. There is power in positive peer pressure. The Scriptures challenge us to stimulate one another to love and good deeds (Heb. 10:24). To build up one another. To admonish one another. To speak to one another with psalms, hymns, and spiritual songs. This is part of how we hold one another accountable for our lives and keep us all heading in the right direction in our marriages.

In the mid-1980s as FamilyLife began to develop Bible study guides on marriage for small-group use, we used those four objectives to make sure the small-group experience would involve more than just knowledge. What we designed is the HomeBuilders Couples Study, a series of small-group studies for married couples. In each of these studies there's an opportunity to interact together around God's Word, for application, in a context where community and account-ability can occur. Each session in each study includes a "Make a Date" assignment that takes place between sessions, so a couple can continue to interact in a more private setting. Then as the next session begins, couples start off by telling each other what happened during their "Make a Date" time.

My conviction is that small groups can provide churches with the best strategy for helping to build stronger marriages, and that build-ing stronger marriages is the front line of the Christian's battle against the flesh (see Gal. 5:16-26). The process of sanctification in the life of a believer most regularly takes place in the crucible of the home. D. L. Moody said, "If I wanted to find out whether a man was a Christian, I wouldn't ask his minister. I would ask his wife. If a man doesn't treat his wife right, I don't want to hear him talk about Christianity. What is the use of his talking about salvation for the next life if he has no salvation for this life?" It's at home in our marriages that the rubber meets the road. When husbands and wives learn how to love each other well, they can love anyone well.

But won't couples get tired of talking about marriage all the time? Won't they want to study other things? They will. But church leaders would be wise to make sure that those couples are regularly coming back to something that will strengthen and refresh their marriages. Because marriages go through phases and transitions every couple of years, we need to bring them in for a regular alignment.

Let me suggest some steps on how a church might begin to launch a small-group ministry for couples focused on marriage. First, you must understand that marriage and family is the preeminent life issue in God's agenda, and you must teach that truth to your congregation. Help them understand that marriage is the first institution that God created, and that it's the picture God has chosen to reveal the mystery of Christ's relationship with His church. Apart from a person's individual walk with Christ, the next most important relationship on which we need to focus in our churches is the marriage relationship. If you believe that, you ought to make building strong marriages your key emphasis. Prepare yourself—if you're committed to making this a priority for your church, you may need to be willing to shut down some existing programs.

Next, call together a handpicked group of folks. Look down the church address list, and figure out how many couples you have whom you could recruit as small-group facilitators. Invite those couples to your home or to the church for a potluck, and tell them you'd like them to be part of a leadership team to help establish a network of small groups in the church. Share with them your passion for cultivating strong marriages in your church. Help them understand that this is a priority, not just another program you are trying to launch. Be ready for their objections—things like, "We're too busy" or "We tried that in another church and it didn't work." Then invite those couples to be a part of the core to help you develop and launch the strategy.

Some pastors never get to this point because when they get out the church address list, they think to themselves, *I don't have many couples who would be qualified to serve as leaders, and my top couples are already busy with other ministry assignments.* Before you give up on the idea, remember the men Jesus selected as His apostles. You don't need Ph.D.s or trained theologians to move ahead—you need a few fishermen and an IRS agent. These people don't need to have perfect marriages. If you have people who are willing, you can find a curriculum that makes it easy for someone to facilitate a small group. Choose people who have a willingness to serve, and invite them to help design the strategy. Ask them to begin thinking about four or five couples in the church they would like to invite to be part of their small group, and have them begin praying for those couples.

Next, begin a sermon series on the subject of marriage—two, three, maybe four Sundays when you teach what the Bible says about marriage but with this as your application point: At the conclusion of your sermon series, you explain to the congregation that over the next two weeks you are going to be forming some new small groups for couples, and you'd like everyone to be involved. Explain that the commitment is for a fixed number of sessions (six to eight sessions will work best) and that everyone will be studying the same material. Introduce the couples you have been working with, and ask them to stand up. Ask people to sign up that morning. Then have your group leaders start calling those who signed up (and those who didn't) to invite people to join their group. They can let the people they call know that they have been praying for them and have been hoping they will agree to join their group. This kind of personal invitation is the key to an effective launch of the strategy.

With the right people working to form the groups, and with this kind of personal invitation strategy, you can wind up with a significant number of your church members involved in a small group from the start. Some will drop out during the study, and some couples will have to miss a few of the meetings. After the groups have completed their first study, the leader can ask everyone if they would like to continue to meet and to go through a second study.

At that point, some groups may fold. Most will continue. Here's the next thing you do: Make sure that in your new members classes at your church, you emphasize your commitment to the small-group ministry. Explain that the key priorities for everyone in the church are being part of the worship on Sunday morning and being part of a small group. Let the prospective new members know that at the end of the class, you'll be connecting them with an existing small group. Instead of making it an option for new members to join a small group, make the new members come up with a reason why they can't be part of a group. Over time you will build a church where everybody is connected as part of a small group.

The challenge at this point is to keep things uncluttered so that people don't have a lot of competing priorities. That doesn't mean you can't offer additional ministry opportunities. It simply means that when you stress involvement in church life, you make sure the priorities of worship and small-group participation are the nonnegotiables. And at least once a year the focus of the small groups ought to be on marriage and family relationships. When couples meet to study what God's Word teaches about marriage and family relationships in the context of a small group, God can use that pattern to prevent some marriage and family problems before they occur. Couples can begin to diagnose and solve their own problems without having to come to the pastoral staff for help.

Mike and Mary Murray—the couple I talked about at the beginning of this chapter—are a living testimony to the power of a small group to turn a marriage around and to preserve a legacy. Today the Murrays have three children—two girls and a boy. As they watch their children grow, they can't help but think that one of those precious youngsters would never have been born if it hadn't been for a small-group meeting where they learned how to apply God's Word to their marriage. The Murrays were on their way to becoming a statistic. In fact, Michael says, "I would have either committed suicide or we would have split up. That's where we were going."

But instead they are together as a family. Michael spends his time, almost full-time now, helping churches in the Vermont area start small groups. They have led a number of groups in their home, telling their story and encouraging other couples to find their hope and help in God's Word. Do you know why? Because Michael is like a guy who found the vial that cures the disease he had, and he can't keep from telling others, "This will heal things. It did for me, and it can for you."

---

1. You've probably heard the statistic that half of all marriages end in divorce. That's a little misleading. For every two marriages that begin this year in Dallas, there will be one divorce filed for. But that doesn't mean that half of all marriages end in divorce, because a number of folks are going through multiple divorces. According to *Time* magazine (September 25, 2000, 77), "more than 40% of first marriages" now end in divorce."

5

Cultivating a Man-Friendly Church

H. B. London, Jr.

————⊗⊗⊗————

I carry in my Bible a picture of my great-grandfather whom I never knew and my great-grandmother whom I knew in passing because she lived to be ninety-seven years of age. I don't know that she ever knew me. But in a couple of his books Dr. James Dobson (my first cousin) tells a story about my great-grandfather who came to my great-grandmother one day and said to her, "The Lord has laid it on my heart that we should give an hour every day to praying for our family." And so they laid aside the time between 12 and 1 every day to pray specifically for their children and grandchildren. Then one day my great-grand-father said, "The Lord has given me another impression, and that is that in our prayers we should claim four generations for the Lord." And so they began to pray for those in their own generation and their offspring and their offspring's offspring. But they also began to pray for generations they would never see or know. Dr. Dobson tells the story that in those generations—four generations—every offspring either was a minister or married one.

I am a trophy of amazing grace, a miracle of God's favor and mercy. Jim Dobson accepted Christ early in his life. He pretty much wore a white hat and was lily-white most of the way through. I, however, went kicking and screaming through all of life and through the beginnings of ministry and even today tend to kick and scream a little.

But through all of that, the Lord has touched my life. When Beverley and I went into ministry, I had been kicked out of college, and she was from a little town in central California and didn't want to go back. So we got married, and then the Lord got ahold of our lives and straightened us out, and soon we were back in seminary. Three and a half years later we loaded a '56 Chevy to the gills and went to our first church in Southern California on the wrong side of the tracks, where folks were not very educated. If they had been smarter, they wouldn't have let me come because I was the most unlikely one to fill the position.

But I noticed in those early days that strong-willed women dominated the church. Now, being a strong-willed woman is not an issue that I'm dealing with here, but I'm just saying that the men in the church had abdicated their roles. They had given up in so many ways their leadership capabilities, to the point where they didn't grow. They just spectated and went through the motions. It was a very radical church. It was so radical that they wouldn't even pay me on Sunday. I had to go to the treasurer's house on Monday to pick up my check, which, such as it was, was not very big. But the treasurer was very imposing—about 6'3" and 280 pounds, and when she came to the door, I'm telling you, I said, "Thank you" over and over.

We stayed at that church for about three and a half years, and then we moved on to Bloomington, California, which was near Fontana, which was near Colton, which was near San Bernardino, which was near Riverside, which was near . . . wherever. Kaiser Steel Mill was still in existence there and going strong. They worked three shifts at Kaiser, and my church was made up of Kaiser Steel workers. Every week the graveyard shift was either missing, or their wives made them come to church before they went to bed. I found in that church that because the men had worked that shift and were into all the things that go along with being in the union, they generally said to their wives, "You do the church stuff, and we'll bring home the check." That's just the way it was. So there were all kinds of problems with children and with identity and with trying to get men to take responsibilities on boards or to teach or whatever.

Then in 1968 I was called to a church in Salem, Oregon, where I stayed for twenty years. I went there as a very young pastor, and I quickly realized it was an interesting situation. On our church board, nineteen were men and one was a woman who was head of the missionary society. All the men wore suits and ties to the board meetings—as conservative as you can possibly imagine. And I realized that also in this situation there was kind of a dogmatism that existed. There was not much liberalism; there was not much creative thought. It was pretty much by the book, and consequently many of these men ruled their homes with an iron hand. There was not a lot of love shown. There was not a lot of love expressed. Somewhere along the way somebody had told them that strong men don't cry and strong men don't hug and strong men don't affirm. And so that's the way they treated their pastor. They didn't hug or love. They just kind of sat there in their suits and ties. And I was young enough that I could make a bunch of mistakes and go sell shoes if it didn't work out.

Sports were a big part of our lives, and as I was playing softball with some guys one day I asked two or three guys after the game if they'd like to go out and get a Coke. They were shocked that a pastor who was all dusty with skinned shins would take time to go out with them for a Coke. And we went. It was the most amazing thing. I didn't turn any of the conversation on me but turned everything to them. I got them discussing their lives and their families, and two hours later these guys were still going at a record clip. I don't think they had ever in their lives had an opportunity where people just stopped and listened to where they were going. And so that night, coming home from a ball game all dusty and scratched up, it came to my mind that here was an opportunity in 1968 for me to pave the way not just for my denomination but for the community, an opportunity for men to be honored and valued and encouraged to take their places of leadership in the local church.

Now you might say, "You mean you didn't go to a Promise Keepers thing and Bill McCartney didn't grab you by the neck and tell you to shape up or you didn't go to Willow Creek and buy a plastic notebook or sit through some boring seminar to discover this?" No.

I discovered at McDonald's, with dusty, scarred knees, that the best economy for building a church is to build around 2 Timothy 2:2, to invest yourself in teachable, likable, trainable, pliable, available men who in turn will teach others. And from 1968 through 1991, when I established programs and changed paradigms, it was always with the men of the church in mind.

Here's the deal. Ninety percent of the time when I would be able to lead a man and help him see how valuable and talented he was and could get him to bow his knee to Jesus and proclaim Him as Lord, the whole family would follow. In fact, it was more than 90 percent of the time. Now please don't think I'm being chauvinistic and weird because I promise you I'm not. But let me tell you what happens. So much of the time when wives come to church and their husbands stay at home, there is a neurosis that sets in. "Poor me, poor us, I don't know how we are going to make it. I just don't know how life could be different." Then at around twelve or thirteen, the children start saying, "Well, Dad's not coming to church, so why should I? If he's going to sit with a beer in his hand watching football on Sunday, why can't I sit with a Coke in my hand and watch it with him? I'd rather be with Dad than in some boring Sunday school class."

A lot of dysfunction starts at the point where all of a sudden the mom begins to think that by her taking the lead, naturally everybody will follow her. And they will for a while because Dad wants them out of the house so he can have the TV to himself for a little bit anyway. That will work for a little while, but finally a division starts because the man all of a sudden realizes that he will never catch up with his spouse as far as biblical knowledge and understanding; but he's embarrassed to even talk about it because he doesn't know what he's talking about. Many times the wives will say that's stupid. Why would he say that?

Let me just give you these statistics.

Men are the senior pastors of nine out of ten Protestant churches; however, a new nationwide survey done by Barna Research suggests that women shoulder most of the responsibility for the health and vitality of Christian faith in America.

Did you get that? Without women, Christianity would have nearly 60 percent fewer adherents.

The survey data shows that nearly half of the nation's women have a faith that classifies them as "born again," compared with just one third of men. In other words, there are between eleven million and twelve million *more* born-again women than there are born-again men in our country. Christianity is still the faith of choice among Americans, but particularly among women. When asked to identify their religious affiliations, nine out of every ten women nationwide said they consider themselves to be Christians.

Here are some more interesting statistics: One of the characteristics of the women that emerges from the research is their high degree of spiritual depth. Nearly eight out of every ten women say the term *spiritual* describes them accurately. Just 60 percent of men do. Almost seven out of every ten female respondents resonated with the phrase, *deeply spiritual*; among men it was only 50 percent.

Perhaps even more indicative of women's sense of spiritual focus, 41 percent of women said they have set specific spiritual goals that they hoped to accomplish in the coming year or two. Only 29 percent of men have identified such spiritual objectives. Women are also more likely to acknowledge a significant faith commitment. Three quarters of women said their religious faith is very important in their lives. This compares to just three out of every five men who indicated that their religious commitment is a critical aspect of their lives.

Now, if that's the case, we are starting at a great disadvantage. When it comes to establishing a man-friendly church, let me walk you through my own experience. I sat there that night realizing that I'd hit on something that is pretty unique. So I moved from that to the thought that if, by the Holy Spirit, I can win the man to Jesus Christ and to the church, I can win the family. So I began to build on that assumption. In the next few weeks I began to spend three to four hours of every day with men. Breakfast, lunch, on their turf, in the office, in the shop, even on the farm. Many times I walked behind a wagon picking up onions that had fallen out just to try to identify with a farmer who had been hurt by a pastor a long time ago and had no interest in the church. By me showing interest in him, he began to identify that maybe every pastor isn't a jerk.

I invested twenty hours a week to men's ministry. Not at Promise Keepers events or some kind of pancake breakfast, but in individual lives. This is so simple that I'm sure people will think I'm not very smart, but sometimes simplicity is smart. And I based my relationship with them on three things.

(1) In my time with them I tried to establish their level of spiritual background. It wasn't the "if you died right now, would you go to heaven?" thing. It wasn't grabbing somebody by the lapels and telling them they would burn in hell if they didn't change their ways. It was general conversation and then just kind of dropping out of the sky with just the phrase: "Did you ever go to Sunday school as a kid?" That phrase can tell you more in five minutes than all kinds of deep theological interaction. "Did you ever go to Sunday school as a kid?" "Aw, you know my folks didn't go to church very much," or "Are you kidding? My parents dragged me to church every Sunday. They'd get there and act all holy and then go home and beat up on each other." Follow-up questions included, "Did your parents go to church with you? Did you have a pastor that influenced you? A youth pastor that loved you? Were you ever disappointed by the church? Was there ever anything that caused you to turn your back on the church? Is there any reason why you don't like to go today?"

See, here's the thing with men. Most often most men are never listened to. The TV's on at home. The dinner table centers around the children. In the areas of deep concern, men either blow up or hold it in. They never just get a chance to talk. The whole philosophy around my ministry to men was to give them center stage. "You are the most important person in my life right now." And so we would discover and build on their spiritual background.

(2) We established common ground for shared interests. And that meant I got the guy talking about himself. What turned him on? What did he like? Cars? Wrestling? Hunting? Fishing? It was never a time of me letting him tell his story so I could tell one to beat his. Guys never have a chance to win because somebody always has a bigger

story or a more important event or whatever. So if they talked about their kid hitting a home run in a Little League game, I wasn't about to tell him that my kid hit two. The conversation was totally based on them. I looked them in the eye and asked leading questions. When they just answered with a two- or three-word answer, I said, "What did you mean by that?" I'd get them talking.

(3) We established the groundwork for ongoing relationships. Here is the key. If you establish a relationship with a man and then disappoint him, you might as well kiss the relationship good-bye. If you promise a man something and don't deliver as a pastor or a Christian leader, you might as well say, "See ya later." If a man trusts you and believes in you and is vulnerable with you but then is betrayed by you, that's like getting cut from a team or going hunting with a bunch of guys and getting cut out of the quail hunt. It's an embarrassment a man is never able to get over.

Let me illustrate that. In Oregon we had a very high-ranking senator, Mark Hatfield, who wrote a book, *Between a Rock and a Hard Place.* He was a conservative Baptist, and when he went to church and stood in the foyer, people would beat him up because they thought he was either too liberal or not liberal enough or they didn't like the way he voted on something. So this senator and his aide started coming to my church, sitting in the balcony when nobody else was sitting in the balcony. They'd come a little early and leave a little early. One day I got a letter from the senator asking me to be his guest at the National Prayer Breakfast. I was a twenty-something pastor, green behind the ears, and I was blown away by that. I went, and I remember walking into this pin-striped, button-down world. Coming from Oregon I had on a bright sport coat, slacks, and boot-like shoes, and my hair was real long. I walked into this world, and the senator looked me in the eye and shook my hand, saying, "I'm so glad you're here. Let me introduce you around." We went downstairs to where a little train takes you from the Senate building to the Capitol. He introduced me to all the guards and senators who walked by.

He went into this little room off the rotunda in the Capitol, and he said, "I'd like to pray for you." At the little altar there this high-ranking senator got down on a little kneeler beside me, put his arm around me, and prayed for me. Then he led me onto the train again, and we went into the Senate dining room where he served me "Senate bean soup." All around me were these guys I'd seen on television, and he was introducing me to them. When we went back upstairs, he looked me in the eyes and said, "Pastor, thank you for coming. You've honored me by your presence. If there's anything in the world I can ever do for you, you have my number. All you have to do is call me."

That changed my life. I thought to myself for a moment that maybe it was a play or an act, but you couldn't have convinced me of that because when he looked me in the eye he told me that what happened to me mattered to him.

At any kind of effective ministry to men, we have to tell them that we are not there to use or abuse them or preach to them, but that we are there to join them on the journey. We all have the same needs and the same frailties. "What happens to you matters to me."

A successful men's ministry is not just events—it's relationships that are sincere. I want to share one more story with you. I was intimidated by a very reputable surgeon in our church. He was pretty outspoken, and he dressed weird. He came to my office one day and made small talk. He crossed one leg, then crossed the other; then fifteen minutes later he left. I was so relieved he had gone because I didn't know what to say to the guy. Maybe "How was your latest incision?" An hour later my phone rang, and it was this doctor. He said, "Pastor, I needed you today, and you weren't there for me. I'm going through one of the most traumatic times with my two sons that we've ever had. Can you imagine coming into my office, sitting on the examination table for fifteen minutes, and me never asking what I can do for you? I came to your office today because I needed you. You failed me once, but I'm going to give you one more chance. I'll be over in thirty minutes."

I wasn't intimidated by anyone ever again. As men, regardless of our position in life, we all carry the same baggage and the same pain and hurts and needs. For me to look another guy in the eye and be intimidated by him says there is a weakness in my own life that I have to work on.

Now, I know that we all have different personalities, and I know that all of our personalities have little chinks in them. One of the gifts that God has given me is that I am not afraid of people. I may be a little standoffish. I'm not like a lot of pastors who just dive into the crowd. That just drives me nuts. And I don't like coming in late to anything. If I have to leave early, I sit in the back so everybody doesn't see me walking out. That's part of my personality. But if I can get a guy one on one, I feel like I can talk to him about anything that he is willing to talk about and not be put off by it.

A successful men's ministry does not begin with a big event or a pancake breakfast or a softball tournament. A successful men's ministry begins when the men in the church who are in leadership positions are willing to invest themselves in other men. Men's ministry does not begin with a busload of guys going to Promise Keepers. Men's ministry begins when the people of the church are willing to say, "I'm going to invest myself in teachable, pliable, available men who in turn will teach other people." I believe that with all my heart. And I think that many men's ministries start and fail because the investment has not been made at the proper level. It has been more at an event level than at the individual level.

With that in mind, let me go to the next point: Keep it simple. Successful men's ministries are built around food because in most cases guys like to eat. Many times I'd go to a guy's office and take a bag of doughnuts or cookies. It's amazing how many inhibitions are destroyed over food (especially a Krispy Kreme doughnut!). In these breakfast or lunch meetings (and there were many days when I'd have two breakfasts or two lunches), I would never come on as Dr. or Pastor or Reverend. I would always come across as a sinner saved by grace, sharing a journey. I've found that most people see ministers not as male, but as something else. People don't know what to do with us. They don't know what to call us. I've had a lot of people say, "What should I call you at lunch?" "Well, my name's H.B."

Let me hit you with this study done at Abilene Christian

University. It's the first cross-generational study that measures the father's positive and negative influence upon teens spiritually. It found that the dad's role as teacher came out to be the most important predictor. It said:

> We are not suggesting there aren't many other players in spiritual formation; among the other top predictors of adolescent spiritual maturity as related to dad were his commitment to Christ, his spiritual well-being, his ability to verbalize love, his ability to appropriately touch, his warmth, his prayer life, his boldness in discussing issues of faith, his genuineness and his emotional closeness. Of those teens whose fathers expressed their love well, 84% had a high spiritual maturity but among teens whose fathers had difficulty doing so, only 39% had a high spiritual maturity.

Isn't that awesome? Do you see the great responsibility that falls on the shoulders of fathers who don't have a clue on how to express love, to express tenderness? Many of them are first-generation Christians. They don't have any modeling to guide them through. And so here we are at these big conferences saying, "You need to be the spiritual leader, and you need to lead the devotions." They don't know the difference between Genesis and Gen-X. They don't know what it's all about. So they freeze!

So my role and my staff's role in their lives was to give them freedom to say, "I don't have a clue what I'm doing. I don't know how to pray. My kids know the Bible better than I do." And my role in these breakfast/lunch meetings was to say to them, "I give you freedom to be a dummy. I give you freedom to fail, to be afraid. You will never learn until you find out where your areas of weakness are." And amazingly, these guys came out of these meetings asking for material to help them. They wanted to be a part of it all because somebody said it was okay to stub their toes.

A second important factor is accountability. We tried to establish three levels of *accountability*. First, a prayer breakfast accountability. For twenty-two years I met every Tuesday morning at 6:30 A.M. with over one hundred men for low-level accountability. They would usually always sit in the same place, talk to the same guy; but through it all, it wouldn't be high-level teaching. It wouldn't be something that when they left at 7:30 A.M. they were pondering the dimensions of the ark or something. It dealt with practical, real-life issues. The pornographic issues. The language issues. The interaction issues. The forgiveness issues. All the kinds of things that guys deal with.

Another thing I established was a covenant relationship. This was based on this one fact: "Every time I pray for you, I will pray for you by name." We would meet together one-on-one once a week for twenty or thirty minutes at most. We didn't talk about cars or sports. We talked about applying Scripture to our lives, accountability, issues we were dealing with in our lives, prayer requests; then two times during the week we would contact each other. But the covenant was that each time I prayed, I would pray for him. The covenant to me was the most important aspect of my life because I couldn't fake him out or hide sin. If I was going to be part of the covenant, I had to be honest. We built the covenant upon the David-Jonathan relationship in 1 Samuel 18—20. Read that passage from several translations to get the gist of the wording. I built my men's ministry upon twenty aspects of the David-Jonathan relationship.

Third, I would try to get them to build *an accountability system with their wives.* I would tell their wives that they needed to be accountable to their husbands and to speak the truth in love. If they saw anything going on, they needed to scream from the rafters until they got their husband's attention.

So I had a men's ministry breakfast on Tuesday, a one-on-one covenant relationship during the week, and an open relationship with my wife, Beverley. I had those three accountability systems in place and shared openly and honestly about them. I shared my failures as well.

Groups of men that related to each other would begin their own breakfasts together, and as much as I could, I would have staff members available at those breakfasts to let the men know that the pastoral staff was supportive of them. Those staff members wouldn't teach but would be there to be a source of encouragement to any guys who wanted to talk afterwards. Most of the time we would not have the breakfast in the church but in a restaurant. I tried to take it away from the ecclesiastical setting so the men would be more comfortable.

In addition to the breakfast and the accountability settings, we had an athletic program. Younger men especially need the chance to flex their muscles and use some of the energy that is stored up from their high school and college days when they were athletes; they still need the chance to prove themselves.

I've had some terrible times playing sports. In my first church I was leading a lot of ragtag guys that I had almost gotten out of the gutter. I would hand them a basketball and a jersey, and off we'd go. In our very first game we had a rumble right there on the basketball court, and I found myself in the middle of the pile wailing away. I totally lost it, and I had the longest time living that one down. I can still see the guys smiling at me when I'd talk about being a peacemaker.

Then when I got to the church in Salem and had fancy jerseys and all, I knew that one guy was out to get me. I figured I'd make the most of it and just plowed into him. I didn't realize that he and his brother were two of the toughest guys in town, and they didn't care if I was a pastor. The first thing I heard was, "Number 22, you're out of the game!" I got kicked out of the game in front of my whole congregation! I was on the side of the court, and I literally crawled under the bench. When I got home I said, "Beverley, take my tennis shoes. I will never wear them again!" But you know what? I became a hero to the men in my church. "Did you hear the pastor got kicked out of the game last night?" It's the weirdest thing, I know, but they could relate to me after that. When we are not preaching, we need to be able to remove all the ecclesiastical trappings and just be a man—not Brother or Reverend, but just a man. The after-game camaraderie is more important than the game itself. I really believe that the game is secondary; it is simply a tool. It's not about the trophy or the play-offs. It's about the lessons you learn and the friends you make and the families that come together as a result.

Another must is activity. Here's why most men's ministries only last a little while or why the same guys are always there: Guys get bored. If you are not changing things around or putting new challenges out there, they will lose interest. I remember the first Bible study I started. I coerced about four guys to come. One was a dentist who hated life anyway. Another was a retired guy who had plenty of time and wanted to talk all the time. It was quite a mix. We got up early and sat at this restaurant for four or five weeks wavering over this or that Scripture. One day the dentist called me and said, "H.B., I don't mean to put you down, but that's the most boring thing I've ever been to in my life. It's a waste of my time, and I'm not coming anymore." I'm sure I was a boring teacher, but don't kid me, you know you've bored a lot of people in your ministry too.

So I asked him what he wanted us to do. He asked me why I had to talk all the time. Why did I? Weren't their thoughts just as important as mine? So now in our breakfast there is something different going on every twelve minutes. Testimonies, song, Scripture, an illustration, an application, whatever. Every twelve minutes something new happens. Then the men are asked to bring a friend if the time has been helpful to them. And they know that when their friends come, they won't be bored. A lot of people don't care about sports or Promise Keepers, and you can't build everything around those things. Many guys are super at woodworking or super at this or the other, but unless you find their interests, you will never be successful in ministering to them.

The last principle has to do with discipleship. Men who succeed in the church need to feel a sense of importance. So often the same people do everything. Men who can sing need to sing. Men who can usher need to usher. Men who can teach need to teach. They need to be trained and coached. But they need not to go solo too soon. They need to show signs of spiritual growth. They need to be encouraged. They need to be relieved from time to time. They need to know they are making a difference. They need to know they are winners. That's what a strong men's ministry will do. We need to establish within these men that they are important.

You may ask, "Why haven't you talked about all the ways to organize men's ministries?" Because that's not what I'm about. I'm about organizing men's ministries around one-on-one encounters that become gatherings of three, four, five, six, and seven. I'm not interested in the big event. Those happen anyway. You will always have Promise Keepers, couples' conferences, etc. I'm interested in pastors and Christian laymen learning how to walk up to an individual, look him in the eye, and simply say, "You matter to me." Give men the stage, give them an opportunity to reveal their weaknesses, and then minister to them rather than walk away from them.

Yesterday I talked to a man who is dying of prostate cancer. He was in my church in Oregon before I got there. At that time he had a failure in his life that could have destroyed him. He came into my office and sat on the couch and dissolved in tears. He said, "My job, my family, my life—it's all gone. It's gone." And I said to him, "No, it's not. You may think it's gone, but I promise you that I'm going to walk through this with you every step of the way. And when you feel comfortable, there will be other guys to help hold you up." That was in 1971. Yesterday, talking to him on the phone, dying from the cancer that is all through him, he could barely talk. He said to me, "H.B., you're the best friend I've ever had." I haven't been his pastor for fifteen years! Why did he call me his best friend? Because I wasn't scared or pushed away. I looked him in the eye and told him I would stick with him, no matter what. And we made it. And everything's intact. And he's going to heaven with a smile on his face because people believed in him when he didn't believe in himself.

Now this last point I share with all my heart: Stick with it. So many men's ministries have started and stopped, and men get discouraged when you start and stop. They need dependability. Don't ever tell a man you love him and then not have time for him when he calls. Be a man who's worthy of trust.

I really believe that was why Jesus had such success in His outreach to men. He spoke the truth to them. He looked them in the eye. He cared for them in a way that was genuine and not surface, and in the end He gave His life for them. The words of Paul to young

Timothy echo the life that Jesus lived. The church today is still an echo of His presence and power in their lives.

Once again, my friend, embrace Paul's admonition: "And the things you have heard me say in the presence of many witnesses entrust to reliable men who will also be qualified to teach others" (2 Tim. 2:2, NIV).

I promise you it will pay huge dividends for your ministry and the greater body of Christ.

6

SINGLE ADULTS IN YOUR MINISTRY: WHY THEY STAY AND WHY THEY STRAY

Dick Purnell

———

What kind of ministry do you have for single adults?"

We were sitting in the TV studio behind the camera waiting for our turn to be interviewed. The man next to me was a nationally known pastor of a mega-church on the west coast of America. Since his scheduled interview was only a few minutes away, I took the opportunity of asking this man what his church was doing to meet the unique needs of single adults.

"I have no idea," he responded. "I think we are doing something, but I am not sure."

"No idea." "Not sure." I was stunned because hundreds of single adults probably attended his church. Do you know how many single adults sit in your congregation each Sunday? Recently I was speaking in a church to three thousand people. I asked for all the people who were unmarried and twenty-two years old or older to stand up. Over a thousand people stood up! The audience was surprised and gasped at the large number—and then they broke out into a spontaneous applause.

Do you realize that the number of single adults in America exceeds the total national population of all but eleven of the world's

192 nations? How shocked would you be to discover that the number of single parents is greater than the entire population of Colorado and Tennessee combined?[1]

According to the 2000 U.S. census 40 percent of all adults eighteen and older (forty-eight million) are single. We are seeing a tremendous shift in American social values. The median age of a first-time marriage is now twenty-five among women and twenty-seven among men. The fastest growing family type is single parents. Fifty percent of all children born today will live in a single-parent home at some time by the time they are eighteen, which means millions will go through the trauma of divorce. Kids bury their fears and confusion inside themselves. But years later when they try to develop a relationship of their own, they are unsure how to build one that will last longer than their parents'.

If your church is in an urban area, the percentage of single adults living near you is much higher than in a rural area. Singles gravitate to the cities for jobs, things to do, and others to meet. They are searching for connection and community. The biggest negative emotion single adults experience is fear. They are often afraid of loneliness, commitment, and isolation. Most of those under thirty have never been married. The average age of a married person's first divorce is thirty-four. That means that after years of marriage, they are thrown back into the dating scene. They feel awkward and unprepared. They face the same relationship challenges that teens face, but they feel out of place.

One woman said to me, "I am now single, but I feel married. I don't want to be single, but that was forced on me." They have been out of the dating world for so long that they have very little idea what to do. And no one is helping them or even having a discussion about some of these issues.

Most singles are invisible to churches. The reason is that they look like everybody else. There are no distinguishing features. They represent every economic stratum you can image—everything from presidents of major corporations to the unemployed and all in between. Fifty-three percent of all unchurched adults are single.

But our churches are built on a mind-set of marriage, and singles are often neglected. They are the "Great Invisible Mission Field." However, businesses are very aware of singles. If you look at the advertising on television or in magazines, you will find that a huge number of the ads are geared to attract single people. Sports clothing, cars, beer, cell phones, and a myriad of other products are marketed to singles. They have the largest amount of discretionary income. But the church in general has a difficult time attracting them and capturing their attention and commitment.

Many single adults believe that the church excludes and ignores them. They feel like the church is either neglecting them or is just not interested in them. So single adults vote with their feet. They come to church for a few months or years; but when their needs are not addressed or they never hear a sermon addressed to their unique issues, they fade away and go somewhere else—or stop going to church altogether. They hear sermons preached on topics such as "How to be a Godly Husband" or "Becoming a Godly Wife." But they have never heard a sermon on "How to be a Godly Single Adult."

Some churches say, "Well, the singles are flaky. They don't get involved in the life of the church. They come for a while and then disappear." However, the singles respond by saying, "There is very little for us there, and there is nothing in church that challenges us to a deeper level of involvement and commitment." They don't stay because there is no emotional glue to keep them there. They are not the "squeaky wheel" that is going to ask the pastor to give a sermon directed toward them or to pound on the door of the budget meeting pressuring for more funding. They just fade away.

Are you desperate to attract single adults to your ministry and get them involved? Here is my top ten list on "Why Single Adults Are Turned Off by the Church."

Number 10: Frivolous jokes degrade the single lifestyle. Grandparents, parents, pastors, and married friends all have jokes about singles. All the married people laugh, but the single buries the snub under a weak smile.

I was single for forty-two years. When I served as an assistant pastor in my middle thirties, I heard lots of good-natured jokes, but often the ribbing was not funny to me. "Hey, are you afraid to take the responsibility for a mate?" Here I was in charge of several significant ministries in the church, and they tell me I'm afraid to take responsibility? "Maybe you are just too picky. Are you looking for a perfect wife?" In other words, if you lower your standards, you may get somebody. "You're not getting any younger, you know." That was supposed to pressure me to get moving? Sometimes I would get the big one: "What are you waiting for?" Like I better hurry up before I miss the "right one." But isn't there a sovereign God? His timing may not be my timing—or the timing of the people who ask me to hurry up.

In trying to encourage me, people would give what I call romantic testimonies: "I finally gave everything over to God, and six months later I found the right one." But I was forty years old and had been a full-time minister for over fifteen years. Was there something I had not given up to God that some married twenty-year-old had already given up to God? All the marriage formulas that people give singles may be individual experiences they had, but those formulas are not normative for all believers. Why should I seek the holy grail of marriage if God wants me to be content in every situation?

After four years as a pastor, I resigned from my church. Even though I no longer was the pastor, I continued to attend the church. A single female friend of mine from Kansas came to our city one weekend to visit some of her college buddies. I brought her to the 11 A.M. church service. As we were walking down the aisle, an elderly usher led us to a front row for seating. The organ was softly playing, and everybody was kind of quiet. When we stopped to turn into the row, he handed my friend a bulletin and said to me loudly so most of the people could hear, "Hey, Dick, when are you going to marry her?" I wanted to die right there, but first I wanted to punch his lights out.

These kinds of jokes will not attract singles to your church! No way! They degrade single life as if the only bright future is for married people. That idea is not found in the Bible. Even the apostle Paul stated that an unmarried person can have undivided devotion to the Lord (1 Cor. 7:32-35). He did not consider singleness a joking matter.

Number 9: Church leadership is mainly interested in the interests and needs of married people. The pastor and leaders are usually all married with very little significant empathy or understanding of the unique needs and concerns of single adults. Single Christians are rarely eligible to be members of the governing board. There are very few single senior pastors. The silent criterion of marriage eliminates singles from serving in many aspects of the typical church. If you carry that to a logical conclusion, the apostle Paul would not be qualified to be a pastor or an elder. Even Timothy would be shut out of the opportunity for leadership.

After four years as an assistant pastor, I wanted to become a senior pastor. I had a total of fifteen years experience in the ministry and two Master's degrees. However, when I sent my resumés, not one church ever asked me to candidate, because I had to write on the front page of the resumé my marital status: "Single." Who wants a senior pastor who is single?

It was a bitter experience. I was unqualified to be a senior pastor of a church because I did not have the "Mrs." degree. Many men graduating from seminary have tremendous pressure put on them. If they want to rise above the level of youth pastor, they must be married. Why is marriage the unspoken golden key that unlocks the door to pastoral advancement?

Number 8: Budgeted funds for single ministry are usually inadequate or nonexistent. Many churches don't budget anything for singles. When the churches that have budgeted some funds for singles ministry must cut the budget somewhere, the singles ministry often is the one that gets the ax. "Singles are adults—they can handle it," the budget committee says. But the message that gets across is, "You are not as important as other people in our church."

Many of my friends used to be single adult ministers. Their job description kept changing because the church leadership told them other needs in the church took precedence. Additional responsibilities were added until the singles minister was pulled far from his passion to serve the single adults in the church. Such a pastor eventually has his fire put out, gets discouraged, feels unappreciated, and gives up. The singles get shortchanged and leave.

The message the singles hear is loud and clear: "You are the lowest on the totem pole. Your needs come last. You are not worth our paying a minister who can meet your needs." Therefore, singles respond with their feet. They say, "I'm out of here."

I am seeing all over America a dwindling of singles ministries. The numbers of singles attending is declining. Sure, there are a few churches doing great things, but they are in the minority.

Number 7: Singles feel the church neglects them. They feel like they are barnacles on the side of the church ship—there but forgotten. Marriage is espoused as the norm, and singles just don't fit the model.

I have conducted over three hundred single adult conferences throughout America, Canada, and twelve other countries. Yet only nine senior pastors stopped by to observe and/or greet the crowd. The event was in their church, in their building, and these are adults. I remember each of the nine because they are so rare. The eighth pastor was located in Canada. Over 250 singles attended the conference, located in the sanctuary. The pastor chose to address the crowd. After he thanked the people for coming, he introduced me. While he was walking off the platform, I said, "Pastor, just a minute." He was shocked as he turned toward me.

"I want you to come on back up here." I am sure he did not know what was coming. I put my arm around him even though I had never met this man before in my life. I didn't know how big a name he was. I didn't really care. I just wanted to show my appreciation.

"Sir, I want these people to know that I appreciate your heart and your attitude. You took these few minutes from your busy schedule just to come to greet us." Then I addressed the audience. "Men and women, this pastor has a heart for you. He came here to show he cares for you. You are welcome in this church." Two hundred and fifty adults gave him a standing ovation.

Sure, pastors have a gazillion things to do. But a little bit of interest and time given toward singles will speak loudly and clearly that the church is interested in meeting some of the singles' needs. You would be amazed at how they will respond.

Number 6: There is a perception that single adults are morally loose. If a person is not married by mid-twenties, there is something wrong, it is generally thought. A particular church was in the process of trying to hire a youth pastor. Since they could not find one for over a year, they held a congregational meeting to explain the progress they were making. The elder in charge presented all kinds of reasons for the delay in locating the right person for the position. At the end of his explanation, I stood up and asked, "Does the person you are looking for have to be married?"

You could have heard a pin drop on the carpet. People gasped. It was the unthinkable question. The elder hemmed, and he hawed, and he slithered all over the platform. All I wanted was a yes or no. He was obviously unnerved by my question. Finally some lady in the very back said, "What we need is a role model for the young girls. So I think he should be married."

"You mean to tell me, in this entire congregation there is not one woman who's a role model for the girls?" Silence.

"I tell you what I think the real reason is. You are afraid that a single pastor would be sexually frustrated and have sex with one of the teenage girls. Out of all the pastors I have known personally, four have had affairs and left the ministry in disgrace. Each of them was married. Almost all the pastors I have read about in magazines and books who have committed adultery were married. True, married people do not have a corner on the market in becoming immoral. But you should not be prejudiced against a single adult simply because he is single."

I tried to tell them that some of the best youth pastors in America are single. I wasn't a very popular guy after that. The elders eventually hired a youth pastor. Yes, he was married.

Some churches won't allow singles to teach Sunday school for fear these men and women will succumb to sexual temptation. That is unfounded fear. We all need the power of God to overcome temptation. Don't single out single people as the most likely to succumb. That is unfair and inaccurate. Single adults want to be respected and trusted. Let them show by their faithfulness that they have a genuine relationship with God.

Number 5: Marriage is portrayed as normal for everybody. If someone is not married by thirty something, there must be something wrong with him or her.

I have heard pastors say, "If you have the desire, then God has someone for you to marry." But is that true, or is it simply an assumption? The Bible never says a word about that. In fact, many of the biblical characters were unmarried, or at least nothing indicates that they had a spouse.

Here are some of the singles in the Bible: Jesus, Paul, Timothy (probably), Mary, Martha, Lazarus, Jeremiah, Hagar, Ruth, Naomi and Anna (and countless other widows), Simeon, the Ethiopian eunuch (and all the other unnamed eunuchs in Bible times), Jephthah's daughter, and Tamar. Queen Vashti was dumped and divorced because she was honorable. Isaac did not get married until he was forty years old, and Moses followed his example. Nothing is mentioned about Nehemiah, Daniel, and Mark having families. The Bible does not portray marriage as the norm. If it did, all of the above would be abnormal and unappreciated.

I desired to be married throughout my twenties, thirties, and into my forties, but God didn't bring anybody into my life whom I cared to spend the rest of my days on earth with.

Some of my single friends are in their sixties, and they still want to get married. God just hasn't brought anyone into their lives. The sovereign God has not revealed to me why some people do not get married. But marriage is not for everyone. Population statistics reveal there are more women than men. Not everyone will get married. Yet I believe a person can be fulfilled without being married. The message of the Bible is that Christ is our sufficiency.

Number 4: The emphasis on "family church" really means couples and kids. Now I am all for a family church, but as far as I can see, it is the family of God church, not the family of married people church.

A church near my home placed a huge sign on the front lawn: "This year is the Year of the Family." I tried to tell the pastor that the hidden message was "Singles unwanted for twelve months." Announcements are enthusiastically presented in the church service:

"We are going to have our annual family gathering. Bring your whole family." The singles look at each other and say, "I guess they don't want us."

Churches annually celebrate Mother's Day, Children's Day, and Father's Day. Flowers are presented to the mothers. Special sermons are given for fathers. People smile and giggle listening to the children's choir. When are the singles celebrated and honored?

Number 3: All singles are lumped into the same category as "unmarried." But single adults cannot be put into a box like that. They are not a homogeneous group. What does a twenty-six-year-old never-married person have in common with a women who is sixty-eight years old, three times divorced, and a grandmother of fourteen?

On the other hand, married people are very homogeneous. The young newly married couples have things in common. All those who have little children have common interests and needs. Couples in different stages of married life have similar interests and challenges. So you can have a program that appeals to young marrieds without children and all the young marrieds without children will come.

But when a church starts a program for singles, what group of singles does it target—never married, divorced, widowed, separated? To what age range will the appeal be made? A dynamic church will have to rethink how the people are going to meet the needs of people—all people, including singles. You can not take the marriage paradigm of a typical church and model a singles ministry after it.

How will the church endeavor to approach almost half of the adult population? The majority of single adults have rejected the church and are unaffected by the programs geared toward the married half of the population. The average single goes to church only six times a year. Open your eyes to the "Great Invisible Mission Field" and see the vast numbers surrounding your church. They live behind apartment doors. They live inside gates that isolate condos from the passing public. They work at the grocery stores, schools, hospitals, construction projects, and a myriad of other places that are within driving distance of your church. How are we going to reach them? How are we going to meet their unique needs?

Number 2: Divorced persons feel rejected. Divorce is rarely pleasant. Couples outside and inside the church split up and battle over custody of their children. As tragic and horrible as divorce is, it is not the greatest sin. Even adultery and immorality are not the greatest sins. The greatest sin is rejecting Jesus Christ.

I believe that marriage is a lifetime commitment between a man and woman. Since I am a marriage counselor and not a divorce counselor, I emphasize the healing power of the Holy Spirit to bring warring couples back together. There is always hope in Christ to restore brokenness.

However, the reality is that couples will divorce. Yet in our response to the tragedy of a broken home and broken vows, people in the church often ostracize the husband and/or wife. To effectively reach out to the divorced, the church must repair shattered lives with love, concern, and biblical teaching.

Ministering to the divorced brings difficult questions that church boards may not want to address. What are the biblical grounds for a divorce? What about remarriage? Where can a divorced person serve in the church? How can we help children of broken homes?

How a church answers these questions will signal to singles whether they are truly welcomed. They want to be an integral part of the whole life of the church. As a church opens its arms and hearts to singles, many will hear and begin to attend, confident they will be welcomed and fed spiritually.

Number 1: Singles often feel left out. Bottom line: Thousands never enter a church because there is very little there that relates to them. Sure, you can point to the few who attend your church to "prove" that you are attracting single adults. But what about the thousands who live within a few miles of your church? Even many of the ones who attend your services feel misunderstood, out of place, and isolated from the mainstream of the church. Unless a person is married, his or her place in the life of the church is questionable.

At a Sunday service in a particular church of which I was a member, the pastor announced the status of the building program financial campaign. In his presentation he displayed a chart on a huge screen depicting the results. The title was, "Giving by Family Units." At the conclusion of the service, I approached him with this question: "What do you mean by the phrase 'giving by family units'?"

"It means the average amount a family has given," he replied.

"Do you want single adults to give to the fund-raising program?"

"Certainly!"

"Well, they do not consider themselves family units. By dividing the church into family units, you have excluded all the singles. They feel like the church does not want their contribution. You made it pretty plain that you don't want them at all." He huffed as he walked away. He never got the picture, and neither did the elders.

Single adults are a vital part of the Body of Christ. They want to be accepted and appreciated on an equal basis with everyone else. They want to be challenged to give their all for the sake of Christ. They have time, education, experience, talents, and finances to help expand the church.

How can the church utilize and motivate this vast resource? There is an invisible glass wall around the church that keeps single adults out. It needs to be smashed so the masses can come in.

What will attract single adults to your church? What will motivate and challenge them to participate and lead? Here are fifteen simple ideas that you can incorporate into your ministry to show the community you are becoming "single friendly." Without spending one dollar, you and your ministry can open the doors to over 40 percent of the adults in your area.

1. Emphasize the family of God church.

The church is for all people, not just those who are married. When it comes to really understanding and reaching single adults, the people who know the most about singles are the singles themselves.

Churches need single adults on their governing boards. They want to participate in the whole life of the church and become examples for other singles to get involved in every aspect of the church. When singles hit a brick wall of indifference before they even begin, they will probably lose their desire to become involved. Challenge them to total commitment to Christ. Motivate them to go on mission teams and volunteer for ministry opportunities. They have the time, the funds, and friends who can send them and finance them. When they are challenged and motivated, they can spend lots of time working in a variety of ministries in the church.

If you begin to get the heartbeat of single adults, they are going to flock to your church, because there is nobody else (or nearly so) in the whole city who is competing with you for them. When you build a family of God church, pretty soon the news is going to filter out to singles throughout the community. Believe me, they have a large network of friends. It may take a few months, but they will come to a church where they are appreciated and where singles are involved in all areas of ministry and leadership.

When the proclamation is "Everyone can become a vital part of our church family," you will appeal to all groups. If you have specific opportunities for singles to feel at home in your ministry, they will be attracted and will get involved with a thankful heart of joy.

2. Ask God to open your heart to reach singles for Christ.

I know people ask you to pray about lots of stuff. But I am amazed at the lack of passion that pastors and laypeople demonstrate for reaching singles. We get passionate about needy people in foreign lands or the plight of little children. But singles leave us cold. They are just as needy, but they don't tug on our heartstrings. Ask the Lord to open your eyes to see the fields already ripe for harvest in the "Great Invisible Mission Field."

Singles are desperate for relationships. They want to be connected. In our culture we have become so used to controlling things. We control what we want on our computer. We use the remote to choose what we want to see and hear. We have all sorts of gadgets to do our bidding. We can push a button and get the results we want. However, when it comes to relating to another human being, we can't manipulate a loving relationship.

Many singles are seeking loving relationships but have very little idea how to get them. They may feel comfortable in front of a computer, but not in front of a person of the opposite sex. Here they are, adults in responsible positions in their work or profession, but they don't know how to build a love relationship that will last.

The church could become a beacon light to thousands of people. Singles want to be part of a family—the family of God. And they want to meet other godly single people. They are tired of the bar scene. If the church begins to understand how to appeal to the heart of single adults, your church will experience an influx of people who are looking for a community in which to get involved.

3. Institute an annual Singles Day, similar to Mother's Day, Father's Day, Children's Day, Secretary's Day, and every other kind of special day. Ask several singles to give testimonies of what Christ means to them and how He guides their lives. Do some special things for them that make them glad to be in the center of God's will for their lives.

4. Preach one sermon a year especially directed toward single adults. Teach about Paul's admonitions in 1 Corinthians 7. Paul said, "I wish that all men were even as I am"—that is, single. Why would he make a strong statement like that? Proclaim the standard of fulfillment found in Christ. Motivate singles to godly living in the midst of a perverse world.

5. Plan special things for single parents. Encourage the youth group to volunteer to baby-sit for the children of single parents so they can enjoy a night out. Set up support groups and Sunday school classes that deal with issues that will appeal to them, such as coping with a former spouse, financial planning for a single parent, and raising children by yourself. Establish a fund to assist them financially. I tell you, you will win the heart of every single parent in that whole church.

6. Speak to the singles Sunday school class or evening meeting. A month before you address them, ask the singles to write down questions anonymously for you to answer at a future meeting. What are the top twenty questions from women and the top twenty questions from men? Explain the differences. If you are married, ask your wife to answer some of the questions. The singles hear you all the time; they want to hear her side of the issues too. They want to see how a couple deals with the issues that they confront. Singles are looking for models of how to put together a lasting love relationship.

7. Develop and train single adults to become leaders in your ministry. Make it a part of your discipleship process to actively prepare mature single adults to become elders, deacons, Sunday school teachers, small-group leaders, and mission team captains.

Select a compassionate layperson, pastor, or elder to shepherd the single adults. In one church where I have spoken several times, there was an old plumber who was a grandfather. His kids were grown and gone, and the grandkids weren't around. He and his wife wanted to have some people eat Sunday lunches with them. The only people who came consistently were the single adults. So each Sunday they invited the singles for lunch. After a period of time twenty-five or thirty singles would sit around the house eating and talking.

The church elders asked him to spend more time with the singles, offering to pay him to spend a quarter of his time teaching and encouraging the singles. The singles throughout the area started flocking to the gatherings. He started a Sunday school class with a handful. As the ministry grew, the elders increased his time until he was full-time. His Sunday school class built up to over three hundred singles. Isn't it amazing—he gave up his plumbing to become a full-time single adult minister, and the place filled up with singles?

Pray that God will raise up someone with a passion to reach out to singles. Besides a heart, they need training. Give that person opportunities to study and learn how best to teach and motivate singles.

8. Discourage jokes about single adults needing to get married. If you hear people making jokes, pull them aside. "Do you know how singles are affected by jokes like that?" I am not saying to go around telling people, "Don't joke. No laughing." Have an atmosphere of fun, but don't say things that put others down.

9. Incorporate sermon illustrations that apply to single adults. When you talk about resolving conflicts, bring up the topic of dealing with a roommate or an ex-spouse. Use the same principles as interacting with a spouse or coworker.

Sermons on holidays need extra thought. The three hardest days for single adults are Christmas, Valentine's Day, and Mother's Day. These are special holidays for lovers and families. If you look at all the statistics about psychology and depression, more people get depressed at Christmastime than any other time during the year. Everyone talks about and sings about warm, nostalgic relationships. But many singles don't have a family, or their family is spending the holidays with their ex-spouse. You can help them deal with feelings of loneliness, rejection, and discouragement.

When you speak to the women on Mother's Day, include all categories of women. Preface your remarks by saying something like, "Today is Mother's Day, and we are going to honor mothers; but I know there are women in this service who do not have children. Some of you are not married and wonder if you will ever have a husband and family. God loves you. Just because you don't have a spouse and children doesn't mean you are forgotten by God. In fact, there are women in the Bible who were single and childless—for example, Martha and Mary. God has your future in His hands. Others of you are married and would love to give birth to a child but cannot for some reason. God loves you too. Hannah, Sarah, and several other women in the Bible had struggles in this area. They trusted God, and so can you."

If you say something simple like that, you will win the day with every woman in the audience.

Some of the great hymns were written by singles. One of my favorites is the hymn "O Love That Wilt Not Let Me Go," written by George Matheson in 1882. Although it cannot be verified, many people think he wrote the song after his fiancée left him just before their wedding when he told her he was going blind. He wrote to express the deep anguish of his soul and the deeper love of Christ to hold him close. I sang and cried Matheson's song through many lonely nights, and God covered me with His love. The Lord Jesus understood my loneliness and met my deepest needs like no one else could.

10. Encourage singles to get involved in every area of your church. Give appeals that are directed particularly to singles. Motivate married couples to invite single adults to their homes for Sunday lunch. Put together a planning group where singles and marrieds discuss how to reach their entire community for Christ.

11. Publish a list of ministry opportunities that single adults especially could fill. There are many places where they would love to get involved. Highlight them. Post a job opportunity sheet in a room where singles meet. You don't have to say these are for singles, but describe mission trips, visits to the elderly in their homes, helping out with various activities with the youth, and small accountability groups that incorporate singles.

12. Present sermon topics and Sunday school class subjects that attract single adults. If you want to get some ideas, visit my website (www.DickPurnell.com) for more than one hundred topics, books, and other materials that singles like. Pick out some of these titles or some of the descriptions to utilize in your ministry.

Some of these topics include financial planning for singles, single-parent issues, adult dating, sex and the single adult, resolving conflicts, how to care for elderly parents, and finding the right one. Put together a panel discussion on an interesting or controversial topic, such as dating vs. courtship. Missions and evangelism are great topics. Challenge these singles to participate in local ministry outreaches or short-term missions. Motivate them to take a two-week vacation with a significant purpose where God can use them for His glory.

13. Give sermons on building a marriage before you get married. A lot of churches err when they offer premarital sessions. What this often means is, "If you are already engaged, find out if you are compatible."

By the time people are engaged, they are lost. Their hearts have been given away, and they are simply looking for confirmation of their engagement, not investigation to learn if they are marrying the right one. Have you ever reasoned with an engaged couple hoping they will question if their chosen partner is really the right one? By that point they may look at you as if you had just put on a red suit with a tail, carry a pitchfork, and are throwing barbs at God's obvious will for their lives.

Preempt the situation. Teach a series featuring how to build a quality relationship with the opposite sex. Sponsor a single adult conference on dating, relating, and becoming the right person.

14. Highlight single adults in the Bible. Show how they handled their circumstances and the consequences of their actions. Encourage singles, and married people, to benefit from their portraits. Teach about Absalom the rebellious single, Anna the elderly widow, Daniel the single politician in the middle of national pressure, or Hagar the abandoned single parent.

Preach a sermon on eunuchs. The Ethiopian eunuch is a good one to start with. I know that doesn't sound like a popular topic. But in Matthew 19:12 Jesus speaks of "eunuchs who have made themselves eunuchs for the sake of the kingdom of heaven" (RSV), which seems to speak of men who decided, because they loved God so much, that they were going to remain unmarried (and thus be "eunuchs" figuratively, not literally become castrated), so they could serve God only. Elevate their commitment—the Bible does.

Isaac was single until he was forty or so. What pressures did he face? Jeremiah was a very powerful single. John Mark was the young single who went on a missionary trip with Paul and Barnabas but chickened out when the going got tough. But later he turned his life around and ventured out again with Barnabas. Joseph, the single prisoner, did not get married until he got out of prison. For all those years he was alone, though the Lord was with him. I think his singleness added to some of the difficulties that he faced.

Lazarus was a close friend of Jesus. Martha was a hardworking single, while Mary was a gregarious socialite. The latter liked to be with people, especially Jesus. Moses was single until he was forty years old. Naomi, an angry widow, had a daughter-in-law named Ruth, an industrious widow. Her hard work and faith paid off. There are two Tamars in the Bible. Both had sexual problems; each was single because of circumstances. The Word of God says a lot about widows. Talk about God's commands to the church to care for widows and orphans.

15. Conduct brainstorming sessions with single adults on how to develop a powerful ministry to singles in your area. Listen intently to their good ideas for activities and publicity that would attract other singles. Get several married and single people to discuss how to do things together and utilize everyone's gifts and talents.

All the ideas above don't cost any money. However, here is an idea that will. But it will give you great returns: *Increase your annual budget for singles ministries to at least the level of your youth ministry.* Make the singles program alive, attractive, and encouraging. It will be an investment in the lives of people who can give back tremendously in leadership, missions, evangelism, prayer, time, and finances.

There are thousands of singles waiting for someone like you to give them a cup of living water.

1.   George Barna, *Single Adults* (Ventura, CA: Issachar Resources, 2002), p. 8.

7

FATHER HUNGER AMONG A LOST GENERATION: THE PASTOR'S OPPORTUNITY

Timothy B. Bayly

———⚬⚬⚬———

> *Yet most I thank thee, not for any deed,*
> *But for the sense thy living self did breed*
> *That Fatherhood is at the world's great core.*
> GEORGE MACDONALD[1]

Some years back when I first entered the pastorate, I sat in a small-town café listening to the son of a prominent church member summarize his relationship with his father: "Nothing I did ever pleased him." In his late twenties, the son was a ne'er-do-well; divorced and not able to hold down a job, his children were shunted back and forth, week by week, from one broken home to another.

He came to church only on Christmas and Easter; so our breakfast appointment was about the only chance I had. His eyes revealed the last flicker of what once had been the bright flame of father hunger—that hunger God places in the heart of every son. None of my seminary professors had mentioned this hunger to me, and I was at a loss as to how to cure his soul. Not knowing how to respond to this great sadness, I was silent.

Six years later, another young man began to attend our church. He was married, had a houseful of children, and worked to support his family, but he was a hard-drinking womanizer. After attending church for a few weeks, he called midweek and asked me to pray that he would quit drinking. Admitting his sin, he explained that his father had always told him he would never amount to anything.

"I was going to show him wrong," he said, "but he died on me."

Songs written about the unrequited love of a man for a woman are a dime a dozen, but when Harry Chapin sang "Cat's in the Cradle," the tears of a fatherless child marked our nation's conscience.

The church I currently serve is in a university community, so we have a steady stream of students joining our congregation. Not a few of the young men struggle with gender identity issues, including homosexual desires. What is the common denominator among such men? Father hunger.

These illustrations are no denial of the formative influence of mothers in the lives of their children, but the harm suffered by children who have been raised in a home where the father is absent, cruel, or silent is an open sore in the church. As a pastor grows in his awareness of this tragedy, he also will grow in his love for the promise that brings the Old Testament to its close:

> Behold, I am going to send you Elijah the prophet before the coming of the great and terrible day of the LORD. He will restore the hearts of the fathers to their children and the hearts of the children to their fathers, so that I will not come and smite the land with a curse.
>
> —MAL. 4:5-6, NASB 95

God cares about the bonding of fathers and children, and His servants ought to share this commitment. The recovery of fatherhood in the church, home, and society should not simply be ceded to social scientists or Dr. James Dobson; rather, it must be central to the strategic agenda of the church as she witnesses to the Father, Son, and Holy Spirit.

What is fatherhood, and why does it matter? The subject is inexhaustible, but let's focus on two aspects of fatherhood—the fatherhood of God over all creation and that of pastors and elders in the church, the household of faith.

GOD THE FATHER, FROM WHOM ALL FATHERHOOD GETS ITS NAME

To get to the meaning and purpose of fatherhood, we must start with the fatherhood of God. Our Lord taught us to pray, "Our Father, who art in heaven . . ."

When we address God as "Father," we are confessing that He is the archetypal father and has imprinted His fatherhood on all creation. This is the significance of the apostle Paul writing, "For this reason I kneel before the Father [*pater*], from whom all fatherhood [*patria*] in heaven and on earth derives its name" (Eph. 3:14-15, NIV marginal reading).

Note that God does not get the name father from earth, but earth gets the name father from heaven. The late F. F. Bruce wrote, "God is the archetypal Father; all other fatherhood is a more or less imperfect copy of his perfect fatherhood."[2]

A decade ago Carl F. H. Henry was asked what doctrine he thought most merited the attention of young evangelical theologians. He answered, "First, the doctrine of God. Evangelical theology tends to treat the doctrine of God devotionally. That in itself is certainly not to be disparaged—but it does so to the neglect of the intellectual significance of the doctrine in the contemporary conflict of ideas."[3]

Nowhere is this more evident than with this doctrine of the fatherhood of God. We pray, "Our heavenly Father," we meditate on the privilege of sonship shared by all those God has adopted, we preach on the sacrifice of love made by the Father when He sent His only begotten Son to die for sinful man, but our focus on God's fatherhood rarely goes beyond personal devotion. We would be hard-pressed to describe its meaning and significance, let alone defend it, as the war over sexuality rages around us.

At the center of today's battles over sexuality is the nature of manhood and womanhood, but Christian leaders seem blind to the fact that the doctrine of the fatherhood of God and the doctrine of man stand or fall together. Bible translators are quick to reassure us that no changes have been made to the fatherhood of God and the sonship of Jesus Christ in their latest Bible, but some translations have cut out the male marking of hundreds of texts, deleting the manifestation of God's fatherhood in the life of man.

The language of fatherhood is not merely an expendable human habit. This language is God's decree, rooted in His very nature and therefore universally binding on His creation. David Lyle Jeffrey comments:

> In *theological* terms . . . 'God the Father' is not really a metaphor at all—at least not in the minds of the writers of Scripture or early interpreters in Christian tradition. . . . As Jaroslav Pelikan puts it: "Using the name Father for God was *not* . . . a figure of speech. It was only because God was the Father of the Logos-Son that the term father could also be applied to human parents, and when it was used of them it *was* a figure of speech." (emphases in the original.)[4]

Similarly, John Calvin writes: "It is customary . . . for God's names to be transferred to creatures insofar as he exerts his power in them. Thus he himself is alone Lord and Father, but they are also called fathers and lords whom he dignifies with this honor."[5] And Hendrikus Berkhof adds: "When certain concepts are ascribed to God, they are thus not used figuratively but in their first and most original sense. God is not 'as it were' a father; he is the Father from whom all fatherhood on earth is derived."[6]

What glory, that we have been granted the privilege of approaching the living God in prayer: "Our Father, who art in heaven!"

We forget what a terrible gulf has been bridged for us by our Lord, who gives to all those who believe in Him the power to become the sons of God. But that gulf comes into focus when we stop to consider, for instance, the world of Islam. Were we to overlook Islam's idolatry and claim that Allah is the God of Abraham, Isaac, and Jacob, an exchange at an ecumenical gathering of over 100,000 held in Berlin, West Germany, back in 1989, would be a rude awakening.

One of the Protestant leaders, Professor Antony Wessels of Amsterdam, called for a spirit of unity between all religions: "I hope we are all Moslems and live in submission to the one God. And I hope we are all Christians and follow Jesus."

There was no such blurring of the nature of the Islamic and Christian God, though, on the part of the invited Islamic participant, theologian Nigar Yadim, who announced that she opposes mixing religions: "I cannot pray Christianity's Lord's Prayer, because Islam does not think of God as Father."[7]

The fatherhood of God is a peculiarly Christian understanding, revealed from heaven and given as comfort to those who believe in the Father's only begotten Son. How precious a truth this is to all believers, particularly those who have never known any benevolent manifestation of fatherhood in their own human families. Christians ought to rejoice in our freedom to know God as Father; we ought to fight for the protection of this divine trait and all its manifestations in the language of Scripture, worship, and life. Many forces are aligned against its beauty; we must study those forces and oppose them in the power of the Holy Spirit, realizing that this battle is just one more area where the feminist heresy lays siege to God's truth.

We must also, though, work to present to the world living fatherhood that points to God Himself. There are many places where such fatherhood may be demonstrated, but for sons and daughters robbed of it in their own childhood, it is most important that it be restored within "the household of God, which is the church of the living God" (1 Tim. 3:15, NASB 95).

FATHERHOOD WITHIN THE HOUSEHOLD OF FAITH

Some years back I began a sermon series on the Ten Commandments and, coming to the fifth commandment, "Honor thy father and mother," as was my habit, I turned to Thomas Watson's exposition and read, "the king . . . is a political father. [And] these fathers are to be honored."[8]

Sitting there at my desk, worlds exploded as I thought of the implications of this simple truth: Kings, presidents, governors, judges, law enforcement officers, mayors, principals, teachers, and professors bear the image of God's fatherhood. Elders and pastors are fathers after their heavenly Father and are to demonstrate His character as they shepherd His flock. Thus Question 124 of the *Westminster Larger Catechism* reads:

> Question: Who are meant by 'father' and 'mother' in the fifth commandment?
>
> Answer: By 'father' and 'mother,' in the fifth commandment, are meant, not only natural parents, but all superiors in age and gifts; and especially such as, by God's ordinance, are over us in place of authority, whether in family, church, or commonwealth.

It is this understanding of the paternal nature of the eldership upon which the apostle Paul bases his intimate family appeal to the church in Thessalonica:

> *You know how we were exhorting and encouraging and imploring each one of you as a father would his own children, so that you would walk in a manner worthy of the God who calls you into His own kingdom and glory.*
>
> —1 THESS. 2:11-12, NASB 95

God has provided for every one of His children's needs, including their need of flesh-and-blood fathers who will make visible to them some small portion of the perfections of their heavenly Father. Such fathering is a critical part of the ministry of the Word and Sacrament, but also of the eldership.

Since the earliest days of the wilderness wanderings of the sons of Israel, when Moses, following the counsel of his father-in-law, Jethro, appointed elders over every group of ten (Exod. 18:13-27), to the apostolic age when the apostles appointed elders over the church in each city (Titus 1:5), those who belong to God are settled in the household of faith, where their heavenly Father has provided them spiritual fathers; and those fathers have the wonderful privilege of ministering to their spiritual children.

The apostle Paul ministered in this way to the members of the Corinthian church, referring to them as his "children" and to himself as their "father":

> *I do not write these things to shame you, but to admonish you as my beloved children. For if you were to have countless tutors in Christ, yet you would not have many fathers, for in Christ Jesus I became your father through the gospel.*
> —1 COR. 4:14-15, NASB 95

Fatherless Timothy (likely the son of an unbelieving father)[9] also received such ministry. Adopted by God, he was placed in the household of faith under the care of the apostle Paul who corrected, rebuked, encouraged, and loved him as a father does his son, tenderly referring to Timothy as his "beloved and faithful child in the Lord" (1 Cor. 4:17, NASB 95).

Still today, every believer is given the gift of membership in this same household, where he or she is granted the privilege of receiving fatherly care from pastors and elders, and it is the calling of those ordained to these offices[10] to study this aspect of our work.

While reading Charles Eastman's autobiographical account of his American Indian childhood recently, it struck me that across culture and time children copy parents and sons copy fathers and elders:

> What boy would not be an Indian for a while when he thinks of the freest life in the world? This life was mine. Every day there was a real hunt. There was real game. Occasionally there was a medicine dance away off in the woods where no one could disturb us, in which the boys impersonated their elders, Brave Bull, Standing Elk, High Hawk, Medicine Bear, and the rest. They painted themselves and imitated their fathers and grandfathers to the minutest detail, and accurately too, because they had seen the real thing all their lives.
>
> We were not only good mimics, but we were close students of nature. We studied the habits of animals just as you study your books. We watched the men of our people and represented them in our play, then learned to emulate them in our lives.[11]

Our sports were molded by the life and the customs of our people; indeed, we practiced only what we expected to do when grown. Our games were feats with the bow and the arrow, foot and pony races, wrestling, swimming, and imitation of the customs and habits of our fathers.[12]

According to the *Westminster Larger Catechism*, the fifth commandment requires of the child "imitation of [his parents'] virtues and graces."[13] The New Testament records similar imitation. For instance, the apostle Paul writes, "You know how I lived the whole time I was with you," and "I urge you to imitate me" (Acts 20:18, NIV; 1 Cor. 4:16, NIV). And the Hebrews are commanded, "Remember your leaders, who spoke the Word of God to you. Consider the outcome of their way of life and imitate their faith" (Heb. 13:7, NIV).

Combine these statements with Eastman's account of his childhood, and we begin to have a picture of the work of pastors and elders rarely considered or taught; namely, whether or not we are aware or plan for it, we will be an assembly line for character, filling in for absentee fathers and producing sons of our own who someday will themselves be fathers. And although to our untrained ears it seems impious to talk about imitating anyone other than Christ, those of us called to be pastors and elders (this applies to older women too[14]) must be conscientious in this work.

Recognizing that the choice is somewhat arbitrary, let's focus on two aspects of fatherhood that are of critical importance: discipline and tender affection.

DISCIPLINE

If we return to the men mentioned at the beginning of the chapter and probe more deeply into their heartsickness, we will find that their fathers failed to provide their sons with proper discipline. This is not to say their fathers never spanked, punched, yelled at, mocked, or belittled them, but that any punishment their sons received was a product of their father's irritation and anger rather than an effort to form the son's character. It might even be that the father was completely passive, neither raising his voice nor bullying his son, but allowing the young man perfect freedom to develop willy-nilly, as he chose.

What can be said about such a son? By the authority of the Word of God we must acknowledge that this son is not loved by his father:

> *In your struggle against sin, you have not yet resisted to the point of shedding your blood. And you have forgotten that word of encouragement that addresses you as sons: "My son, do not make light of the Lord's discipline, and do not lose heart when he rebukes you, because the Lord disciplines those he loves, and he punishes everyone he accepts as a son." Endure hardship as discipline; God is treating you as sons. For what son is not disciplined by his father? If you are not disciplined (and everyone undergoes discipline), then you are illegitimate children and not true sons. Moreover, we have all had human fathers who disciplined us and we respected them for it. How much more should we submit to the Father of our spirits and live! Our fathers disciplined us for a little while as they thought best; but God disciplines us for our good, that we may share in his holiness.*
>
> —HEB. 12:4-10, NIV

Were I to speak to pastors and elders about nothing else, I would be content with impressing upon them the crucial witness of loving, firm discipline within the Body of Christ, carried out by men who themselves have known, and welcomed, the loving discipline of their heavenly Father.

There is a book in this, but let me simply hit the basic themes. In Acts 20 we read the apostle Paul's farewell charge to the Ephesian elders. There Paul characterizes his own work among the flock at Ephesus as follows: he "serv[ed] the Lord . . . with tears and with trials"; he "did not shrink from declaring to [them] anything that was profitable, and teaching [them] publicly and from house to house"; he spoke of "repentance toward God"; and "night and day for a period of three years [he] did not cease to admonish each one with tears." Then summing up his work, he makes this stunning claim: "I testify to you this day that I am innocent of the blood of all men" (Acts 20:17-31, NASB 95).

Honestly, who among us could think of making such a claim—
that we have no bloodguilt because we have been faithful shepherds
warning our sheep house to house, day and night, with tears? Yes, the
apostle Paul is quite popular among Bible-believing Christians today;
he is our *alma mater*, feeding us the great doctrines of the church. But
while our shelves groan with the weight of theological treatises exam-
ining almost every aspect of his work, one aspect of that work is
neglected—fatherly discipline.

Why this neglect? Is it because we are trying to demonstrate the
doctrines of grace in our pastoral relationships; is it because we are
seeking to lead our flock to the one who is meek and gentle of heart,
in whom we shall find rest for our souls?

No. Rather, I fear that too often our talk of grace and a parallel
neglect of discipline are the products of our aversion to conflict, our
fear of a drop in attendance and giving, and our dread of dismissal.
Richard Baxter understood pastors when, back in 1656, he first published his classic work *The Reformed Pastor*. Concerning pastors' neglect
of discipline, he wrote:

> It is a sad case, that good men should settle themselves so long
> in the constant neglect of so great a duty. The common cry is,
> "Our people are not ready for it; they will not bear it." But is
> not the fact rather, that you will not bear the trouble and hatred
> which it will occasion?[15]

Pity the home and church where fathers, finding in their hearts
no love for their sons, cast them off without benefit of discipline. And
pity the sons who grow up yearning for this proof of their sonship.

Fifteen years ago God taught me a lesson about the connection
between discipline and father hunger, and that lesson has since been
a cornerstone of my work. At the time I was the pastor of a yoked
parish serving two congregations eight miles apart, one in a small town
and one out in the country, sandwiched between dairy farms just off
the right-of-way of the state highway. The country church had for
years been keeping on its membership rolls families that never

attended church, except maybe an occasional Easter morning or Christmas Eve.

Sensing our biblical responsibility to go house to house warning these souls, the elders undertook their duty with fear and trembling. Splitting up the names and families, we started to visit each home. With diligence we worked through the list, speaking to each person about his soul and inquiring whether something or someone within our congregational life had offended him, causing him to stop attending. Before leaving, we read a fitting portion of Scripture and prayed for the family, but also made it clear that we expected to see him in church in the weeks to come.

Certainly none of us involved in this work would claim that we did our visits perfectly. Our word choice wasn't always the best, and we failed to demonstrate the depth of love that Christ showed to His own disciples. As we did our work, we were jars of clay, but jars of clay seeking to be faithful in all our responsibilities—not just the easy ones. And so we set out to discipline our flock, including those who felt that having their names on the roll of a Christian church and returning to that church each time they had babies to be baptized, sons and daughters to be married, and grandmothers and grandfathers to be buried was the normal Christian life and guaranteed their soul's eternal protection.

The results were predictable. Immediately some souls returned to the sheepfold, where they were greeted with joy. Others needed another push, six months to a year later, before they returned. Some returned at first but then became sporadic in their attendance and were visited again and again; the spirit was willing, but the body was weak. Some cursed us and began gossiping in the community, lying about what had been said and how it had been said.

When some who heard this gossip called the elders, those elders explained that none of us wanted to see these persons leave the church; in fact, just the opposite—we were trying to restore them to our fellowship. We commended our consciences to every man as we had occasion, reminding the congregation of their membership vows and their duty to keep those vows. We went back to the offended parties, delicately trying again to explain our concern over their souls and our desire that they return to the fold. But with a number of those offended, it was to no avail.

After several years of pursuing this work, the time came to remove the names of ten or fifteen people from the list of active members. The authority for this lay within the board of elders, but one family decided to come to the annual meeting that year and publicly oppose the elders' action.

The day arrived and, following our potluck meal, I called the meeting to order, and we proceeded through our agenda. Eventually it was time for our clerk of session to report on our membership, and the battle was joined. Using every tactic at hand, the offended family stood and fought, accusing the elders of being unchristian, unloving, hypocritical, judgmental, and even un-American. With meekness and humility, though, the clerk of session (speaking for all the elders) held his ground.

Two things came of this, one predictable and the other astounding. Predictably, a number of people left the church. We knew this was a probable consequence of our work, but we still found it painful. As our overall attendance declined, though, one subgroup began to grow until its presence within the church was the most noticeable thing about our fellowship. Each Sunday morning, halfway back on the left side of the church, young men between the ages of fifteen and twenty-five began to fill up a row and a half of pews.

It was stunning, really, since a number of these men had not been raised in the church. We noticed their presence and began to talk about it, trying to figure out why they were there. Yes, we had a vital youth ministry that extended beyond our own congregation to the youth of a number of community churches, but that had been going on for several years and couldn't be the whole story. And yes, we had a family in our fellowship that lived in a nearby town and ministered to the young people of that town, inviting them into their home and around their table; but again, that had been going on for some time and couldn't be more than a small part of the explanation.

Then it hit us: These young men started coming after the infamous congregational meeting. They had heard about the fathers of the church disciplining their congregation, and the father hunger in them led them to a congregation where there were real men showing faithfulness in discipline, even at significant personal cost.

Watch *Hoosiers*, my state's favorite movie, and you will see this same theme: As the coach restores discipline to his basketball team, the townspeople gnash their teeth, but the players fall in love with their coach and begin to win. So when a vote is taken to fire the coach, the players defend him and he stays on. As we watched the movie, my daughter observed that the coach as father is at the center of the sports movie genre.

The purpose of the story of the membership rolls is not to argue that elders across the country ought to go and do likewise. There are many different forms of polity within our congregations, and disciplinary action appropriate in one church may well be inappropriate in another. Rather, I tell this story as a testimony to the power of God to use sinful men who are willing to be obedient to their duty to discipline God's flock. Ezekiel records the warning God gave him as a prophet, and that same warning has direct application to the work of pastors and elders today:

> *Son of man, I have appointed you a watchman to the house of Israel; whenever you hear a word from My mouth, warn them from Me. When I say to the wicked, "You will surely die," and you do not warn him or speak out to warn the wicked from the wicked way that he may live, that wicked man shall die in his iniquity, but his blood I will require at your hand. Yet if you have warned the wicked and he does not turn from his wickedness or from his wicked way, he shall die in his iniquity; but you have delivered yourself.*
> —EZEK. 3:17-19, NASB 95

Is it not God Himself who has taught us the disciplinary nature of true fatherly love, and has not His discipline proven to us that we are His adopted sons? And what about Paul; did he not exhort the Ephesian elders to be faithful in discipline?

Be on guard for yourselves and for all the flock, among which the Holy Spirit has made you overseers, to shepherd the church of God which He purchased with His own blood. I know that after my departure savage wolves will come in among you, not sparing the flock; and from among your own selves men will arise, speaking perverse things, to draw away the disciples after them. Therefore be on the alert, remembering that night and day for a period of three years I did not cease to admonish each one with tears.

—ACTS 20:28-31, NASB 95

Why then is there such an oppressive silence in our seminaries, bookstores, pulpits, and church boardrooms on this subject of discipline? Can it be that Christians have evolved to the point that we no longer need this proof of our heavenly Father's love?

If we ourselves have had the privilege of knowing the disciplinary love of God, let us reclaim that same ministry of discipline for our flocks, giving ourselves wholeheartedly to this duty. And let us trust that God's servants doing God's work using God's tools will never lack God's blessing and protection.

TENDER AFFECTION

As the men mentioned at the beginning of the chapter lacked their fathers' discipline, so also their fathers failed to nurture them with tender affection.

This is not to say their fathers never tucked them in at night or gave them a playful jab on the shoulder, but rather that as these sons grew they never had the privilege of burrowing into the fertile black soil of clear outward demonstrations of affection—the kind of thing that every son is mortified to see other fathers doing, but wishes his own father would give him.

Back in the mid-eighties, my father was speaking at a chapel service at Wheaton College. In passing, he mentioned his conviction that college students wanted their fathers to hug and kiss them. To his surprise, the comment provoked a standing ovation.

Happily, my father practiced what he preached. He was a frequent traveler, and how distinctly I remember meeting him in the middle of the concourse at O'Hare, throwing our arms around each other and kissing in front of hundreds of starched shirts and suits. And, standing there in my father's loving embrace, I confess sometimes I thought, *Eat your hearts out, men; I love my dad, and my dad loves me.*

American men are so stingy with their affection, robbing their sons of the warmth of human fatherly contact so necessary to their sons' emotional well-being. But this is not the way of Scripture.

Look into the Bible and see how its pages are filled with emotion—with tears, affection, and love. See Joseph as he falls on Jacob's shoulders crying tears of joy upon his reunion with his father (Gen. 46:29-30). See Jesus as He weeps at the grave of His dear friend, Lazarus (John 11:35); see Him again as He receives (and defends) the tearful and unseemly ministrations of the sinful woman at the home of Simon the Pharisee (Luke 7:36-50); see Him as He pleads with the three beloved disciples to stay awake, to watch and pray with Him as his hour draws near (Matt. 26:36-46). See Paul as he bids the Ephesian elders a final farewell on the beach at Miletus. We read that after giving them their charge, Paul "knelt down and prayed with them all. And they began to weep aloud and embraced Paul, and repeatedly kissed him, grieving especially over the word which he had spoken, that they would not see his face again. And they were accompanying him to the ship" (Acts 20:36-38, NASB 95).

On this scene, John Calvin comments:

> When the Spirit . . . commends their tears . . . he is condemning the thoughtlessness of those who demand from believers an iron and inhuman firmness. For they falsely suppose that the feelings, which God has implanted in us as natural, proceed only from a defect. Accordingly the perfecting of believers does not depend on their casting off all feelings, but on their yielding to them and controlling them, only for proper reasons.[16]

What signs of tender affection do our congregations see passing between their pastor and elders? Would there ever be an occasion when they might see a scene in our own church foyers or parking lots similar to the scene of Paul's departure from the Ephesian elders?

Somehow the church has been misled into denying the legitimacy of feelings and emotions. What then are we to do with the record left for us in the New Testament of the tender affection that permeated the apostolic church? Speaking to Timothy, his son in the faith, Paul writes: "I thank God . . . as I constantly remember you in my prayers night and day, longing to see you, even as I recall your tears, so that I may be filled with joy" (2 Tim. 1:3-4, NASB 95).

Fatherhood proves itself through discipline and tender affection, and sons of the church who have grown up in harsh and loveless homes lacking discipline will respond to spiritual fathers who correct, rebuke, and encourage them with tenderness and love.

In celebration of Father's Day 2002, *The New Yorker* carried an autobiographical essay by the actor Steve Martin that began:

> In his death, my father, Glenn Vernon Martin, did something he could not do in life. He brought our family together.
>
> After he died, at the age of eighty-three, many of his friends told me how much they loved him—how generous he was, how outgoing, how funny, how caring. I was surprised at these descriptions. I remember him as angry. There was little said to me, that I recall, that was not criticism. During my teen-age years, we hardly spoke except in one-way arguments—from him to me. I am sure that the number of words that passed between us could be counted. At some point in my preteens, I decided to officially "hate" him. When he came into a room, I would wait five minutes, then leave. . . .
>
> Generally . . . my father was critical of my show-business accomplishments. Even after I won an Emmy at twenty-three as a writer for "The Smothers Brothers Comedy Hour," he advised me to finish college so that I'd have something to fall back on. Years later, my friends and I took him to the premiere of my first movie, "The Jerk," and afterward we went to dinner. For a long time, he said nothing. My friends noted his silence and were horrified. Finally, one friend said, "What did you think of Steve in the movie?" And my father said, "Well, he's no Charlie Chaplin."[17]

Picture Martin (or millions of young men like him) walking through the doors of the church and finding in her fellowship the fatherhood of God in all its beauty, lived out by older men ready to give the encouragement and affection Martin's father lacked the strength to provide.

In the congregation I lead, located in the shadow of a research university, we've decided that one of our mission priorities will be to invest ourselves in raising up, training, and sending out church leaders, both men and women. The repercussions are large in terms of time and money, and the work is often daunting, but we've never regretted this commitment.

Over the years scores of women and men have left this fellowship ready to be spiritual mothers and fathers themselves. And though it's painful when they leave, immediately a new crop of young souls springs up hungry for the fatherhood of God. So we return to our simple commitments: early-morning and late-evening discipleship groups, students around our dining room tables and flopped on our living room floors, young men preaching in our evening services . . . Only God knows the full extent of the harvest this work has produced.

CONCLUSION

But those willing to give themselves to this work must not be naive. There are some in our congregations who, due to the destructive influence of their own father, stepfather, professor, pastor, or priest, have been hardened in their hatred of fatherhood. But fatherhood has never been for the timid. It's been said, "There's only one adventurer in the world . . . the father of a family. Even the most desperate adventurers are nothing compared with him."[18] Under the guise of pastoral sensitivity, pastoral leaders will be tempted to make concessions to the spirit of our age, but our courage must not fail.

The center of our culture's sexual anarchy is a rebellion against the fatherhood of God, but those who would come to God and worship him as He is, rather than as they wish He might be, must meet and embrace His fatherhood liturgically, confessionally, and ecclesiastically. To refuse to worship him as Father, Son, and Holy Spirit is idolatry.[19]

Thus the faithful shepherd will lead the sheep in his flock to confess, with all Christians everywhere, "I believe in God the Father Almighty." And having led this confession, he will work hard to discipline and love his sheep to the end so they will come to grow in their love for the Father from whom all fatherhood gets its name. Father hunger presents Christians with a wonderful opportunity to testify that fatherhood is, indeed, at the "world's great core." May we confess this, our faith, with sensitivity and courage, refusing to turn away in shame.

1. From the unpublished, handwritten dedication of MacDonald's first book, *Within and Without*, to his father, in 1857.
2. "Ephesians 3:14 probably means that God is 'the Father [*pater*] from whom every fatherhood [*patria*] in heaven and on earth is named' . . . every *patria* is so named after the *pater*." Colin Brown, ed., *The New International Dictionary of New Testament Theology*, 3 vols. (Grand Rapids, MI: Zondervan, 1976), s.v. "Name," by Frederick Fyvie Bruce, 2:655.
3. "Interview of Carl F. H. Henry," *Theological Student's Fellowship Bulletin*, March-April 1987, 16-19.
4. David Lyle Jeffrey, "Inclusivity and Our Language of Worship," *Reformed Journal*, August 1987.
5. Commentary on Colossians 1:16.
6. As quoted in Donald G. Bloesch, *The Battle for the Trinity: The Debate over Inclusive God-Language* (Ann Arbor, MI: Servant, 1985), 25.
7. Harold O.J. Brown, *The Religion and Society Report*, August 1989, Vol. 6, No. 8, 3.
8. Thomas Watson, *The Ten Commandments* (Carlisle, PA: Banner of Truth, repr. 1981), 122.
9. "For I am mindful of the sincere faith within you, which first dwelt in your grandmother Lois and your mother Eunice, and I am sure that it is in you as well" (1 Tim. 1:5).
10. Baptists and congregationalists might have a similar understanding of the office of deacon.
11. Charles Alexander Eastman, *From the Deep Woods to Civilization Including Excerpts from Indian Boyhood* (Chicago: R. R. Donnelley and Sons [Lakeside Press], 2001), 7.
12. Ibid., 43.
13. *Westminster Larger Catechism*, Question 127; thank you, Phil Henry.
14. Titus 2:3-5 indicates the responsibility of older women to teach younger women in the Church.
15. Richard Baxter, *The Reformed Pastor* (Carlisle, PA: Banner of Truth, 1974), 47.

16. Commentary on Acts 20:37.
17. Steve Martin, "The Death of My Father," *The New Yorker*, June 17 and 24, 2002, 84.
18. Charles Peguy, as quoted by James Bemis, *The Wanderer,* June 6, 2002.
19. For a helpful discussion of the confessional nature of speaking of God as Father, see Donald G. Bloesch, The *Battle for the Trinity: The Debate over Inclusive God-Language.*

8

THE MARRIAGE CEREMONY: A CORNERSTONE IN BUILDING GODLY FAMILIES

Timothy B. Bayly

⸻⸗⸻

Recently Miss Manners took pastors to task for a lackadaisical approach to wedding ceremonies:

> In a house of worship, which figure represents the higher authority—the presiding member of the clergy or the wedding coordinator?
>
> Miss Manners would not have thought this to be a particularly thorny protocol question. She would be mistaken. Everyone gets the answer wrong.
>
> The wedding coordinator, whether she is in the business professionally or for the purpose of being married, thinks it is she. And if the clerics don't actually voice agreement, an amazing number of them behave as if they regretfully believe this to be the case.
>
> "There's nothing we can do," they wail when admitting that some of the arrangements strike them as being undignified, if not sacrilegious. "That's what people want nowadays."
>
> Well, sure. People want to commit all kinds of sins, not just against etiquette, but that doesn't mean that the clergy must condone it. They themselves may be tempted to do the

wrong thing for the noble sake of accruing income or popu-
larity for their congregations, but they are supposed to resist
temptation. . . .[1]

Scripture presents us with few accounts of weddings in biblical
times. Yet consider what this record of the marriage of Rebekah and
Isaac says concerning Christian marriage:

> *Isaac went out to meditate in the field toward evening; and he lifted
> up his eyes and looked, and behold, camels were coming. Rebekah
> lifted up her eyes, and when she saw Isaac she dismounted from the
> camel. She said to the servant, "Who is that man walking in the field
> to meet us?" And the servant said, "He is my master." Then she took
> her veil and covered herself. The servant told Isaac all the things that
> he had done. Then Isaac brought her into his mother Sarah's tent,
> and he took Rebekah, and she became his wife, and he loved her;
> thus Isaac was comforted after his mother's death.*
>
> —GEN. 24:63-67, NASB 95

Commenting on this text, Matthew Henry wrote, "Rebekah
behaved herself very becomingly, when she met Isaac: understanding
who he was, she alighted off her camel, and took a veil, and covered
herself, in token of humility, modesty, and subjection."

Similarly Calvin wrote, "Moses also says that she took a veil:
which was a token of shame and modesty. For hence also, the Latin
word which signifies to marry, is derived, because it was the custom
to give brides veiled to their husbands. That the same rite was also
observed by the fathers, I have no doubt. So much the more shame-
ful, and the less capable of excuse, is the licentiousness of our own age;
in which the apparel of brides seems to be purposely contrived for the
subversion of all modesty."[2]

What a contrast to our own wedding culture in which brides seem
to compete with one another for the dubious honor of having the
largest bridal party, the lowest-cut bodice, or the cutest flower girl. I
remember the day I stood in my living room laughing at the sight of
a stretch limousine getting a jump start from an old trashy Pinto
parked nose to nose in the church driveway; what pastor does not feel

the need for relief from the conspicuous consumption that overwhelms our weddings?

And yet if the spiritual graces of modesty, submission, and fidelity are missing from our ceremonies, we have no one to blame but ourselves. Pastors must reckon with the fact that we are responsible for the abandonment of those timeless elements of wedding liturgies that led the bride and groom, their families, and all those assembled to think sober thoughts about God's commands concerning marriage and to plead for His grace to fulfill those commands. In such a climate, is it any wonder so many of our marriages end in dissolution?

The wisdom that God gave the church in past centuries can help us regarding marriage ceremonies today. For hundreds of years pastors have presided over wedding ceremonies in such a way that the God who instituted marriage was honored and His Word proclaimed. Great care was taken to "tie the knot" with precision, and nothing was left to chance. By their habituation to the words of the liturgy, each successive generation was reminded of God's timeless truths governing this union of man and wife.

Let us examine parts of the wedding ceremony most frequently used across the English-speaking world for almost five centuries now. This ceremony was assembled from several sources, including the thirteenth-century Sarum Rite, by Anglican Archbishop Thomas Cranmer.[3] First published in 1549 in the *Book of Common Prayer*, the ceremony's content finds an echo in Baptist service books as well as in the truncated garden ceremonies that are a staple of Hollywood movies.

THE FORM OF SOLEMNIZATION OF MATRIMONY[4]

Instructions: First the banns ("banns" were public announcements of intended marriages) must be published three Sundays, during the time of the morning or evening service, the people being present, after the accustomed manner. And if the persons that would be married dwell in different parishes, the banns must be published in both parishes, and the Curate of the one parish shall not solemnize matrimony between them, without a certificate of the banns being three times pub-

lished by the Curate of the other parish also. At the day
appointed for Solemnization of Matrimony, the persons to be
married shall come into the body of the church, with their
friends and neighbors. And there the priest shall thus say . . .

Place and Time

It is clearly stated at the beginning that this wedding is not secret or
clandestine; the bride and groom will take their vows with both God
and the assembled congregation as their witnesses, and future viola-
tions of those vows will carry the weight of condemnation those witnesses imply. In fact, Malachi 2:14 reminds us that "the Lord was
witness" in the marriage covenant "between you and the wife of your
youth."

However, throughout the Middle Ages, men and women sought
to avoid bringing their marital unions under public scrutiny. Entering
into secret matrimonial agreements or "clandestine" marriages for a
variety of reasons, some wanted to avoid the public scrutiny implied
by the reading of the banns, knowing their choice of spouse was forbidden by the laws of incest or consanguinity. Others sought to escape
accountability for past promises of marriage to a man or woman other
than their intended. Still others wished simply to avoid the expense of
throwing a large party for those in attendance.

Whatever the reason, both informal promises of marriage and
clandestine wedding ceremonies were the cause of endless conflict,
and both civil and ecclesiastical authorities did their best to bring such
practices to an end. Consider the following statement by John Donne
from a wedding sermon he preached in 1621: "As marriage is a civil
contract, it must be done so in public, as that it may have the testimony
of men. As marriage is a religious contract, it must be done so as it may
have the benediction of the priest. [Without public testimony and religious benediction it] is but regulated adultery, it is not marriage."[5]

A proper wedding was held only after the banns had been published three consecutive weeks within both communities where the
bride and groom resided, thus giving those knowing of any impediments to the marriage ample opportunity to come forward. If they had

missed these opportunities, the liturgy of the wedding itself provided them one final moment to speak or forever hold their peace.

There were pastors and priests who, for a fee, were willing to officiate at clandestine weddings. Larger cities like London offered such anonymity with clergy known to be accommodating. Even local clergy were known, at times and for a certain fee, to turn a blind eye to marriages early in the morning or late at night, away from the community's prying eyes; but they officiated at some risk to their position since clandestine weddings violated church law.

Weddings were public affairs, involving not simply the union of one man and one woman, but two extended families and their respective communities; the bride and groom were to wed in such a way as to assure the health and continuity, not just of their own home and immediate family, but also the church and civic community.

To this day there is no doubt that elopement produces a valid marriage, but at considerable risk to the future well-being of the married couple and their children. The bride and groom are intentionally avoiding the choreography surrounding wedding days, a large part of which is intended to assure the greatest chance of a harmonious union of two family systems and their respective communities. For all the jokes made at the expense of the mother of the bride, there will be no escaping her after the ceremony, and weddings present an excellent opportunity to work through the first tensions of this marriage in a context assuring the greatest possible success. Invitations have been sent out, gifts have been purchased, vacation dates have been altered; think of how embarrassing it would be to postpone or cancel the big event.

Demonstrating, again, that the wedding ceremony united whole communities and not only the groom and his bride, many of the early reformers (including Calvin, Knox, and the first Scottish *Book of Worship*) placed the wedding in the context of the corporate worship of the Lord's Day, just before the sermon.[6] So too, Cranmer begins the ceremony with the simple instruction that "the persons to be married shall come into the body of the church, with their friends and neighbors," and all things are done "in the sight of God, and in the face of his congregation."

Dearly beloved friends, we are gathered together here in the sight of God,
and in the face of his congregation, to join together this man and this
woman in holy matrimony, which is an honorable estate instituted of
God in paradise, in the time of man's innocency, signifying unto us the
mystical union that is between Christ and his Church: which holy estate,
Christ adorned and beautified with his presence and first miracle in
Cana of Galilee, and is commended of Saint Paul to be honorable
among all men: and therefore is not to be entered into, nor taken in hand
unadvisedly, lightly, or wantonly, to satisfy men's carnal lusts and
appetites, like brute beasts that have no understanding; but reverently,
discreetly, advisedly, soberly, and in the fear of God.

Words of Institution

As is common practice with baptism and the Lord's Supper, the wedding ceremony also begins with a recitation of the biblical precedents for this worship service, and in each case this biblical basis is referred to as the "words of institution." Although the Reformed fathers rejected the sacramental status claimed for marriage by the Roman Catholic Church, Protestant weddings continued to be held in church,[7] introduced by a short summary of marriage's scriptural warrant.

"Matrimony . . . is an honorable estate instituted of God in paradise, in the time of man's innocency." Thus it is part of God's perfect plan, not some second-rate compromise arising from the Fall. What an excellent theme to strike in a day when marriage is being redefined under civil law such that its permanence and heterosexuality are denied! By pointing the assembled congregation back to the institution of marriage in "paradise" when man was in his "innocency," we are reminded that marriage has from the beginning been heterosexual, and that all of marriage's attributes are binding across time because they are not products of sin but graceful gifts from the Father who sends "rain on the just and on the unjust" (Matt. 5:45, KJV).

Neither heterosexuality nor lifelong monogamy nor the headship of the husband are principles binding on God's covenant people alone; rather, having been instituted in the Garden of Eden, they are binding on all mankind. And although we certainly cannot expect those without the Spirit of God to demonstrate in their marriages the selfless and sacrificial love of Christ for His Church, we must not give in to efforts today to strip marriage of its constituent features ordained by God. The French poet Charles Peguy wrote, "We will never know how many acts of cowardice have been motivated by the fear of seeming not sufficiently progressive."[8]

Monogamous, lifelong, heterosexual, husband-led marriage is binding on all people and nations, and Christian judges, legislators, and citizens must work not only to protect these truths from the encroachments of civil law, but also to proclaim them unashamedly in the public square as faithful witnesses to our Lord and His truth.

Warning

By warning against the "carnal lust and appetites [of] brute beasts," the liturgy reminds those assembled that man bears God's image, and that this once-in-a-lifetime step of marriage is to be taken only with the greatest caution and in "the fear of God." There are times to remind Christians of the Father's authority and of the consequences of dealing lightly with His Law. Scripture warns us concerning the danger of taking vows lightly,[9] and marriage vows today need, again, to be taken in the context of Scripture's warning, "It is a fearful thing to fall into the hands of the living God" (Heb. 10:31, RSV).

Too many weddings held in evangelical churches are characterized more by flippancy, romanticism, and sentimentality than by the sobriety and reverence here commended. Certainly there is a time and place for joyous celebration, but anyone married for more than a few days recognizes how much those taking vows need to have impressed upon them the responsibilities and duties that, from this point forward, will be their constant companions. This worship service ought to be characterized by sober reminders of God's transcendent attributes and of our necessary dependence upon Him for faithfulness.

As the bride and groom recess, let the partying begin, and let it be every bit as warm and joyful as that wedding in Cana attended by our Lord. And while joy is present in the ceremony also, the principal note

struck there should be a holy reverence as we meditate on the nature
of the vows being taken. So let us fall on our knees before God,
acknowledging our sinfulness and pleading with Him to give us the
grace to obey what He commands.

> *Duly considering the causes for which matrimony was ordained.*
> *One cause was the procreation of children, to be brought up in the fear*
> *and nurture of the Lord, and praise of God. Secondly it was ordained*
> *for a remedy against sin, and to avoid fornication, that such persons as*
> *be married, might live chastely in matrimony, and keep themselves*
> *undefiled members of Christ's body. Thirdly for the mutual society,*
> *help, and comfort, that the one ought to have of the other,*
> *both in prosperity and adversity. Into which holy estate*
> *these two persons present come now to be joined.*

Three Purposes of Marriage

Part of a wise and reverent approach to marriage leads, here in the ceremony, to a recitation of God's intent for this institution. Historically,
the Church has recognized three purposes taught in Scripture, and
these purposes have appeared in Protestant statements of faith down
through the centuries. Here they are summarized by the *Westminster
Confession of Faith*:

> Marriage was ordained for the mutual help of husband and
> wife; for the increase of mankind with a legitimate issue, and
> of the Church with an holy seed; and for preventing of
> uncleanness.[10]

It's discouraging to see how many contemporary marriage ceremonies lack any statement of these purposes. In the past, one of these
purposes was occasionally left out of the liturgy, but this was not due
to any opposition to the biblical basis of that purpose; rather, certain
ecclesiastical leaders, squeamish about explicit references to sexuality,
left the "preventing of uncleanness" unstated.[11] But even then, no one
would have thought of leaving out of the liturgy all mention of the
purposes to which God ordained marriage. There is a different kind

of attack on the purposes of marriage today, and this attack seems to have staying power.

Back while serving as a pastor within the mainline Presbyterian Church (USA), I was studying our *Book of Confessions* and discovered that the *Westminster Confession's* chapter on marriage had been altered; in 1953, all reference to "the increase of mankind . . . and the Church with an holy seed" had been deleted.[12] Since making this discovery, I've often wondered whether our reluctance to rehearse the biblical purposes of marriage might not be tied up with our uneasiness over the place of fertility in God's plan for sexuality.

For decades Christians have been harangued for their purported belief that the only legitimate purpose of sexual intimacy is procreation, and many scholars have claimed that our church fathers believed sex to be dirty. Add to this the secular pressures to lower fertility in the face of the threat of overpopulation, and Christians have too often abandoned any mention of God's command given in the Garden of Eden, after the Flood to Noah, and later to Israel to "be fruitful and multiply."[13]

We need never be ashamed of God's truth, least of all in this area where man's wisdom has so clearly been disproved. It is widely acknowledged that the true threat facing the western world today is *under*population, and no one is ready to make a prediction exactly where and when the fertility rate will cease its precipitous decline.[14] A recent article in *The Atlantic Monthly* began with these words: "Fifty years from now the world's population will be declining, with no end in sight. . . . This view is coming to be widely accepted among population experts, even as the public continues to focus on the threat of uncontrolled population growth."[15]

It is God's good plan that sex not be thought of, principally, as a legitimate way to get a rush, but rather as God's way of bringing man and wife to the point of greatest unity and, through that unity, propagating (for Himself) "a godly seed" (Mal. 2:15, KJV). Thus fertility rightfully holds its own as one of the three purposes of marriage revealed in the Bible, and pastors cannot go wrong repeating each of these purposes during marriage ceremonies.

Therefore if any man can show any just cause why they
may not lawfully be joined so together: Let him now speak,
or else hereafter forever hold his peace.

And also speaking to the persons that shall be married, he shall say:

I require and charge you
(as you will answer at the dreadful day of judgment,
when the secrets of all hearts shall be disclosed)
that if either of you do know any impediment,
why ye may not be lawfully joined together in matrimony,
that ye confess it. For be ye well assured, that so many
as be coupled together otherwise than God's word doth allow:
are not joined of God, neither is their matrimony lawful.

At which day of marriage if any man does allege any impediment
why [the bride and groom] may not be coupled together in matrimony:
And will be bound, and sureties with him, to the parties,
or else put in a caution to the full value of such charges
as the persons to be married do thereby sustain
to prove his allegation: then the Solemnization must be deferred,
until such time as the truth be tried.[16]

Final Reading of the Banns

The pastor here gives one last opportunity for "impediments" to the marriage to be brought forward with the sober warning that, although such impediments may be hidden to the eye of man, God sees all, and any hidden matter—such as a prior private promise of marriage given to someone other than one's intended—will become clear on the "dreadful day of judgment, when the secrets of all hearts shall be disclosed."

Why is a similar warning not given today? Is it because fornication is absent from our congregations? Is it because young men and women no longer promise lifelong love as a prelude to their secret pleasures? Is it because promises no longer matter?

Regardless of the reason, as a pastor approaches the liturgy and sees these strange words that insert such an ominous and foreboding note into a happy day, it is the work of a moment to delete this from the order of worship, to everyone's intense relief. Who in their right mind actually expects a bride or groom to announce a prior covenant that prevents the taking of a new one? And who wishes on any bride the fate of Jane Eyre who, standing at the altar, finds out that her groom is already married?

From Hollywood's rather limited romantic perspective, this section of the liturgy has no purpose other than to give true love one last opportunity to speak or forever hold its peace. So at the conclusion of *While You Were Sleeping* we all breathed a sigh of relief when Sandra Bullock avoided a loveless marriage, marrying her true love instead.

Lest there be any confusion, though, the celebrant goes on to warn the congregation that any bride and groom joined "otherwise than God's word doth allow: are not joined of God, neither is their matrimony lawful." During either the rehearsal or wedding proper, it is my habit to add a simple explanation to this part of the liturgy, that no matter what the legislators and judges of any particular state or country have decreed, it is the law of God—not man—that is the final word concerning the legality of any marriage. In our day of no-fault divorce and homosexual "covenantal unions," a reminder that civil laws are subordinate to the laws of God is timely and wise.

If no impediment be alleged, then shall the Curate say unto the man:

N. Wilt thou have this woman to [be] thy wedded wife,
to live together after God's ordinance in the holy estate of matrimony?
Wilt thou love her, comfort her, honor, and keep her in sickness
and in health? And forsaking all others keep thee only to her,
so long as you both shall live?

The man shall answer:
I will.
Then shall the Curate say to the woman:

N. Wilt thou have this man to [be] thy wedded husband,
to live together after God's ordinance, in the holy estate of matrimony?
Wilt thou obey him, and serve him, love, honor, and keep him
in sickness and in health? And forsaking all others keep thee only
to him, so long as you both shall live?

The woman shall answer:
I will.

Declaration of Consent

It always seemed to me that vows are exchanged twice during the wedding liturgy; first, here where the bride and groom are asked whether they will have each other, then again a few minutes later. Why the duplication of promises?

Over the centuries weddings were seen to consist of three non-negotiable elements: parental approval, the free consent of the groom and bride to the impending marriage, and the giving and receiving of promises that finalized the marriage. Other elements were added and subtracted, as need be, but these three remained constant. Generally speaking, parental permission and the free consent of groom and bride were a function of the betrothal, whereas the giving and receiving of promises were the marriage proper, immediately following which the marriage was consummated.

It was between betrothal and marriage that, by the power of the Holy Spirit, the Virgin Mary conceived, and throughout the Middle Ages it was typical for betrothal to precede marriage by somewhere around twelve months. What has happened to the betrothal ceremony today?

It's been compressed into the wedding ceremony proper, taking the form of what we now refer to as the declaration of consent when the bride and groom are both asked whether they are entering into this marriage of their own free will, fully intending to tie the knot. The major difference between the declaration of consent and the vows proper is that the former is answered in the future tense, whereas the latter is answered in the present. In the first case the bride and groom respond, "I will," in the second, "I do."

Thus, until recently the process of the establishment of the consent of the parents to the coming marriage, as well as the man and woman contracting together to exchange vows at some future date, had been known as betrothal. More recently, though, betrothal has been broken down into two parts: first, engagement where the stakes are much lower than betrothal; and second, the declaration of consent that now is clamped onto the front end of the marriage ceremony itself.

Then shall the Minister say:
Who giveth this woman to be married to this man?

Transfer of Authority

There is evident irony in the continued asking of the question "Who gives this woman to be married to this man?" in weddings today, and although we think we've dealt with this archaism by the father replying, "Her mother and I do," the question itself runs cross-grain to our individualist, egalitarian ethos. After all, why should anyone give away the bride but not the groom?

As in many parts of the liturgy, here too past generations transfer to us their biblical understanding that father-rule is at the heart of the Christian home. Father Abraham sent his servant off to find a wife for his son, Isaac, and the law of Moses decreed that fathers and husbands had veto power over the vows of their daughters and wives (see Num. 30:1-9).

Such laws made it impossible for a daughter to contract her own marriage against her father's will, and still to this day when a father gives his daughter's hand in marriage with the words, "Her mother and I do," whether consciously or not, he is illustrating to the assembled congregation his biblical headship. From this moment on the father's authority is transferred to the new man in his daughter's life, her husband, who will be the "head"[17] of her new home.

Summing up the essential elements of Jewish marriage contracts from the fifth century B.C., John J. Collins writes, "The contract was formally an agreement between the groom and the person with authority over the bride . . . [and] marriage contracts were settled with the father or person in authority even when the bride was mature."[18] Similarly, during the Middle Ages, "The woman was 'given' in marriage by her father or by an adult male friend, in a silent but potent symbolic transfer of authority."[19] The Puritan divine Richard Greenham thought this part of the liturgy "a laudable custom in the church and a tolerable ceremony . . . both to show his authority over her and to witness his consent in bestowing her."[20]

While it may not pay to quibble over the wording of the transfer since, in a real sense, the mother of the bride is also relinquishing—indeed, must relinquish—her authority over her daughter from the time of the wedding on, it is worth calling attention to the bridal party that these words have biblical precedent and communicate important scriptural truths concerning both the necessity and nature of authority in the Christian home. And in this connection, has it not been heartening to all those with biblical commitments to see a renewal of the practice of men going to the father of their intended, requesting his daughter's hand in marriage even before securing the agreement of his beloved and placing a ring on her finger?

It's interesting to note that the Reformers commonly referred to the necessity of parental or "paternal" permission for marriage in their exposition of the fifth commandment. For instance, note this question addressed by Turretin under his exposition of the fifth commandment: "The question is can children shake off the subjection and obedience due to parents and withdraw themselves from paternal authority? . . . We deny it."[21]

And the minister receiving the woman at her father or friend's hands:
shall cause the man to take the woman by the right hand,
and so either to give their troth to [the] other:

The man first saying:

I N. take thee N. to [be] my wedded wife, to have and to hold
from this day forward, for better, for worse, for richer, for poorer,
in sickness, and in health, to love and to cherish, until death us do part:
according to God's holy ordinance: And thereto I plight thee my troth.[22]

Then shall they loose their hands, and the woman taking again
the man by the right hand shall say:

I N. take thee N. to [be] my wedded husband, to have and to hold
from this day forward, for better, for worse, for richer, for poorer,
in sickness, and in health, to love, cherish, and to obey,
till death us do part: according to God's holy ordinance:
And thereto I give thee my troth.

Exchange of Vows

The vows are the heart of the wedding, and here, if nowhere else, it's imperative that the bride and groom have a sense that they are not engaging in a romantic act in which creativity is of paramount significance, but are rather submitting themselves to the ages and walking in lockstep with those who have gone before. For a couple of decades now it has been in vogue for couples to write their own declarations of consent and vows, but such efforts pale in comparison to those bequeathed to us by Cranmer and his predecessors. Consider these promises taken from the weddings of celebrities:[23]

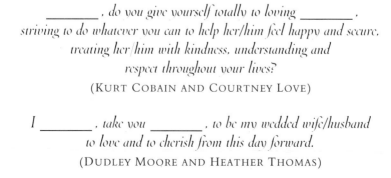

_____, do you give yourself totally to loving _____,
striving to do whatever you can to help her/him feel happy and secure,
treating her/him with kindness, understanding and
respect throughout your lives?
(KURT COBAIN AND COURTNEY LOVE)

I _____, take you _____, to be my wedded wife/husband
to love and to cherish from this day forward.
(DUDLEY MOORE AND HEATHER THOMAS)

I, _____ , take you _____ , for my lawful wife/husband,
from this day forward, to have and to hold, as equal partner in my life,
to whom I give my deepest love and respect.
I humbly open my heart to you as sanctuary of warmth and peace
where you may find a refuge of love and strength.
(Tom Selleck)

A couple of things may be said about these vows: They are lacking in gravity, and they are unisex—one size fits all. Although each one of us has expressed similar sentiments to our own husband or wife, they are understood to be more fitting for birthday and anniversary cards than the taking of matrimonial vows. Sure, we all want to "help our spouse feel happy and secure," to "treat him with kindness [and] respect" as our "equal partner," and to "open our heart" to him as a "sanctuary of warmth and peace," but such sentiment is woefully inadequate to keep the home fires burning through years of living with an alcoholic husband or a wife who has Alzheimer's.

No, at such times the meaning of the words "for better, for worse, for richer, for poorer, in sickness and in health . . . till death us do part" become clear, and nothing else will do.

Since our fathers had both been ordained to the pastoral ministry, my wife and I were pleased to ask them to co-officiate at our wedding ceremony. A day or so before the wedding, my father came to me privately and told me he expected us to promise publicly that we would never consider divorce as an option in our marriage. Then he added that if we were not willing to make this promise, he would withdraw from officiating at the wedding.

Immediately I went to Mary Lee and told her what Dad had said. She responded, "Well, of course we don't expect to get divorced, but who knows what's going to happen years from now?"

"Well," I responded, "unless we make the promise, he won't marry us."

That promise was made twenty-six years ago, and over the years we have repeated this story many times to couples in troubled marriages. We are so grateful that my father had the wisdom to require us to publicly promise lifelong fidelity, committing ourselves never even to consider divorce as an option. Like all marriages, ours has been through troubled times; but no matter how heated the arguments or how deep the moments of despair, because of our public promise we were free from any thoughts or threats of divorce. What stability it has given us to have this whole option simply removed from the table! (And may I add that marriage yields a good number of its greatest treasures only after the passing of decades—not five, ten, or even fifteen years.)

That Word "Obey"

Yet there remains a part of Cranmer's wedding liturgy that my father never mentioned, and that still to this day is rarely a part of even the most traditional services. I'm speaking of the insertion of the promise to "obey" that has, historically, differentiated the bride's declaration of consent and vows from those of the groom.

Ordained to the pastoral ministry in 1983, I had officiated at scores of weddings before I was aware of this differentiation. Then in 1995 I was going through the wedding service with a couple about to be married when the bride, having looked over the liturgy, asked me if I would object to adding a promise to her wedding vows—to obey her husband.

Caught flat-footed, I said I'd look into the matter, and so began my study of wedding liturgies. The more I read, the more I became convinced that there simply is no biblical justification for the removal of the word "obey" from the bride's declaration of consent and vows. Any summary of Scripture's teaching concerning the duty of the wife and husband, one to the other, must begin with the duty of the husband to "love" his wife and the duty of the wife to "obey" her husband.

For this reason Christian marriage rites down through history have contained vows for the bride that acknowledged her biblical duty to honor and obey her husband.

At the request of this godly young woman, I returned the promise to "obey" to its rightful place in my wedding liturgy, and to this day each marriage ceremony I preside over includes the word "obey" in the bride's vows.

Sermon

At the end of the liturgy, Cranmer includes a short summary of Scripture's teaching on marriage that the pastor is instructed to read aloud in the event that he has no other sermon prepared. Only six hundred words long, this homily does nothing other than to rehearse Scripture's teaching in Ephesians 5, Colossians 3, and 1 Peter 3 concerning the duty of husbands to love their wives and of wives to submit to their husbands. What a revolution there would be in the household of faith if pastors again proclaimed these biblical themes with equal simplicity! We ought to feel considerable remorse remembering how often we have exhorted husbands to love their wives while neglecting to mention the bride's concomitant biblical duty to "reverence," "submit to," and "obey" her husband.

CONCLUSION

Think of the explicit commands that Moses, speaking for God, gave the sons of Israel concerning their duty to carry on the Passover tradition. Each part of the observance was to be kept intact, but not silently and thoughtlessly; rather, each celebration and each ritual was to be accompanied by a full explanation of that tradition's significance passed on with great intentionality and discipline from father to daughter, father to son:

> *And you shall observe this event as an ordinance for you and your children forever. When you enter the land which the LORD will give you, as He has promised, you shall observe this rite. And when your children say to you, "What does this rite mean to you?" you shall say, "It is a Passover sacrifice to the LORD who passed over the houses of the sons of Israel in Egypt when He smote the Egyptians, but spared our homes."*
>
> —EXOD. 12:24-27A, NASB 95

Today how are we passing on the truths of God's Word related to the divine institution of marriage? Are we keeping the pattern of sound words concerning the solemnity of vows, the wickedness of divorce, the blessing of fertility and children, the duty to honor fathers and mothers, and the specific duties of husbands and wives?

Ask the man in the street what a pastor does, and he'll say, "Marrying, burying, and preaching." Ask the pastor in the street which of those duties he least enjoys, and he'll answer, "The marrying." I have two brothers who also are pastors, and my brother, David, has made a habit of asking groups of pastors what their least favorite task is. He reports that most of them answer, "Weddings."

Why? Because of broken homes; because of ostentation and pride; because of materialism; because of the focus on appearance rather than substance, on sentiment rather than truth; because of unrealistic expectations; because weddings are the place where, as much as any other aspect of pastoral ministry, we are asked to do things that infringe upon or violate our consciences; because even our preaching is not immune but suffers under the expectations that everything said during the ceremony will be entirely innocuous.

Yet the difficulty of the task does not excuse the worker from his duty. Given the full-scale assault within our culture against the principal doctrines at the center of this divine institution (fertility, heterosexuality, monogamy, and father-rule), is it any surprise that we pastors find this aspect of the work so dispiriting and perform our duties in such a lackluster manner?

We must recover a biblical understanding of marriage, renewing or reforming our wedding ceremonies in such a way that every part of this service aims at the mark of honoring and pleasing God—not man, or more likely the mother of the bride. Indicating the solemnity of this service in which vows are taken, Dietrich Bonhoeffer wrote:

> Your love is your own private possession, but marriage is more than something personal—it is a status, an office. Just as it is the crown, and not merely the rule, that makes the king, so it is marriage, and not merely your love for each other, that joins you together in the sight of God and man. It is not your love that sustains the marriage, but from now on, the marriage that sustains your love.[24]

God Himself decreed that it is not good for the man to be alone, and it was He who made woman from man's side, to be his helper and to be loved and cherished by him so long as they both shall live. If this love is to survive marriage's summers, but also its many winters, it must hark back to this hour when the bride and groom both had the honor and dignity, in the presence of God and many witnesses, to place themselves in the crucible of vows, the better to perform their duties. From that moment forward these lovers will remember that their primary accountability is not to themselves but to all those who witnessed their vows—and most particularly the One who decrees that what He has joined, no man may sever.

BIBLIOGRAPHY

Baldwin, Claude-Marie. "Marriage in Calvin's Sermons." In *Calviniana,* ed. Robert V. Schnucker. Vol. 10: *Sixteenth Century Essays and Studies.* Kirksville, MO: Sixteenth Century Journal Publishers, Inc., 1988, pp. 121-129.

Benes, Peter, ed. *Families and Children, The Dublin Seminar for New England Folklife Annual Proceedings 1985.* Boston: Boston University, 1987.

Clark, Gillian. *Women in Late Antiquity: Pagan and Christian Lifestyles.* Oxford: Clarendon Press, 1993.

Cressy, David. *Birth, Marriage, and Death: Ritual, Religion, and the Life Cycle in Tudor and Stuart England.* Oxford: Oxford University Press, 1997.

Daniel-Rops, Henri. *Daily Life in the Time of Jesus.* Ann Arbor, MI: Servant Books, 1962.

Davies, Horton. *The Worship of the English Puritans.* Westminster, England: Dacre Press: 1948; reprint, Morgan, PA: Soli Deo Gloria Publications, 1997.

Emmison, F. G. *Elizabethan Life: Morals and the Church Courts.* Chelmsford: Essex County Council, 1973.

Genevan Book of Order: The Form of Prayers and Ministration of the Sacraments, etc. used in the English Congregation at Geneva: and approved by the famous and godly learned man, Iohn Caluyn. Geneva:

1556. More commonly known as *John Knox's Genevan Service Book*.

Jeremias, Joachim. *Jerusalem in the Time of Jesus*. Philadelphia: Fortress Press, 1969.

Ovard, Mark. *Do-It-Yourself Ceremony Selections, Plus the Vows of the Stars!* Dallas-Fort Worth: DFWX.com, 1998. Available from http://www.dfwx.com/ 177selections.htm. Accessed December 18, 1999.

Stevenson, Kenneth. *Nuptial Blessing: A Study of Christian Marriage Rites*. New York: Oxford University Press, 1983.

Taylor, Denise. *Seventeenth Century Wedding Customs*. Living History Reference Books Series. Bristol, England: Stuart Press, 1997.

Thompson, Roger. *Sex in Middlesex: Popular Mores in a Massachusetts County, 1649-1699*. Amherst, MA: University of Massachusetts Press, 1986.

Turretin, Francis. *Institutes of Elenctic Theology*, 3 vols. Phillipsburg: Presbyterian and Reformed Publishing Company, 1994. 2:104-111.

"Form for the Confirmation of Marriage Before the Church," in *The Psalter with Doctrinal Standards, Liturgy, Church Order, and Added Chorale Section*. Grand Rapids, MI: William B. Eerdmans, 1999.

"The Directory for The Publick Worship of God," in *Westminster Confession of Faith*, 1646. Reprint, Glasgow: Free Presbyterian Publications, 1994.

1. Judith Martin, "In Church Weddings, Who's in Charge?" in *St. Louis Post Dispatch*, April 11, 2001.

2. "There is evidence . . . the veiling of the bride was part of the marriage ceremony. In Akkadian the bride on her wedding day is called *kallatu kutumtu*, 'the veiled bride.'" Nahum M. Sarna, *The JPS Torah Commentary: Genesis* (Philadelphia: The Jewish Publication Society, 1989), 170. Also, "Rebekah, as soon as she saw the man in the field coming to meet them, sprang from the camel to receive him, according to Oriental custom, in the most respectful manner." C. F. Keil and F. Delitzsch, *Commentary on the Old Testament*, 10 vols., Vol. 1: *The Pentateuch*, trans. J. Martin (three volumes reprinted in one) (Grand Rapids, MI: Eerdmans, 1973), 261.

3. See Kenneth Stevenson, *Nuptial Blessing: A Study of Christian Marriage Rites* (New York: Oxford University Press, 1983), 134-152.

4. The text is a compilation of texts from http://justus.anglican.org/resources/
   bcp/BCP1549.htm and http://www.recus.org/BCP/1662bcp.htm. For readability, words and spelling have been altered.

5. As quoted in David Cressy, *Birth, Marriage, and Death: Ritual, Religion, and the
   Life-Cycle in Tudor and Stuart England* (London: Oxford University Press,
   1997), 295.

6. Stevenson, *Nuptial Blessing*, 130.

7. A small number of Protestants sought to deny the church any role in weddings,
   but the overwhelming testimony of the church has been that it is proper for
   couples to repeat their vows within the Body of Christ, with a pastor officiating and asking for God's blessing. Cf. Horton Davies, *The Worship of the English
   Puritans* (Morgan, PA: Soli Deo Gloria Publications, 1997), passim, esp. 44-45,
   55.

8. As quoted by Joe Sobran in *SOBRAN'S—The Real News of the Month*, August
   2001, Vol. 8, No. 8.

9. "When you make a vow to the LORD your God, you shall not be slack to pay
   it; for the LORD your God will surely require it of you, and it would be sin in
   you. But if you refrain from vowing, it shall be no sin in you. You shall be careful to perform what has passed your lips, for you have voluntarily vowed to the
   LORD your God what you have promised with your mouth" (Deut. 23:21-23,
   RSV).

10. *Westminster Confession of Faith*, XIV:2.

11. Stevenson, *Nuptial Blessing*, 151-152.

12. In 1983, the breach between northern and southern Presbyterians caused by
    the Civil War was healed. The two branches reunited, taking the name
    "Presbyterian Church (USA)." One curiosity produced by that reunion was
    the new denomination's issuing a new *Book of Confessions* in which the
    Westminster Confession's chapter on marriage was broken into two parallel
    columns, one listing all three historic purposes for marriage, while the other
    column listed only two. It was the column inherited from the northern
    Presbyterians that lacked the purpose of procreation.

13. Genesis 1:22, 28; 8:17; 9:1, 7; 35:11.

14. "The British economist Thomas Malthus's prediction that population growth
    is bound to outrun food production, condemning societies to perpetual mis-
    ery and starvation, is much more than plain wrong. It has been an enduring
    source of error and self-bamboozlement for almost every day of the 201 years
    since the young Malthus hit on the idea." Nicholas Wade, "Why Malthus Was
    Mistaken," *New York Times*, September 19, 1999, WK5.

15. Max Singer, "The Population Surprise," *The Atlantic Monthly*, August 1999,
    22-25.

16. The one bringing forth the accusation against the legality of the marriage must
    be willing to bear the cost of postponement, should his appeal not be sustained.

17. For a helpful discussion of the significance of the Greek word translated
    "head" in Ephesians 5, see Wayne Grudem, "The Meaning of Kephale

("Head"): An Evaluation of New Evidence, Real and Alleged," in *Journal of the Evangelical Theological Society* 44 (2001), 25-65.

18. John J. Collins, "Marriage, Divorce, and Family in Second Temple Judaism," in *Families in Ancient Israel*, eds. Leo Purdue, Joseph Blenkinsopp, John Collins, and Carol Meyers (Louisville: Westminster John Knox, 1997), 108-109.
19. Cressey, *Birth, Marriage, and Death*, 337.
20. Ibid., 340.
21. Francis Turretin, *Institutes of Elenctic Theology*, 3 vols., trans. George Musgrave Giger, ed. James T. Dennison (Phillipsburg, NJ: P & R Publishing, 1994), 2:105.
22. To "plight" means "to promise by a solemn pledge," and "troth" means "faithfulness."
23. Vows taken from http://www.dfwx.com.
24. As quoted by Richard John Neuhaus in "The Public Square: A Continuing Survey of Religion and Public Life," *First Things*, May 2001, No. 113, 79-80.

9

CHURCH DISCIPLINE: GOD'S TOOL TO PRESERVE AND HEAL MARRIAGES

Ken Sande

———

Redemptive church discipline is one of the most sorely needed yet grievously neglected ministries in the church today. As a result, thousands of marriages that might have been preserved are instead ending in divorce.

The marriage-saving potential of discipline is well illustrated by a story related to me by a young pastor.

This pastor had been under attack for calling his church to discipline a man who was divorcing his wife without biblical grounds. The man had hardened his heart, left the church, and proceeded with the divorce. To make matters even worse, since the church's previous pastor had avoided discipline, the congregation was immature in this area and viewed church discipline as being judgmental and unloving.

After a particularly grueling congregational meeting where several people criticized the pastor's leadership in this area, one man approached the discouraged pastor and said, "Pastor, don't back off on this. Church discipline saved my marriage."

The pastor scratched his head and said, "John, we never disciplined you. I didn't even know your marriage was in trouble."

John replied, "A year ago it was in trouble. It was about that time that you called the church to discipline Max because he would not break off the affair with his secretary. I was just beginning to get involved with someone at my office. When I saw what happened with Max, it shook me up so much that I broke off the relationship and confessed my sin to my wife. She forgave me, and we finally got into the counseling we needed to deal with the problems in our marriage."

This story reveals both the redemptive power of church discipline and the trap we fall into when we try to measure its effectiveness. We tend to measure success according to the response of the person who faced discipline and how well our church supports it. If the offender responds well and our church condones the process, we say we have succeeded, but if the offender leaves the church or several people object to it, we conclude, "It doesn't work!"

But we err in two ways. To begin with, we try to measure success in terms of results. If we do not see immediate repentance in the person under discipline and if we do not experience widespread congregational support, we think we have failed. We forget that God does not measure success in terms of immediate results. Unlike us, He defines success in terms of faithfulness—faithfulness to His Word regardless of the immediate results or consequences (see Heb. 11).

We also fail because we look only at the short-term visible effects of discipline. As the opening story reveals, however, we can never know this side of eternity how many marriages are saved because people in the pews witness discipline in action and are challenged to repent of their sins before they become public.

If faithfulness to God's Word is the true measuring rod for success, then many churches are utter failures in His eyes when it comes to obeying His clear and repeated commands to restore straying saints through redemptive church discipline. In this chapter we will take a careful look at this problem and then explore ways to restore this vital ministry to the church, especially when it comes to preserving and healing struggling marriages.

DIVORCE IS RAMPANT IN THE CHURCH

During the last century, divorce in the United States increased over 400 percent. Tragically, the church has kept perfect step with the culture around us. A recent survey by George Barna revealed that the divorce rate among born-again Christians is disturbingly high.[1]

This is shocking news! Of all the people you would expect to be faithful to their vows and to fight for their marriages, Christians should be at the top of the list. We know that God instituted marriage as a lifelong covenant. We understand the implications of sin; we can draw on the power of the Gospel. We have so much to motivate us and strengthen us. And yet our marriages are failing with the same frequency and in the same ways as those in the world are failing! The effects of this massive, church-wide failure are enormous. Christian families are disintegrating before our very eyes, often through bitter court battles that leave lifelong wounds. Thousands of Christian children are robbed of the security and unified guidance that God intended their parents to provide, and they learn at an early age that vows to God are less important than seeking personal pleasure. Many adults and children who have gone through divorce leave the church altogether. And all the while, the world is given yet another convenient excuse to label Christians as hypocrites and to laugh in our faces when we try to tell them about the redeeming grace of God.[2]

THE FOUR CLAMPS ARE GONE

The church's failure to fight for its marriages comes at the worst possible time. Marriage has always been somewhat of a pressure cooker. Two sinners come together to share life's experiences, and shortly after the honeymoon, their sinful desires begin to clash (cf. Jas. 4:1-3). Conflict erupts, producing heat and pressure that may threaten to blow the marriage apart.

For many years, there were four clamps that helped hold the lid on the pressure cooker until people cooled down and decided to work out their differences. In order to get a divorce, you had to overcome legal hurdles, social disgrace, financial pressures, and church scrutiny. These four obstacles worked together to slow angry people down, force them to count the cost, and motivate them to try once more to overcome their marital problems. As a result, even though most marriages went through times of great disappointment or anger, the lid usually stayed on long enough for people to get past their intense emotions and see the benefit of working together to save their marriages. As a result, most American couples ended their lives with their original life partner, usually thanking God for getting them through the rough spots along the way.

Unfortunately, even though modern marriages are still pressure cookers, all four of the clamps have disappeared. No-fault divorce laws have removed legal barriers to divorce. Society pays no attention one way or the other to people keeping their marriage vows. Many women already have an income from work outside the home, and husbands rarely face lifetime alimony payments. Worst of all, instead of fighting compassionately yet firmly for their members' marriages, most churches today stand silently by as their members head off to divorce court.

A growing number of people think it is time to put some of these clamps back into place. Sociologists, legislators, and feminists are beginning to face up to the disastrous financial and social costs imposed by divorce. As a result, some states are reconsidering their no-fault divorce laws, while others are experimenting with new laws that give couples the option of making a more binding marital covenant. But these changes will come slowly and sporadically. There is only one institution that can act promptly and decisively to restore one of these vital clamps, and that institution is the church. If even one clamp could be placed back on the pressure cooker, countless marriages could be saved from divorce.

MINISTERING TO PEOPLE IN DIVORCE

There are four qualities that church leaders must exercise, by God's grace, if they are going to rescue their people from divorce. Most importantly, they need an enormous amount of *compassion*. When a marriage is on the rocks, people have often been struggling with sin and discouragement for years. Some of them are calloused and hard-hearted, while others are weary and hopeless. It is all too easy to condemn the former and to give simplistic exhortations to the latter. Again and again the Lord has had to convict me of such attitudes, leading me to pray, "God, this attitude will prevent me from ministering to this man or this woman. Please give me the compassion that Jesus had for the lost and the weary." It is only as we put on the compassion of Christ that we can effectively obey the timeless counseling instructions provided in 1 Thessalonians 5:14-15 (NIV): "And we urge you, brothers, warn those who are idle, encourage the timid, help the weak, be patient with everyone. Make sure that nobody pays back wrong for wrong, but always try to be kind to each other and to everyone else."

Divorce intervention also requires *conviction that comes from knowledge*. Many pastors are unwilling to stand up to divorce because they have forgotten how strongly the Bible supports the sanctity of marriage, or they do not believe that God will bless their labors to fight for marriages. Thus they deserve the rebuke that Jesus gave to the Sadducees: "You are in error because you do not know the scriptures or the power of God" (Matt. 22:29, NIV). If you are going to go into battle against divorce, you need to dig into the Bible and develop a firm conviction as to what God says about divorce. Then you need to develop a clear and unequivocal policy about marriage, divorce, and remarriage. Finally, you need to teach it to your people so they know what God and the church will call them to. Such teaching is especially important to correct the worldly ideas on marriage and divorce that infiltrate Christian homes through every form of media. Our people desperately need clear guidance on this issue.

As Jesus warned the Sadducees, however, knowledge alone is not enough. You must also have *faith* that God will back up the commands of His Word with the power of His Spirit. Fear throws up a multitude of objections to exercising discipline. "People will get angry." "They will call you legalistic." "It won't work." "It's a waste of time." "You might be sued." One of the greatest disappointments in my work with churches is to hear leaders say, "I know the Bible says this, but . . ." No Christian should ever put a "but" after "This is what God's Word says"! The only thing we should say is, "Scripture says this, and here is how we will do it." Yes, we need to be thoughtful and careful, but we must never let the fear of man cause us to compromise God's Word. We must ask God for faith and then move ahead, believing that

He will bless our obedience. "Therefore, my dear brothers, stand firm. Let nothing move you. Always give yourselves fully to the work of the Lord, because you know that your labor in the Lord is not in vain" (1 Cor. 15:58, NIV).

A fourth and related quality is *prudence*. Divorce intervention often involves legal risks. These risks can be substantially reduced if a church takes precautionary steps to get its house in order legally before a crisis erupts (Prov. 22:3). Among other things, this involves updating your bylaws and guidelines on church discipline so they address the legal pitfalls that have been created in recent court cases that granted church members more latitude in suing their churches. I am not aware of a single denominational book of church order that has kept pace with these legal developments, and I have seen very few sets of church bylaws that were not completely deficient in this area. As a result of this neglect, most churches are unnecessarily exposed to being sued when they exercise discipline. Now is the time, before the storm erupts in your church, to bring your core documents and policies up to date. An ounce of prevention today (which I will describe in detail later) can literally save you twenty thousand dollars in legal fees tomorrow.

FORMATIVE AND CORRECTIVE DISCIPLINE

When people hear the phrase *church discipline*, they usually think of a formal process that may result in excommunication from the church. But this is actually only a small portion of what discipline is all about. The Bible calls us to think of discipline in broad and generally informal terms. This has led me to develop the following definition for church discipline: *the church involving itself in people's lives to bring them to maturity by teaching and holding them accountable to God's Word*. This definition may be divided into two specific categories of discipline: formative discipline and corrective discipline.

Formative discipline encompasses the teaching and fellowship ministries of the church that help believers grow into maturity. It includes preaching, Sunday school, personal study and prayer, fellowship, small groups, and all of the other day-to-day activities of the church that enable believers to grow in the knowledge of God and inspire them to follow His ways (see 2 Tim. 4:2; Heb. 10:24-25; Jas. 5:16).

A church can use formative discipline to strengthen and preserve marriages by providing thorough teaching on God's design for marriage, on ways to nurture and mature, and on how to deal with problems that arise in the marital relationship. Through Sunday school classes and small-group Bible studies, the church can provide members with opportunities to discuss questions and difficulties. Mandatory premarital counseling can help couples deliberately prepare for the challenges of marriage. And through informal fellowship, younger couples can learn from older couples as the latter model the attitudes and skills that lead to a solid marriage.

Corrective discipline is practiced less frequently, and only when a believer strays from God and needs help getting back on track. As Paul explained it to the Galatians, "Brothers, if someone is caught in a sin, you who are spiritual should restore him gently" (Gal. 6:1, NIV). Jesus Himself lays out the general framework for corrective discipline in Matthew 18:12-20 (NIV):

> *"What do you think? If a man owns a hundred sheep, and one of them wanders away, will he not leave the ninety-nine on the hills and go to look for the one that wandered off? And if he finds it, I tell you the truth, he is happier about that one sheep than about the ninety-nine that did not wander off. In the same way your Father in heaven is not willing that any of these little ones should be lost. If your brother sins against you, go and show him his fault, just between the two of you. If he listens to you, you have won your brother over. But if he will not listen, take one or two others along, so that 'every matter may be established by the testimony of two or three witnesses.' If he refuses to listen to them, tell it to the church; and if he refuses to listen even to the church, treat him as you would a pagan or a tax collector. I tell you the truth, whatever you bind on earth will be bound in heaven, and whatever you loose on earth will be loosed in heaven. Again, I tell you that if two of you on earth agree about anything you ask for, it will be done for you by my Father in heaven. For where two or three come together in my name, there am I with them."*

As this and related passages teach, corrective discipline has three primary purposes. The first is *to restore fallen Christians to usefulness to God and fellowship with His church* (see Matt. 18:12-14; 2 Cor. 2:5-11; 7:8-10; Gal. 6:1-2; Jas. 5:19-20). The second is *to guard and preserve the honor of God* (see Rom. 2:24; 1 Cor. 10:31). And the third purpose is *to protect the purity of the church* (see Rom. 16:17; 1 Cor. 5:6; 1 Tim. 5:19-20). As we will see, corrective discipline generally begins in private, but may involve as many people as are necessary to achieve repentance and restoration (see Matt. 18:15-20; Gal. 6:1-2; Col. 3:16; Jas. 5:19-20; 1 Cor. 5:1-13; 2 Thess. 3:14-15; 2 Tim. 4:2; Heb. 13:17). The rest of this chapter will be devoted to discussing the exercise of corrective discipline.

TEACH AND APPLY THE "SLIPPERY SLOPE"

Corrective discipline is much easier to administer and to receive if people have been taught about it before it becomes necessary. The trouble is that many Christians have an automatic aversion to the concept of discipline, thinking of it only in formal and extreme terms, such as *excommunication*. One way to get past this aversion is to show that formal church discipline is only a small part of a wider and more informal process for promoting discipline and resolving conflict. Peacemaker® Ministries has developed a simple diagram that can make this teaching process easier. It is called "the slippery slope of conflict."[3]

This diagram illustrates the various ways people respond to conflict. On the left side of the curve are the "escape" responses: denial, flight, and even suicide. In most cases, escaping from a conflict only makes matters worse. Occasionally it is appropriate to flee from a conflict to get help or to get away from imminent danger, but in most cases escaping only delays a proper resolution to the problem. Sadly, this is the way many people respond to conflict—quitting a job, changing churches, filing a divorce. They may get temporary relief, but they usually take their problems into future relationships.

On the right side of the slippery slope are the "attack" responses, which are used when people are more interested in winning a conflict than in preserving a relationship. These responses can involve litigation, verbal or physical assault, or even murder, all of which are generally forbidden by Scripture[4] (see 1 Cor. 6:1-8; Eph. 4:29; Exod. 20:13). Obviously, attack responses are almost always destructive to relationships.

Instead of escaping or attacking, Christians are commanded to respond to conflict in six constructive ways, which are shown on the top of the slippery slope. These responses include three "personal peacemaking" responses: overlooking minor offenses (Prov. 19:11); discussing personal offenses that are too serious to overlook, which involves confession, confrontation, and forgiveness (Matt. 5:23-24; 18:15); and negotiating substantive issues (Phil. 2:3-4). If personal peacemaking does not solve the problem, we can ask others to help us through "assisted peacemaking," which may include mediation (Matt. 18:16), arbitration (1 Cor. 6:1-8), or formal church discipline (Matt. 18:17-20).

When a congregation is well trained in these concepts and skills, most conflicts between members, including marital conflicts, can be resolved through informal corrective discipline and without direct involvement by the leaders.[5] When members have problems, they can go to each other more easily and try to work them out themselves. Moreover, when they see someone else in a harmful situation, they will know that it is biblically appropriate to go and talk about it. This alone could prevent many divorces in the church. I have been involved in many divorces where a friend of the couple later told me, "I noticed that he was getting a little close to that woman at work. But I told myself it wasn't any business of mine." If you teach your people that God commands them to go to each other when they see someone falling into a sin, much questionable behavior could be confronted and changed before it causes great harm.

As you teach these concepts, remind your people that if they are unable to handle a conflict on their own, they should seek assistance. A woman named Patsy did this in a courageous way. She literally dragged a friend into my office. The friend, who was married, had confided in Patsy that she was getting involved with a man at work. When Patsy was unable to persuade her to break off the relationship, she asked the friend to come in and see me. When she refused, Patsy asked her out to lunch. As they walked past the building I was in, Patsy said, "I need to go in here." When they got to the door outside my office and the other woman saw the sign, she balked. Patsy grabbed her by the arm and literally dragged her into my office. Holding tightly to her friend, she said, "Ken, we need to talk to you." I was caught completely off guard, but God gave me the words to encourage this young woman to sit down and tell me what was happening. Although we had an awkward beginning, she seemed to realize that God was giving her a last chance to turn aside from an adulterous affair.

As a result of our conversation, she broke off the relationship and got into counseling with her husband. Years later they walked up to me in a church I was visiting to thank me again for being used by God at that critical time in their lives. With them were two youngsters, and the wife held a baby in her arms. She said, "These children are God's reward to us for staying together." I could only thank God for His goodness, which included a woman named Patsy who had the love and the guts to get involved in another person's life at a critical moment.

So train your people to be peacemakers! They are your best workers. They mingle together in their homes, neighborhoods, Bible studies, and places of work; so they are often the first to see signs of conflicts and marital problems. If they have been taught how to respond to conflict biblically, they will often be able to deal with problems in their early stages, thus avoiding the need for formal church discipline and preserving precious relationships in your families and church.

ESTABLISH A POLICY ON DIVORCE

One of the most valuable gifts a church can give to its people is clear biblical guidance on the nature and permanence of marriage. This will necessarily require developing a principled position on when a Christian may legitimately file for divorce. This is not an easy question to answer, which is why many sincere Christians differ in their response. Some believe that divorce is not permissible under any circumstances, while others would allow it if one partner no longer loves or finds fulfillment with the other. Personally, I am persuaded that there are at least two legitimate grounds for divorce. The first is adultery, when one spouse has been sexually unfaithful to the other (see Matt. 5:31-32). The second is desertion, when an unbelieving spouse physically leaves the marriage and indicates that he or she no longer wants to be part of the marriage (see 1 Cor. 7:15-16).

Abuse within a marriage presents special challenges. Referring to God's love for justice and His concern for the oppressed, some people argue that abuse also constitutes grounds for divorce. I have not yet been persuaded of this argument, but I certainly recognize the need for the church to take serious measures to deal with abuse. This may involve formal church discipline and even calling in civil authorities to protect the family and force the abuser to face the seriousness of his sin.

Many books available today discuss various views on what constitutes grounds for divorce. Unfortunately, there is so much diversity on this issue that after much reading you can still be confused on what the Bible teaches. In the midst of these many conflicting books, I have found two resources that seem to be the most biblically rigorous and practical. One is Jay Adams's book *Marriage, Divorce, and Remarriage*.[6] The other resource is a detailed study done by Alfred Poirier called "What the Bible Says about Divorce and Remarriage."[7]

Both of these resources offer an excellent theological starting point from which a church can develop a policy on marriage and divorce.

SLOW THE DIVORCE DOWN

If a couple in your church is headed toward divorce, you should try to slow the process down so you have time for informal corrective discipline. The first and most important step in this process is to pray for God's intervention. Be specific and be biblical. For example, if the divorcing spouse is involved in an affair, you can draw on the book of Hosea as you pray: "Lord, put a hedge of thorns around this woman. Make her time with this other man distasteful to her." You can also pray for God to act as David describes in Psalm 32: "Lord, make Your hand heavy upon her; sap her strength as in the heat of summer; let her bones ache. And every time she walks away from this man, make her feel dirty and unhappy." That is not a hateful prayer; it is a loving prayer, because it is asking God to bring temporary consequences to her to save her from far more serious lifelong consequences.

Since many divorces arise impulsively or out of anger, delays will often work in favor of reconciliation. As people cool down, they may reconsider their decision, especially if there has not been a great deal of personal and legal damage already. If papers have not already been filed, you can appeal to the couple to hold off for a few days or weeks while they reconsider their actions. If papers have been filed, you can urge the other spouse to have his or her attorney slow the process down by not filing answers until the very end of the required time periods and using other legitimate delaying tactics. You do not want to push this too far or you may see an angry backlash from the divorcing party, but a good attorney can often buy several weeks or even months in which to find a way to turn the divorce around.

You should be aware that there is a potential downside to delaying the divorce process. If someone wants out of a marriage, he or she may feel guilty initially and as a result be more generous on property settlement, alimony, or child support. As time goes by, especially if he or she gets aggravated, some of that guilt may dissipate and his or her heart may harden and be less generous to the person he or she is divorcing. Therefore, you need to pray for wisdom about whether the delay is likely to bring about a turn toward reconciliation or cause a heart to be hardened.

During a delay you should reach out to the person who wants the divorce and try to minister to him or her personally and informally, which may often make formal discipline unnecessary. Your goal is for the person to realize that you really care about him or her and may be able to help with this crisis. If the person is not inclined to listen to you out of respect for your spiritual authority, you will need to appeal to his or her self-interest. There are several things you can say that may induce someone to talk with you. You can indicate a sincere interest for the person's well-being, for the pain he or she must be going through, and for the effect this must be having on the children.

Sometimes I have persuaded someone to talk with me by saying something like this: "I know you are determined to go ahead with the divorce and don't think there is any way your marriage can be saved. Even if that is true, I would appreciate your assistance in helping your husband understand where he blew it. He's willing to continue counseling regardless of what you do. He wants to deal with the issues in his life that contributed to the breakdown of your marriage. He has told me a lot of things, but I know he can't be entirely objective. I don't know of anyone else who could tell me more accurately what he does wrong than you. Would you come in and visit with me about this? We don't even have to talk about you. Just tell me where you think he needs to change."

I have found that many people are willing to talk with me on this basis. As we talk, I am continually praying that God will build trust between us. After spending time getting the information about the spouse, I say, "I appreciate your coming in. You've given me a lot of helpful insights. I was pleased to see that some of the areas you mentioned are areas your husband has already described, and we are working on them." In saying that, I want to show her there is hope that he will change. Then I will usually say gently, "You know, in most cases in which I get involved there are usually struggles on both sides. You are probably aware of some things you have done to contribute to this situation as well. You don't have to talk about those things, but if you'd like to, I would be happy to listen." She will usually hesitate, at which point I will say, "If your marriage ends, the chances are you're going to be with someone else someday. If you don't deal with your own attitudes and habits now, you will carry them into a future relationship. Maybe now is a good time to address them."

I will also try to draw people into counseling by encouraging them to think about their children. I might be fairly frank and say, "What will you say to your daughter eighteen years from now when she asks, 'Mom, your divorce threw my entire life upside down. Did you do it impulsively, or did you really try to save your marriage with Dad?'"

Depending on how much I think a person can take from me, I may paint some pretty vivid pictures of what will happen if the couple goes through with a divorce. By the very nature of sin—especially in these cases—people are looking straight down at their feet; they are not thinking even two inches ahead. They are only thinking about the pleasure or the relief that they want now, not about the long-term consequences of their choice. So one of your tasks is to lovingly ask questions that the Holy Spirit will echo in their minds after they leave your office. God willing, those echoes will eventually stimulate honest soul-searching and turn them back from a divorce.

BUILDING HOPE THROUGH CONFESSION

Although divorce can be caused by many things, I have found that hopelessness is the factor that pushes people over the edge. They have often endured years of frustration and disappointment, hoping that things might somehow improve. Then one day something happens, and they just give up hope. "Why should I go on being miserable," they say, "when there is no hope of things ever getting better?"

A hundred years ago people stayed in hopeless marriages out of commitment, but today even among Christians commitment is often not sufficient to see them through tough times. Therefore, one of the most important steps in turning a divorce around is to rebuild hope as quickly as possible. Think of giving hope as a doctor thinks of giving a transfusion to someone who has lost a great deal of blood: Unless this essential element is quickly restored, the patient (or the marriage) will die, and there will be nothing left to work on.

For example, assume you are working with a wife who has decided to leave her husband. When she told him, he was crushed. Trying to get her to change her mind, he said, "I know I haven't been a very good husband. I'm really going to work hard to change. Please stay!"

The wife responded, "I've heard your promises before. You've said this again and again, but you never change. I'm not going to stay in a hopeless marriage the rest of my life."

The husband's bland confession indicates that he doesn't have a clue as to how he needs to change. Empty promises and broad generalizations will not turn things around. The best way he can persuade her to give him another chance is to clearly demonstrate that he has truly come to grips with his sins and is earnest about making concrete changes to be the kind of husband God wants him to be.

This calls for serious and accelerated counseling. Through the prayerful application of God's Word and the working of the Holy Spirit, the husband needs to see how his own selfish desires have ruled his heart and destroyed his marriage (see Matt. 15:19; Jas. 4:1-3). He needs to be truly broken before God. He needs to clearly identify his sinful desires and habit patterns—the self-centeredness, the idolatry, the pride—that contributed to the disintegration of their relationship. And he needs to do this without trying to diminish his guilt by focusing on all of the ways she contributed to their problems.

As he comes to grips with his own sin, you can help him plan how to confess them to his wife in a thorough and specific way. Make sure he understands that the purpose of his confession is not to manipulate her or force her to come back, although you pray together that God will use it to give her hope. He needs to confess because he is guilty and God commands it, regardless of how his wife responds. One way to do this is to use what I call the "Seven A's of Confession":

- **A**ddress everyone involved (Ps. 41:4; Luke 19:8).
- **A**void saying if, but, and maybe (Ps. 51).
- **A**dmit specifically.

- **A**cknowledge the hurt (express sincere sorrow for the way you affected that person).
- **A**ccept the consequences (Luke 15:19; Num. 5:5-7; Luke 19:8).
- **A**lter your behavior (Eph. 4:22-32).
- **A**sk for forgiveness (Gen. 50:17).

I would walk through each element of the confession with the husband, helping him prepare his confession and even role-playing it with him. If his heart has truly been broken before God, and if he has properly prepared, he will give a very different confession to his wife than he did before. Instead of the bland "I haven't been a very good husband," he will say, "Connie, I've sinned against God and you. I haven't lived up to the standard He gives me. He says I'm supposed to love you as Christ loved the church. I haven't even come close to that. I've loved myself and my own desires far more than I've loved you or God. I've made my job into an idol, and I gave myself to it. I've neglected you, and I've broken my word again and again. I have not kept my vows to you. I have left you with the whole burden of raising the kids because I'm too selfish to turn off the TV and help. I can understand why you are so hurt and disappointed and why you feel like you can never be happy with me. I have wronged you in so many ways. . . ."

Time after time when I have been with a couple as the husband makes such a confession, I have sat and watched the color come back into the wife's face. In many cases the cold, hopeless look is replaced by a softer expression. As she hears her husband's words, the Holy Spirit uses them to put hope back into her heart. She begins to realize that something really is different and to believe that things might truly change.

As hope is rekindled, the disillusioned spouse will often be willing to postpone the divorce and to try to work out the problems that have plagued their marriage. This is seldom a quick process. The sinful desires and behavior patterns that led people to the point of divorce usually require weeks or months of counseling to understand and change. But at least they are moving in the right direction, and as God works through the church, most couples can experience a genuine reconciliation and steady improvement in their relationship.

THE DEVIL'S HANDBOOK ON DIVORCE

Some people are so determined to get out of an unpleasant marriage that no amount of confession on their spouse's side will slow them down. The divorcing spouse will often use one of several excuses to justify his or her decision to leave. I have heard the same excuses so often that I have wondered whether Satan has published a little booklet on how to justify a divorce. The excuses comprise what may be called a "popular divorce mythology."[8] If you want to stop divorces, you need to be prepared to respond to these excuses.

Myth #1: When the love has gone out of a marriage, it's better to get divorced. Although this is the world talking, Christians buy into it. Pastors must address this candidly and help couples see that the basis of marriage is not feelings of love. In God's design, *commitment* is the basis of marriage, and love is the fruit.

Myth #2: It's better for the children to go through a divorce than to live with parents who fight all the time. Although parents in a truly unhappy marriage may sincerely believe this, it is usually a superficial rationalization. One way to test their sincerity is to ask them to read Judith Wallerstein's book, *The Unexpected Legacy of Divorce*, which clearly articulates the many detrimental effects of divorce. If they still decide to go through with a divorce after reading these facts, they usually have to admit that it's not the children they are looking out for, but their own selfish desires.

Myth #3: God led me to this divorce. I repeatedly hear people say, "I know the Bible teaches that divorce usually isn't God's will, but in this case God has given me a real peace that this is right." This statement reveals an underlying problem in popular teachings on spiritual guidance, which elevate a sense of "inner peace" to such a level that it can overrule the clear teaching of Scripture itself. This view of guidance must be specifically exposed and refuted. One way to do so is to help people see that a sense of inner peace is not a conclusive sign of God's approval. I usually ask people whether they think Jesus felt inner peace in the Garden of Gethsemane. If they try to say yes, I take them to the Gospels and help them see that in fact He was trembling with apprehension and agony. If He had walked out the other side of the garden,

He might have had a great sense of relief at escaping from the crucifixion, but in doing so He would have been turning His back on God's will for His life. In a similar way, divorce may promise immediate relief, but in the long run it too is usually contrary to the will of God.

Myth #4: Surely a loving God would not want someone to stay in such an unhappy situation. This myth is based on a humanistic presupposition that God's purpose in life revolves around me and my happiness.[9] One way to expose it is to ask the counselee to unfold what it means to say, "A loving God wouldn't want people to suffer this way." Ask him to imagine that he has gone back in time two thousand years to the days of the persecuted church in Rome. He has been asked by a local church to go to the Colosseum and counsel the Christians who are about to be sent out to the lions. Would he really say to them, "Surely a loving God would not want Christians to suffer like this"? What would have happened to the early church if those Christians had believed such a notion? This kind of word picture will help your counselees begin to understand that they have believed a lie.

It is crucial to help suffering people to understand that God has something far more important in mind for His people than pleasant lives. His purpose is to conform us to the likeness of His Son (Rom. 8:28-29). The Bible teaches that this requires pruning, melting, and purifying to burn away the dross in our lives, and this is often done through the furnace of suffering. Take your counselee to Hebrews 11 or 1 Peter. The Bible contains many passages about the value and purpose of suffering. We can use those Scriptures to encourage people in their painful situations.

Myth #5: I know it's wrong, but God is forgiving. If you have done much pastoral counseling, you have heard this statement again and again. Its antidote is Deuteronomy 29:19-21, where Moses warns the Israelites sternly (my paraphrase), "If you presume that you can sin deliberately and then just say magic words and God will forgive you, how great will His wrath be upon you!" It is a frightful thing to sin deliberately. Point people to the example of King David, who willfully sinned against God. God forgave David, but He left consequences that would grieve David for the rest of his life. "The sword will never depart from your house" (2 Sam. 12:10, NIV). David's baby died, and his sons continued to kill each other. David had to bear that on his conscience to his dying day.

And how do people know that God will actually give them a repentant heart after they persist in willful disobedience (see Heb. 3:7-13; 12:16-17; Eph. 4:30; Prov. 28:14)? How can they be sure that God will not turn His face against them and remove His blessings from their lives (Heb. 10:31; 1 Pet. 3:7, 11-12)?

Another way to pierce this myth is to ask a counselee to imagine that she needs some cash. So she decides to rob a bank. She steals the money, then runs down the sidewalk and into an alley. It is clear that she has gotten away. Then she puts the money down and says, "God, I'm so sorry. It was wrong to rob that bank. Please forgive me. Thank You, Lord." Ask her if she thinks she could just pick up the money and walk away. Most people will admit that they could not. What is the evidence of genuine repentance? Undoing the harm of the original wrong by picking the money up and taking it back to the bank. In the same way, real repentance for a sinful divorce will not be empty words, but a turning around and going back to work things out.

These are only a few of the common excuses people hang onto as they try to justify a divorce. Each of them must be dealt with directly, lovingly, and biblically, so that true motives are revealed and people will turn back to the Lord for help.

MOVING TO FORMAL DISCIPLINE

No matter how loving and persuasive you are, some people will ignore all informal efforts to help them reconcile with their spouses and turn away from unbiblical divorces. When this happens, it will be necessary to move from informal discipline to formal discipline (see Matt. 18:16-17).

Formal discipline can take different forms, depending on the polity of the specific church. In most cases when a person is seeking an unbiblical divorce, formal discipline will require that the spiritual leaders of the church, usually referred to as elders, warn the person that he will face formal discipline if he refuses to be reconciled to his spouse and continues to seek a divorce. This warning should be communicated in a loving yet firm way, preferably in person. If the person refuses to acknowledge or heed the warning, it may be repeated both verbally and in writing.[10]

In some cases the person will simply harden his or her heart and refuse any further communications with the church. But in many cases God will use this warning to shock the person into realizing how serious his or her actions are. When someone realizes that he or she may actually face formal discipline that could lead to being put out of the church, he or she will often pause the divorce process and reconsider the possibility of seeking marriage counseling to resolve the problems in his or her marriage. If so, the church should immediately offer encouragement, accountability, and whatever resources are needed to assist the couple in rebuilding their marriage.

SEEKING AND RESTORING A LOST SHEEP

What can a church do if a member persists in pursing a divorce and even leaves the church itself? The easy thing to do is to say, "Well, we tried" and to give up. But this is not the course that a true shepherd of the flock would take. As Jesus says in Matthew 18:12 (NIV), "What do you think? If a man owns a hundred sheep, and one of them wanders away, will he not leave the ninety-nine on the hills and go to look for the one that wandered off?"

A church on the West Coast provided a superb example of how to go after a wandering sheep. Cindy (not her real name) had been a member of the church and had had an affair several months earlier. She left her husband and resigned her membership in the church. The church's bylaws did not allow it to continue with formal discipline, but the leaders encouraged the members of the church to continue reaching out to Cindy. When members saw her in the laundromat or the grocery store, they would approach her and say, "Cindy, it's so good to see you! I've been praying for you" or "I just want to give you a hug, Cindy. You know, it's not too late. We love you. Come back." Their loving attitude was clearly expressed, and they always said, "Come back. Repent."

After four months Cindy could not resist any longer. She went to the pastor and said, "My conscience is killing me! Is it too late to come back to the church?" He assured her that it was not. She ended the affair, and she and her husband went through counseling with the pastor and some elders, to confirm that she was genuinely repentant.

I was at the church the day they restored Cindy to membership. The pastor gave a beautiful introduction, saying, "Many of you have been praying for Cindy, and I'm delighted to tell you today that she is back with us. The elders and I have been talking with her for the last few weeks. Cindy has something that she wants to say now." The pastor had helped her write a very discreet statement. She did not specifically mention adultery because there were children in the congregation, but most people knew what had happened. She made a beautiful confession and thanked God for the love of that church—how they had not given up, how they had reached out to her. She thanked God for the way His love had brought her back through her brothers and sisters. She confessed her sin and recommitted herself to the Lord.

Then the pastor stood and said, "Cindy has been restored. The elders have accepted her confession, and she has been forgiven. She has been forgiven by us, and that means you also must forgive her. If any of you hold her at a distance or give her the cold shoulder, I will come and talk to you about your sin of unforgiveness." In this way the church leaders put the congregation on notice. That is what Paul wrote about in 2 Corinthians 2. He instructed the Corinthian church to reaffirm their love for the person who had been put out, "in order that Satan may not outwit us. For we are not unaware of his schemes" (2 Cor. 2:8-11, NIV).

The pastor then prayed for Cindy. Before the period was on his "Amen," people were jumping up, running to the front of the sanctuary, and throwing their arms around Cindy. She was fully restored to her church family. This process was a vivid fulfillment of Jesus' teaching in Luke 15:4-7 (NIV): "Suppose one of you has a hundred sheep and loses one of them. Does he not leave the ninety-nine in the open country and go after that lost sheep until he finds it? And when he finds it, he joyfully puts it on his shoulders and goes home. Then he calls his friends and neighbors together and says, 'Rejoice with me; I have found my lost sheep.' I tell you that in the same way there will be more rejoicing in heaven over one sinner who repents than over ninety-nine righteous persons who do not need to repent."

This is the kind of Sunday when you want unbelievers to visit your church, so they can see the Gospel lived out before their very eyes!

GETTING YOUR HOUSE IN ORDER

Church discipline can have major legal repercussions. If church leaders intervene in their members' lives and bring disciplinary matters before the congregation (as churches historically have done), a disgruntled member may try to sue the church for defamation, invasion of privacy, and infliction of emotional distress. A church can dramatically reduce its exposure to such actions if it gets its house in order from a legal perspective before discipline is carried out.

The most important thing to do from a legal perspective is to obtain "informed consent" from your congregation for your disciplinary practices. This requires that all members are fully informed about your disciplinary policies, and that they agree to submit to those policies.

The process of educating your congregation and obtaining informed consent is described in detail in *Managing Conflict in Your Church*, a resource that is available through Peacemaker® Ministries. The basic steps in the process include:

• Provide your members with thorough instruction on the biblical basis and process for corrective church discipline.

• Revise your bylaws and guidelines for church discipline to *explicitly* set forth your church's commitment to carry out church discipline. In particular, specify whether you will inform members of the problem, whether you will continue with the disciplinary process even if someone attempts to resign from the church, and whether you will share appropriate information with another church to which a person under discipline attempts to flee.[11]

• Gain support for and consent to these revisions through a careful educational process, open discussions, and congregational meetings.

• Inform all new members of your disciplinary commitments through a new members' class.

• Refresh the congregation's understanding of and commitment to these policies on an annual basis, possibly through a special Reconciliation Sunday, when the sermon and testimonies celebrate God's goodness to His people through the blessing of formative and corrective church discipline.

This process takes time and effort, but it can secure for the church the protection and freedom it needs to provide the redemptive discipline its members sometimes need. A church that has its house in order both biblically and legally will not have to look over its shoulder fearfully as it seeks to restore wandering sheep. Instead, it will be able to minister boldly and confidently as it works to restore broken relationships and guard its flock from divorce.

CHRISTIANS ARE LOOKING FOR DISCIPLINE

Many church leaders are afraid that teaching explicitly about church discipline will scare potential members away from their church. I am convinced that just the opposite is true. I have talked to many believers who are deeply disappointed by their own church's lack of discipline, which sends the message to adults and children alike that obeying God is optional and up to the individual. Many of these disappointed people were looking around for a church that takes godliness seriously and loves its people enough to hold them accountable to God's Word.

Similarly, I have seen that when a church teaches and models biblical discipline in a principled and loving way, sincere believers respond with appreciation and respect for their leaders. This response is beautifully illustrated in a note a twelve-year-old boy wrote to his elders after he completed the church's membership class, which included detailed instruction on church discipline.

Belonging to a church that practices discipline means a lot to me. It makes me feel secure that someone is caring and watching out for me and tries to keep me from going astray. Just the fact that my brother and I get into so much conflict makes me realize that a church with a lot of members is going to have conflicts, too. Whenever I resolve conflict with my brother, I feel so good that we are reuniting. In that sense I realize how vital church discipline is to the spiritual growth of the church and its members.

It seems to me that this young boy had a more biblically faithful perspective on church discipline than many adult believers. Therefore, it is my earnest prayer that church leaders would do two simple things. First, that they would open their Bibles and study the many Scriptures cited in this chapter to see what God teaches us to do with regard to discipline. Second, that they would trust God and obey what He commands.

The obedient and loving exercise of church discipline in broken marriages can give couples the motivation and help they need to slow down, count the cost, remember God's promises, and look to Him and not to a judge to solve their marital problems. And no matter how dead their marriages seem to be, they can experience the wonderful truth that we serve a God who delights in bringing dead things back to life, for the benefit of His people and the glory and praise of His name!

1. The Barna Research Group, Ltd., August 6, 2001, Survey on Divorce, Marriage, and Remarriage.

    Barna's survey says, "Born again Christians are just as likely to get divorced as are non-born again adults. Overall, 33% of all born again individuals who have been married have gone through a divorce, which is statistically identical to the 34% incidence among non-born again adults." (www.barna.org, survey on divorce, August 6, 2001).

    However, that 33 percent includes a significant number who have come to faith, or have come to church for healing, *after* a divorce. The survey says nothing about whether born-again Christians are *likely* to get a divorce *after* they become born again. Nevertheless, the percentage is disturbingly high.

2. The problem of divorce and its impact on families in our society is staggering. We cannot begin to measure all its effects on our culture, but what we can measure is frightening. Judith Wallerstein's "Children of Divorce" study has shown that divorce is usually detrimental and often catastrophic for children. The impact can be seen in terms of behavior and academic problems, promiscuity, drug use, crime, and difficulty in forming lasting relationships. See *The*

Unexpected Legacy of Divorce: A Twenty-Five Year Landmark Study by Judith Wallerstein, Sandra Blakeslee, and Julia Lewis (Westport, CT: Hyperion Press, 2001). When pastors do not fight for marriages, the lambs almost always suffer.

3. Taken from Ken Sande, *The Peacemaker: A Biblical Guide to Resolving Personal Conflict* (Grand Rapids, MI: Baker Books, 2001).

4. I say "generally forbidden" because there are limited circumstances in which it is appropriate to use physical means in self-defense or to resort to civil courts for redress (see, e.g., Rom. 13:1-6). For a more detailed discussion of the slippery slope and when is it appropriate to use a particular response to conflict, see *The Peacemaker: A Biblical Guide to Resolving Personal Conflict.*

5. Peacemaker Ministries has developed Sunday school resources and small-group Bible studies to help you teach these principles to your congregation.

6. Jay Adams, *Marriage, Divorce, and Remarriage* (Grand Rapids, MI: Zondervan), 1980.

7. This study is available through Peacemaker Ministries at www.HisPeace.org or 800-711-7118.

8. R. C. Sproul does an excellent job of describing these myths in his book *The Intimate Marriage* (Wheaton, IL: Tyndale House, 1986).

9. For an excellent discussion of this issue, see Gary Thomas's book, *Sacred Marriage: What If God Designed Marriage to Make Us Holy More Than to Make Us Happy?* (Grand Rapids, MI: Zondervan, 2000).

10. For a more detailed discussion of how to carry out the disciplinary process, see *Managing Conflict in Your Church,* which is available through Peacemaker Ministries, www.HisPeace.org. or 800-711-7118.

11. As is spelled out in detail in *Managing Conflict in Your Church,* all of these steps are consistent with Matthew 18:12-20 and are sometimes necessary to enlist the support needed to compel a fleeing member to repent and return to the church.

III

THE CHALLENGES TODAY

10

HOW TO ENCOURAGE
HUSBANDS TO LEAD
AND WIVES TO FOLLOW

C. J. Mahaney

———

The engineers at General Electric were baffled. A great complex of machinery had broken down, and they didn't know why. It was the early twentieth century, the Industrial Age was pumping along at full throttle, and this sort of thing shouldn't be happening to a powerhouse like GE.

Uncertain where to even begin, they called in Charles Steinmetz, recently retired from the company, a man whose electrical genius was the stuff of corporate legend. Steinmetz arrived and walked slowly around the interconnected machines, performing various tests. He took a piece of chalk from his pocket and drew an X on one particular component of one particular machine.

When the engineers disassembled that component, it proved to be the precise location of the problem. A few days later GE received a bill from Steinmetz for ten thousand dollars, a seemingly outrageous figure. They decided to return the bill to Steinmetz with a request that he itemize it. After a few days they received the itemized bill, which read:

1) Making one chalk mark—$1.00
2) Knowing where to put it—$9,999.00[1]

X MARKS THE SPOT

Harry sits in the pastor's office, digging his fingers into the arm of the couch. Next to him is his wife, Jill, hands folded, studying the carpet in determined silence. Although just inches away from each other, at no place do their bodies make contact.

This is the first time they have met for counseling with Alan, a young pastor. For forty minutes he has been drawing them out, trying to learn the history behind their six-year marriage. The process has proven more revealing than either Harry or Jill had expected. Still, it is clear to Alan that Harry and Jill love the Lord and one another, they have a due regard for Scripture, and they've been fairly consistent servants in the church ever since joining two years earlier.

After two more appointments, the central problem of Harry and Jill's marriage comes into focus. It isn't pretty, but neither is it very unusual: Jill doesn't follow Harry.

During their engagement, when numerous practical decisions had to be made, Harry's suggestions for the wedding ceremony and reception were frequently dismissed by Jill. After all, she had greater artistic ability and administrative expertise. When Harry did lead in a decision, she would sometimes follow, but with a lack of joy or enthusiasm. At other times, when they agreed on his idea Harry would later discover that "after thinking about it" and getting other opinions Jill ended up pursuing her own mind on the matter. On these occasions Harry would sometimes discuss her failure to follow, but things were usually left with his simply airing his questions and concerns. Meanwhile, Jill kept doing what she thought best.

The pattern established before their wedding has changed little during their marriage. Harry regularly initiates discussions with Jill about their spiritual life, their schedule, their budget, and their children. But unless he makes clear and final decisions, Jill generally does what she pleases. When Harry does make a clear decision, Jill often ends up countermanding it. Left to herself, she always has a reason for doing things differently.

At this point Alan is not quite sure how to proceed with the counseling. He's in need of guidance from a fellow pastor, a more experienced man, a Steinmetz of the soul who can pinpoint the problem. If he came to you for help, what would you tell him? Where on the complex machinery of this sputtering marriage would you draw the X?

Clearly Jill refuses to follow Harry. But marriage is a system ordered and designed by God, and sometimes it is not repaired by attending to the point where it seems most obviously broken. In fact, according to Scripture the proper place to draw the X in this case is not the wife—it is the husband. This is not in any way to excuse the wife's sin. Rather, it is to observe the Bible's emphasis on the importance of the husband's leadership within marriage.

When the problem in a marriage is accurately described by the phrase "the wife won't follow," the wise pastor/counselor focuses his attention initially on the husband. When Harry has understood his biblical role and is exercising his headship with grace and wisdom, at that time Jill's sin will need to become a more central topic of counsel. Until then, the X is placed on Harry. Indeed, most of this chapter will be devoted to Harry, not because Jill's sin is insignificant, but because good followership is far more difficult without good leadership.

Here are five suggestions for helping the husband, followed by some words of counsel for his wife. The goal of your counseling will be to equip this husband to serve his wife in a way that positions her to receive from God the grace to repent and begin the process of change in earnest.

1. Help Him Focus on the Gospel

Most popular Christian materials that address the topic of marriage (at least in my reading experience) exhibit a woefully deficient theology. Of greatest concern is the way these materials treat the Gospel. Typically it is taken for granted, inaccurately described, wrongly applied, or simply ignored. Can there be a greater disservice to any Christian who sincerely desires to improve his or her marriage?

We must never assume that those whom we counsel have a sufficient understanding of or appreciation for the Gospel. The apostle Paul never assumed that. He assumed the opposite! In every one of his letters found in Scripture—regardless of whom he was addressing, whether a young church or a mature and tested leader—Paul's teachings always proceeded from and related to the Cross. *Paul always assumed that his readers needed to be clearly and specifically reminded of the content of the Gospel.*

When the Corinthian church was drifting from the centrality of the Gospel, having been seduced by human wisdom, Paul repeatedly drew their attention back to the Gospel. Toward the close of the letter he wrote, "Now, brothers, I want to remind you of the gospel. . . . For what I received I passed on to you as of first importance: that Christ died for our sins" (1 Cor. 15:1, 3, NIV).

The Gospel was "of first importance" to Paul in his preaching. It was "of first importance" to him as he taught and counseled believers in his letters. Certainly it should be "of first importance" in our counseling as well.

Why is it that we drift so readily from the Gospel? I think part of the reason is that our daily orientation is subjective, not objective. That is, we live by our feelings rather than by truth. Sinclair Ferguson has said, "The evangelical orientation is inward and subjective. We are far better at looking inward than we are at looking outward. We need to expend our energies admiring, exploring, expositing, and extolling Jesus Christ." Similarly, Luther wrote that the Gospel is "entirely outside of you." Do not allow your counselee to become preoccupied with himself. He must look outside of himself by surveying the wondrous cross. Encourage him to expend his daily energies "admiring, exploring, expositing, and extolling Jesus Christ."

We will do well to heed these words of David Powlison, editor of the *Journal of Biblical Counseling*: "Don't ever degenerate into giving advice unconnected to the good news of Jesus crucified, alive, present, at work, and returning. . . . Good principles, gutted of the Lord—de-Christified, to put it clumsily, but precisely—can only function as some form of self-serving."[2]

To offer this husband counsel that is unconnected to the Gospel is to push him into legalism, another daily tendency for Christians. Legalism involves seeking forgiveness from God, justification before

God, and acceptance by God through obedience to God. Legalism is substituting, in essence, my works for Jesus' finished work. Legalism is self-atonement and the height of arrogance. It's living as if the cross of Christ was unnecessary or insufficient. As you counsel this man whose wife will not follow, regularly ask these questions as indicators of legalism.

1. Is he more aware of his past sin than of the finished work of the cross?

2. Does he think, believe, or feel that God is disappointed with him rather than delighting over him?

3. Does he assume his acceptance before God is dependent upon his obedience?

4. Does he consistently experience condemnation?

5. Does he lack joy?

It's important to ask these questions because if the husband is legalistic, he will become preoccupied with and overwhelmed by his sins, his wife's sins, and the consequences of both. Or, in the alternative, his every attempt to serve and win his wife will merely feed his belief that he is making a contribution to his standing before God. That is, he will either become more condemned or more self-righteous and legalistic.

As a protection against both legalism and condemnation, I endeavor to assure myself that the counselee gains and maintains a clear grasp of the doctrines of justification and sanctification. I've often found phrases like these to be most helpful:

• Justification is being *declared* righteous. Sanctification is being *made* righteous.

• Justification is *objective* and a unilateral act of God; it relates to our position before God. Sanctification is *subjective* and a process in which we are daily involved; it relates to our practice before God.

• Justification is *complete*, total, and immediate at the moment of conversion. Sanctification is *progressive*, beginning at the moment we are converted and continuing until the moment we go to be with the Lord.

These two doctrines are distinct, yet inseparable, for God never justifies without also sanctifying. Be sure your counselee is clear on these precious fruits of the Gospel. In that way you will position him to receive grace from God.

2. Help Him Deepen His Understanding of the Doctrine of Sin

A few months later Harry is back in Alan's office, alone. There's been an incident between him and Jill. How it came about is regrettable, but not entirely surprising.

In recent months Harry has been less enthusiastic about doing things with Jill, content to have her make choices and pursue activities that don't necessarily include him. He still makes decisions about matters of the family, but if she disagrees, he won't even bring it up, since "she'll just do what she wants anyway."

One day he comes home to find that Jill has not made the phone calls he'd asked her to handle. Instead she has taken the children out shopping for clothes, using money that he had budgeted for other things. Harry withdraws to his computer, resigned to his wife's lack of submission.

Still, he knows the situation is unacceptable; so he decides they need a weekend away as a couple. He looks into a nearby romantic getaway and makes preliminary plans and reservations. When he tells Jill, she questions the wisdom of this idea. What about baby-sitters? And all the things she needs to get to around the house? And the budget?

In a flash Harry erupts in anger. He confronts her as selfish, insensitive, and unsubmissive. He launches into a tirade about how hard he's tried, how much he's given, and how little she's responded.

"It's really frustrating," he tells Alan. "I know I shouldn't have blown up—I know that was sin—but the main problem here isn't getting any better. She just won't submit to my authority and leadership. Hey, I can't lead if she won't follow!"

At some point any man in Harry's position will be tempted to think and act as Harry has been thinking and acting. And any man who does so will be just as far from the truth as is Harry.

What's the problem? Harry must be reminded—repeatedly, if need be—of the doctrine of remaining sin and progressive sanctification.

He must see that his sin is not created by his wife. She never, for example, "makes him angry." She cannot, for she has no ability to place anger within his heart. Indisputably, his remaining, indwelling sin is already there. Anger *already* dwells in his heart! So does pride and lust and selfishness and much, much more! When he is with his wife, she does not cause him to sin—his sin is *revealed*. God uses his wife to make him actively aware of his own sinfulness. This is an act of divine mercy.

George Orwell once wrote: "We have now sunk to such a depth that the restatement of the obvious is the first duty of intelligent men." Orwell was no Christian, but his statement has great relevance for counselors today. From my limited perspective, the often uncritical acceptance of the therapeutic movement among evangelicals has, in effect, obscured the obvious. And the obvious is this: *Our root problem, our most serious problem, is sin.* J.C. Ryle writes, "Dim or indistinct views of sin are the origin of most of the errors, heresies, and false doctrines of the present day." I submit that dim and indistinct views of sin still abound today in the church.

On the whole, the popular Christian literature I have reviewed locates the source of our problems far more readily in one's parents, one's past, and one's pain than in one's pervasive depravity. Unless you have a firm grounding in biblical teaching, these materials will surely convince you that low self-esteem and unmet needs are the problem, not indwelling sin.[3]

But there is no dim or indistinct view of sin in your Bible. The Savior Himself said, "What comes out of a man is what makes him 'unclean.' For from within, out of men's hearts, come evil thoughts, sexual immorality, theft, murder, adultery, greed, malice, deceit, lewdness, envy, slander, arrogance and folly. All these evils come from inside and make a man 'unclean'" (Mark 7:20-23, NIV).

Even when our Lord is commending the disciples, He doesn't deviate from the doctrine of sin. "If you then, though you are evil, know how to give good gifts to your children, how much more will your Father in heaven give the Holy Spirit to those who ask him!" (Luke 11:13, NIV)

Once regenerated, we are delivered from the penalty of sin and from the authoritative power of sin, but not from the continued presence and influence of sin. Sin is no longer reigning, but it is remaining. And if we yield to sin and consciously act in sinful ways, even as Christians, sin gains more influence over us (Rom. 6:12-16), and that sin grieves the Holy Spirit (Eph. 4:30) and may bring God's fatherly discipline (Heb. 12:5-11; see also Rev. 3:19). Therefore we should always seek to act in ways that are pleasing to God (2 Cor. 5:9; Eph. 5:10; Col. 3:20; Heb. 13:21). These are distinctions your counselee must grasp, and he must see how they apply to two areas: his speech and the desires of his heart.

The words we speak. In your counseling, the influence of the therapeutic movement on language must be monitored most carefully, and gently but boldly challenged. Biblical categories of sin include such morally negative terms as pride, selfishness, lust, laziness, unbelief, and rebellion. But because our capacity for self-deception doesn't end upon conversion, the husband's tendency will be to use morally neutral descriptions and categories for his attitudes and responses toward his wife. Common among these are phrases such as "I was struggling," "I reacted," "I'm insecure," "I became defensive," "I'm oversensitive," "I got frustrated," "I withdrew," and "I'm a perfectionist."

I am not claiming that certain words and phrases used to express human behavior are of no *descriptive* use. They can sometimes help communicate to one who was not an eyewitness of an event something of what took place. But that is where their utility ends.

Such terms are useless to explain cause and effect. One generally becomes "defensive" (a symptom) *because* one is proud (root sin). One generally "withdraws" *because* one is selfish and unloving. Morally neutral terms are universally employed in our culture because they minimize, or even deny, the notion of blameworthiness (sin). Having been coined or co-opted by secular psychology, they emerge from a paradigm that largely rejects the concept of culpability. Having been suffused throughout our culture by the mass media and most educational institutions, they carry an implicit authority and legitimacy that allows one to act sinfully without being seen as sinful. They are mere dodges and excuses masquerading as sophisticated observations on the human condition. The counselor must listen to these terms, receive them as data helping to describe an event, and then—explicitly rejecting their function as blame-buffers—probe beneath them to identify root sins.

The things we love. Often your counselee's speech will reveal his idols; out of the heart the mouth speaks. A man in Harry's position will almost certainly be tempted to allow even a godly desire—the desire for his wife to follow his leadership—to become an inordinate, sinful desire.[4]

> Idolatry is the most discussed problem in the Bible. Yet for Christians today it is one of the least meaningful notions. Idols are not just on pagan altars, but in well-educated hearts and minds. An idol is something within creation that is inflated to function as God. All sorts of things are potential idols, depending only on our attitudes and actions toward them. . . . Idolatry may not involve explicit denials of God's existence or character. It may well come in the form of an over-attachment to something that is in itself perfectly good. . . . An idol can be a physical object, a property, a person, an activity, a role, an institution, a hope, an image, an idea, a pleasure, a hero, anything that can substitute for God.[5]

My favorite explanation of idolatry is John Calvin's: "The evil in our desire typically does not lie in what we want but that we want it too much."

As this husband's counselor, you must regularly help him take an inventory of his own heart. You must help him guard his heart against idolizing his desire, even for such a good thing as his wife's joyful embrace of her biblical role. When that desire, rather than obedience to and faith in God, controls his thoughts and actions, he has crossed the line into idolatry, and you must help him repent and return.

Grace to change. As you help this husband understand and apply the doctrine of sin and sanctification, he will change in four distinct ways. First, he will grow in *humility.* The doctrine of sin will enable this man to follow Paul's example of humility and see himself as the worst of sinners (1 Tim. 1:15).

William Law wrote, "We may justly condemn ourselves as the greatest sinners we know because we know more of the folly of our own heart than we do of other people's. Therefore every sinner knows more of the aggravations of his own guilt than he does of other people's, and consequently may justly look upon himself to be the greatest sinner that he knows."

If this husband does not see himself as the greatest sinner, he will probably be convinced his wife is that sinner—a recipe for relational failure. Without the humility that comes from applying to oneself the doctrine of sin, this couple will make no significant, lasting relational progress.

Second, the doctrine of sin will produce in this husband *conviction of sin*. He will experience godly sorrow, leading to true repentance.

Third, once the husband has experienced conviction of sin, the doctrine of sin will produce *confession of sin*. Confession should be first and foremost to God, but then, as appropriate, to his wife. Genuine confession should be sincere, brief, and clear. Sincerity is critical, for all too often, when insufficiently convicted of our sin, we do not really confess and ask forgiveness. Instead we explain, excuse, and appeal for understanding.

Finally, the doctrine of sin and sanctification will produce *genuine change* in this husband. His growth in spiritual maturity and genuine humility will be evident to all, beginning with his wife.

To emphasize the doctrine of remaining sin is to appeal for a knowledge of ourselves as defined by God. This isn't human speculation or introspection. Nor is it a knowledge of ourselves as defined by modern psychology. It is a knowledge of ourselves as defined by God in Scripture.

It will be crucial for this husband, in seeking to serve and lead his wife, to be able to recognize temptation, identify sin and idolatry, mortify sin, and ultimately cultivate righteousness. As you help him come to grips with the doctrines of sin and progressive sanctification, he will see that the Sovereign God is using his wife as a primary means of sanctification in his life. God will use her to help him discern his heart and to reveal his sin, so that he might understand where he needs to grow in godly character through grace.

The doctrine of remaining sin and progressive sanctification will be an invaluable and immeasurable help to him. It will allow him to see that God's primary intention is to conform him to the image of Jesus Christ, regardless of whether or not his wife ever becomes a faithful follower of her husband's leadership.

3. Teach Him the Meaning of Biblical Leadership

To serve this husband, you as his counselor must be certain that he understands the definition of biblical leadership. This is the only way he can grasp all that God expects of him—and empowers him to perform—in his role as head of his wife. Because this topic is addressed at various other places in this book, I wish only to emphasize a single point.[6]

Your counselee must memorize and meditate on Ephesians 5:25-33, that he might begin applying it. (He should *not* be meditating on verses 22-24.) In verses 25-33, Paul describes love and gives the definitive example of Christ's love for the church. In a word, this love is sacrifice. In seeking to serve this husband, I would ask him what he can do for his wife each day and each week that could truly be defined as sacrifice, for in that way he would be emulating the Savior's love for the church.

4. Encourage Him to Forgive

When I was a teenager, my dentist told me I needed to have three wisdom teeth extracted. Now, I can't stand even the *flossing* phase of a dental appointment; so the prospect of undergoing oral surgery was simply unthinkable. I opted for a plan of indefinite postponement, a brilliant strategy that was simple to implement, involved no physical pain, and seemed to carry no significant consequences.

When I reached my late thirties, wisdom teeth still intact, my dentist began to talk to me about the potential for cancer. That got my attention; so I decided to pursue my last viable, nonsurgical option. I actually began praying for God to remove my wisdom teeth super-naturally. "Lord, remove my wisdom teeth for Your glory," I would plead. He didn't.

So one day there I am, almost forty years old, sitting in the oral surgeon's waiting area with a number of other people. We are an interesting group in that, until I opened the door, the average age in that room is probably about fourteen.

Soon (too soon) I'm ushered deeper into the recesses of the office, to a small room full of various inhuman-looking instruments, and instructed to sit in The Chair. The surgeon arrives shortly in full battle garb. "Okay, we've got three today, Mr. Mahaney," he announces briskly. I'm trying to decide if his apparent cheerfulness is really a good thing, when he holds my X-ray film up to the light, peers at it quizzically, and adds, "You know, the bottom right could be a challenge. I can't really distinguish that one from your jaw." Then he poses a question I'll never forget. "Would you like anesthesia? Would you like novocaine?"

His query stuns me. The question has to be rhetorical, right? But he's still looking at me, waiting. I reply with possibly the most sincere, heartfelt "Yes" that has ever been uttered. Then for the follow-up he asks, "Would you like a local or a general?" With great deliberateness, I respond, "Oh, at least a national, please. In fact, I would like all the drugs that can be legally placed in my body. No offense, doctor, but I don't want to ever recall having met you or even how to find this building. Is that possible? Is that legal?"

We live in a day when surgery need never be accompanied by significant pain. The woman delivering a child can opt for an epidural. Lasers can delicately remove slices of an eye, and the eye feels nothing. Some brain-surgery patients are conscious during the operation. Medical science has at its disposal a host of anesthetics that allow us to be pain-free during otherwise unbearably painful experiences.

Don't you wish there was *relational* anesthesia?

I was able to put off the inevitable removal of my wisdom teeth (clearly a misnomer in my case) for some twenty-five years. The husband whom you are counseling won't be able to postpone his relational pain. There will be times when he finds his wife sinning against him more on the order of every twenty-five minutes, if not twenty-five seconds. Some of her sins will cause him real pain, and you need to prepare him for that inevitability—because when it happens, he will be tempted to engage in bitterness and retaliation due to the self-righteousness that dwells in him (and in you and me and everyone else for that matter).

You must help this husband see that by God's grace there is something better than relational novocaine, and infinitely better than retaliation. It's called forgiveness. This man is called to forgive his wife with the complete, unreserved, unqualified forgiveness with which his sins have been forgiven by God. "Forgive as the Lord forgave you" (Col. 3:13, NIV). He must become very familiar with the core message of Matthew 18: Those who have been forgiven the immeasurable should never be reluctant to forgive the relatively trivial.

At the close of one Sunday meeting at our church, a man shared with me a very grieving, saddening account of his childhood. The worst part was how his father had related to him. Then he said, "I know exactly what you're going to tell me," but he said it humbly, by way of seeking my perspective. "You're going to tell me that I have a responsibility to forgive my dad, to make a decision of my will by grace to forgive him. I know that's what you're going to say."

I replied, "No, that's not where I'd start." He was surprised, and a little perplexed. I said, "In trying to help you, I would first seek to convince you that your sins against God are far more serious than any sins that your father ever committed against you. I'm not trying to minimize your father's sin, but a biblical perspective is that your sins against God are more serious than any sins that will ever be committed against you. And I'd tell you that you will be able to forgive your dad as you first recognize how much you have been forgiven by God."

When someone seeks my forgiveness, my common response is to say something like, "In light of all the sins that I have been forgiven of by God, it is my privilege and joy to forgive you of your sin against me." I take this approach because it places the accent on my sins and how much I've been forgiven, while affirming the importance of confession.

Your job is to help the husband grasp the magnitude of God's forgiveness toward him. Otherwise, when sinned against, his self-righteousness will manifest itself in bitterness and resentment. When I'm self-righteous, I'm saying that your sin against me is ultimately more serious than my sins against God. But Scripture is clear. Because we are the most forgiven people in the world, we should be the most forgiving people in the world. You must labor with this husband to prepare him not only for his wife's inevitable sins against him, but to give him a biblical assessment of his sin and his wife's sin. In that way he can receive God's forgiveness, become aware of just how amazing grace is, and then, without any reluctance or hesitation, extend forgiveness to his wife.

In the twenty-five years I have been involved in pastoral counseling, forgiveness has been a root issue in the overwhelming majority of instances. There is no substitute for forgiveness. There is no alternative to forgiveness. And true forgiveness begins with a recognition of how much you have been forgiven by God.

5. Encourage Him to Glorify God

In all the counsel you offer this man, your goal is to equip him to lead a life that glorifies God. "So whether you eat or drink or whatever you do, do it all for the glory of God" (1 Cor. 10:31).

From the outset, seek to identify his core motivations for participating in counseling. Whom does he see this counseling as being focused on? This counseling may be taking place, in one sense, *because of* his wife. But he must not see it as therefore focused on his wife. It may be that during this process it will be he who undergoes the most change. But he must not see the counseling as therefore focused on himself.

This man must recognize that this process is fundamentally *about God*. Exhort him to align his motive with the purpose of God. His motive must be God-glorifying and God-centered, not wife-centered, and certainly not self-centered. He must ultimately seek to please and glorify God, not convict or change his wife.

This means, in part, that a restored relationship with his wife must not be this husband's ultimate passion and priority. If it is, he's an idolater, and if you let him maintain that perspective, your counseling will only cultivate his idolatry. So you must help him to discern his motive. Then, as necessary, you must help him to realign his motive with God's will and with the chief end of man: to glorify God and enjoy Him forever. As the Puritan Thomas Watson wrote, "The glory of God is a silver thread which must run through all of our actions."

When his motivation is to glorify God, he will be less vulnerable to any manipulation and intimidation—what the Scriptures refer to as the fear of man—that his wife may seek to impose. When his motivation is to glorify God, he will be protected from reacting sinfully if and when she does not respond appropriately to his care, service, and leadership. In both cases, he can be satisfied with and secure in the knowledge that God is pleased with his motive and his obedience, regardless of his wife's behavior.

Finally, if he determines to glorify God, he will be less likely to seek or demand from her what only God can provide. He will be satisfied with and by God, and he will simply seek to serve his wife.

God has so ordered marriage that the biblically ordained head of the home is the primary focal point for all truly Christian counseling. From my experience, the norm is that a wife does eventually respond to a husband's humble and godly leadership. And you should certainly encourage this man with the promises of God and the character of God.

However, if you become convinced that this husband is exercising his headship with grace and wisdom, and if you have opportunity to talk also to his wife, then what can you tell her about submission? Or if a wife comes to you and says that she wants to be obedient to God's Word, but is not sure what that looks like, what can you tell her about submitting to her husband's leadership? Here are some suggestions for words of counsel to wives in the area of submission.

WORDS OF COUNSEL TO WIVES

A Biblical View of Submission

It's a striking fact that every New Testament passage discussing the role of a wife in relation to her husband requires her to submit to him (Eph. 5:22-24; Col. 3:18; 1 Pet. 3:1; Titus 2:5), while no passage indicates that a husband should be subordinate to his wife. Any honest reading of Scripture must conclude that a wife is commanded to submit to her husband.

Certainly few words are more antithetical to the feminist mind-set than *submit*. We should not be surprised if the natural course of human wisdom leads to positions that stand in direct opposition to Scripture. Because this wife has probably, to one degree or another, been exposed to feminist thinking all her life, you may need to help her see that the secular connotations and implications of *submit* are quite different from the consistently positive way this term is used in the Bible.

Full equality. In both her creation and redemption, a wife is fully her husband's equal with respect to her worth and value. True submission in a wife recognizes the husband as her God-ordained authority and has nothing to do with a sense of inferiority.

Joyful obedience. Biblical submission is done intelligently, voluntarily, joyfully, and in faith. It flows from a glad obedience to Scripture, which models the willing submission of the Son of God to His Father, and of the Holy Spirit to the Father and Son, although all three Persons of the Trinity are equal.

Limited specificity. A wife is called to submit to her husband, and only to her husband—not to any other man or to men in general.

Restricted authority. Submission is "as to the Lord" (Eph. 5:22). The only absolute authority over a wife is the Lord Himself, and a wife is truly dependent only on God, not on her husband. A wife should never obey any direction from her husband if doing so would violate Scripture.

Divine enforceability. Let husbands take careful note that this command to submit comes from God; it is not something the husband may demand. The husband is called to teach, remind, encourage, and exhort his wife regarding this command. Exercising all grace, love, and humility, he must refuse to settle for anything less. But it is not his place to enforce God's Law.

Submission and Divine Order

The Christian wife who seeks to honor God in her marriage will be sobered, inspired, and equipped by a clear grasp of Ephesians 5:22-24.

This passage teaches that the respective roles of husband and wife are rooted in the distinctive roles of Christ and His church. Marriage is intended to be a reflection of the divine order in that submission by the wife in marriage reflects the submission of the church to Christ. Help her to see that in neither case is the submission mutual. Christ does not submit to the church, but vice versa, and likewise the husband does not submit to the wife. These roles are not open to redefinition, reinterpretation, or adjustment. Any change represents a deviation from divine purpose, rendering a marriage no longer reflective of the relationship between Christ and the church. Let the wife who loves God and His Word take heart that, in submitting to her husband, she is portraying to the world a reflection of a divine, eternal reality.

A Biblical Understanding of Respect

In addition to submission, Ephesians 5:33 adds that a wife must "respect" her husband. When Jill considers her husband, Harry, are her thoughts characterized by respect? It's sad that, when reminded of this passage, many wives are tempted to respond in ways that violate this very command!

Some of the confusion surely arises from the false belief that respect is essentially an emotion—one deriving, in this case, from a wife's subjective view of how well her husband performs in his multifaceted role. But respect is commanded in Scripture based on a husband's *position*, not his performance.

Headship is a concept woven through all of Scripture. The husband is head of the wife by unchanging divine appointment, not by the choice, preference, or power of any human being. A wife is called to respect her husband because, regardless of his deficiencies, he is her head.

Not long ago there was a President of the United States who lived and behaved in such a way that it was impossible for me to *feel* respect for him. Yet I made every effort to hold him in respect, seeking to think and speak respectfully of him because he held a position of biblical authority that required such behavior of me. God's command that a wife "respect" her husband likewise comes with no qualification—and in that light, disrespect toward her husband equals both disobedience *and* disrespect toward her God.

Here are four practical ways by which a wife can seek to apply the biblical command to respect her husband.

Representation. She should never speak negatively of him to others. He should have no concern about what she may communicate to others regarding him or their marriage. Should she ever need to identify one of his deficiencies to someone else, her doing so should not take him by surprise; the subject should have already come up between them, and he should be comfortable with his deficiency being more widely known.

Consultation. She should not seek counsel from others on important issues until she has discussed them with him. If she disagrees with his position and wishes to get additional counsel on the issue, she should respectfully make him aware of her intention. (See "When a Wife Disagrees with Her Husband" below.)

Attentiveness. When her husband speaks, she should listen attentively to him, making regular eye contact and refraining from correcting him on minor details.

Encouragement. She should adopt a habit of regularly encouraging him in his role as her husband and verbally expressing her respect for him. When appropriate, she should do this in front of their children and in public. When it comes to verbal encouragement, she should understand that Scripture makes no exceptions for temperament, upbringing, or cultural conditioning. If verbal encouragement and expressions of respect seem unnatural to her, she may take encouragement from knowing that these exercises will improve her attitude toward her husband, making her more aware of areas she may have overlooked or failed to appreciate fully.

WHEN A WIFE DISAGREES WITH HER HUSBAND

There will be times when a wife, perhaps for good cause, disagrees with a decision her husband has made or a direction in which he is leading their family. As her husband's equal and as his helper—a gift to him from God—how can the wife appeal her husband's decision, or even challenge it, in a way that honors Scripture? The key lies in honestly communicating her concerns all the while purposing—by grace—never to depart from an active, intentional attitude of submission and respect. As she brings her concerns to her husband, she can do so biblically and honorably by communicating the following:

• Her appreciation that he is taking leadership, even if she disagrees with the direction in which he is leading.

• Her support of him in whatever his final decision will be (excepting, obviously, any decision that would involve a violation of Scripture).

• Her confidence that God is leading their family through him, and her support for him in his leadership role.

As you counsel this couple, remain focused on seeing the glory of God manifested through their lives. In this way, you will prepare them to experience that true, deep, thoroughgoing restoration of marriage that only God can accomplish. As you remind this man of the Gospel, teach him again of the doctrine of sin, define his role as the God-appointed leader in his home, and encourage him about the imperative of forgiveness, you will serve him with the full-orbed counsel of Scripture. As you help the wife grasp the unparalleled beauty and privilege of the role to which she has been called—a model of the Bride of Christ—you will help position her to receive the priceless gift of grace that comes only to the humble. Then, as this husband and wife grow in sanctification, their marriage will increasingly display the glory and goodness of the One who established marriage for that very purpose.

1. Clifton Fadiman, *The Little, Brown Book of Anecdotes* (Boston: Little, Brown, 1985), 523.

2. David Powlison, "Who is God?" *Journal of Biblical Counseling*, Vol. 17, No. 2 (Winter 1999), 16.

3. On this topic of indwelling sin, I must commend the writings of the Puritans. They have been much maligned by the ignorant and ungodly, but the Puritans were passionate about God, and an impressive display of maturity. Why do we need the Puritans? J. I. Packer writes, "The answer in one word is maturity. . . .

The Puritans exemplified maturity; we don't" (*A Quest for Godliness* [Wheaton, IL: Crossway Books, 1990], 22). The Puritans studied the doctrine of sin and sanctification thoroughly and wrote about it exhaustively. They ruthlessly applied it to their lives. On this topic, it would be difficult to improve on the writing of John Owen, especially Volume VI of his *Collected Works*, titled *Temptation and Sin*. An abridged version, *Sin and Temptation*, is available in paperback. And Kris Lundgaard's *The Enemy Within* has, in his words, "kidnapped Owen," bringing his language and thinking into modern English.

4.   Here is a very helpful illustration from an unpublished version of an article (working title, "Basic Biblical Concepts of Human Motivation") from the writings of counselor David Powlison of the Christian Counseling and Educational Foundation. "A woman commits adultery and repents. She and her husband rebuild the marriage painstakingly, patiently. Eight months later the man finds himself plagued with subtle suspiciousness, and the wife senses it and she feels a bit like she lives under FBI surveillance. The husband is grieved by his suspiciousness because he has no objective reasons for his suspicion. 'I've forgiven her. We've rebuilt our marriage. We've never communicated better. Why do I hold on to this mistrust?' What finally emerges is that he is willing to forgive the past, but he is attempting to control the future. His cravings should be stated this way. 'I want to guarantee that betrayal never, ever happens again.' And the very intensity of his craving starts to poison the relationship and it places him in the stance of continually evaluating and judging his wife rather than caring for her and loving her. What he wants cannot be guaranteed this side of heaven. He sees the point. He sees his inordinate desire to ensure the future. Then he bursts out, 'What's wrong with wanting my wife to love me? What's wrong with wanting her to remain faithful to our marriage?' Here is where this truth is so sweet. There is nothing wrong with the object of his desire. But there is everything wrong when it rules his life. The process of restoring that marriage took a long step forward as he grasped a lesson his Shepherd had for him."

5.   Os Guinness and John Seel, eds., *No God but God* (Chicago: Moody Press, 1992), 32-33.

6.   See also John Piper and Wayne Grudem, eds., *Recovering Biblical Manhood and Womanhood* (Wheaton, IL: Crossway Books, 1991).

11

Church Ministry to Persons Tempted by Homosexuality

Bob Davies

━━∞∞∞━━

If you are a typical Christian leader, the admission of homosexuality on the part of someone seeking you out for counseling is probably enough to give you a knot in your stomach. I have certainly talked to a lot of pastors over the past two decades who have found themselves in this uncomfortable situation.

I remember the phone call I received from one such individual. "I really need your help," he began. "There is a fellow coming into my office in twenty minutes, and he's struggling with homosexuality. I don't have a clue how to help him."

"I have really good news for you," I responded. "There are answers. For the next ten minutes I'm going to give you a crash course on how to help this man."

In this chapter I will share the same insights that I gave to that desperate pastor. Even a few simple insights will enable you to move into this type of situation with some confidence and understanding.

MY OWN PAST

I have struggled with homosexuality in my own life and have now been happily married for over fifteen years. In this chapter I want to give you a kind of inside view of the process that God has taken me

210 PASTORAL LEADERSHIP FOR MANHOOD AND WOMANHOOD

through to bring hope and healing. I have also spent the past twenty years giving support to others who struggle with this issue themselves or are close to someone struggling with homosexuality.

This situation reminds me of the verse, "Blessed be the God and Father of our Lord Jesus Christ, the Father of mercies and the God of all comfort, who comforts us in all our affliction so that we will be able to comfort those who are in any affliction with the comfort with which we ourselves are comforted by God" (2 Cor. 1:3-4, NASB). God has comforted me in the midst of homosexual struggles; now I can show you how to offer that same comfort to others.

I first became aware of homosexual feelings when I was entering puberty at about age twelve. This is an important point: "I became aware of . . ." Few men and women consciously choose to have these feelings or attractions. Rather, I believe that they arise from deep inner conflicts that often take root in early life. Many people, like me, are absolutely horrified to make this discovery about themselves.

Several years later I read about something called "homosexuality" in a book for teens on sexuality. I had never heard of such a thing, but as I read this book, the authors seemed to be talking about things I had been experiencing for several years.

Looking back, I can see several problems that "set me up" to experience homosexual attractions. For one thing, I was tall, gawky, and rather unathletic. By the time I got to junior high, I always seemed to be the last person chosen for any sports team. I remember the feelings of deep embarrassment and humiliation just being in those situations. I felt isolated from other boys. I never fit in. I had felt this way for years.

As I moved through my teen years, I realized that the boys and older men to whom I was attracted seemed to have something that I was lacking. Now I know what it was: a firm confidence in their own masculinity. That's what I was lacking, and I was drawn to the boys who had it. I wanted it, but I didn't know how to get it.

As I entered my twenties, I went to college and discovered there was a gay community all around me in my home city of Vancouver, Canada. Back in those days (the early seventies) it wasn't talked about. But homosexuals knew how to find each other, and there were a few bars that attracted a large clientele in the evenings and on weekends.

Now, I had grown up in the church and made a commitment to Jesus Christ about the same time I entered puberty. God had His hand on my life, and I never indulged in homosexual practices. But the inner agony was still severe. I felt the temptations, and I sure wished that the same-sex feelings would go away.

I had drifted spiritually during my late teens, but by my early twenties I was back in fellowship and soon entered Bible college. There for the first time I began to experience healthy same-sex relationships. I lived in the dorm and had a large number of other male students as my friends. I absolutely loved it! I had never experienced such a closeness with other men before, and my homosexual attractions actually receded during this time.

However, after graduation, as I searched for the right career path, I came face-to-face with my inner struggles again. After a stint in short-term missions, I felt the Lord challenging me: "You can't lead others into freedom until you have allowed Me to set you free!" I knew that I'd have to deal with the inner battle that had diminished at times but never been totally won. It was time to deal with my homosexuality once and for all. But how?

ENTERING COUNSELING

In my search for answers, I visited the largest Christian bookstore in my hometown and discovered a book of testimonies of men and women who were seeking freedom from homosexuality through a counseling program associated with Exodus International. I wrote the ministry for more information and felt God's leading to enter their live-in residential program. I moved to the San Francisco Bay area in mid-1979 and entered intensive counseling. What I learned at that ministry changed my life—and my sexual struggles.

During the counseling process I found the answers to some basic questions. One of the most important questions is: Can gays really change?

Yes, they can! One of the most common beliefs in the gay community is: Homosexuality is a genetic condition and therefore cannot be changed. This is something you hear over and over until it becomes a given among active homosexuals and lesbians.

As a Christian, I have two problems with this belief. First, the idea that homosexuality cannot be changed does not take into account the life-changing power of Jesus Christ. He Himself said, "With God all things are possible" (Matt. 19:26), and I believe that verse applies to all the "hard" problems, including homosexuality.

Back in my early days of involvement with Exodus, we used to do a lot of street evangelism in the gay areas of San Francisco. It was a very eye-opening experience. I realized, in talking with men coming out of the gay bars, that there was a shocking number of people in those bars who had grown up in Christian homes.

I would be sharing the Gospel with these gay men, and I'd start quoting a well-known Bible verse. I'd start—and they would finish it for me! Some of these guys knew more about the Scriptures than I did. But they did not know how to apply the Gospel to their sexual struggles.

It's almost as if their lives were divided into two, and the two sections were isolated from each other by a high wall. Perhaps we could label that wall "unbelief" or even "wrong teaching." These gay men did not know how to bring the power of the cross of Christ into the sexual area of their life.

This illustrates one of our biggest struggles as Christian leaders and counselors. We have to show people how to apply the Gospel to their deepest struggles. Otherwise they simply have head knowledge, but not a heart knowledge of the Bible that changes their lives.

I also began to see that there was a real "victim" mentality in the gay community. They had the assumption, "This is something I was born with—and it's something I will die with. Therefore there is nothing I can do about it." These men and women felt powerless. This is a tragedy—and a stronghold that we have to deal with when these people enter our churches. Jesus said that the truth sets us free (John 8:32). That Scripture has a powerful application in this case.

GENETIC?

Let's take a moment to review the common arguments that homosexuality is inborn and genetic. But first, a disclaimer. After twenty years in this ministry, I realize that I don't have all the answers. I am not trained as a genetic biologist. So I cannot prove conclusively once and for all that there is no genetic basis for homosexuality.

However, my lifestyle choices are not dependent upon the latest scientific study. If—and I say *if*—there were proven to be a gene that causes homosexual tendencies, that discovery would not change my moral choices. I would still choose to abstain from homosexual activities because of what the Word of God says about it.

In any case, the studies that have been widely trumpeted by the media are inconclusive. Think about it for a minute: If proof existed that homosexuality was genetic, that news would be on the front page of every newspaper in the country. And the debate would be over. However, the debate is still ongoing, which proves that neither side has offered conclusive proof for its point of view.

Another problem I have with these studies is that in most cases the primary researcher is gay and intent on proving a point. Simon LeVay is a good example. He compared brains in gay and straight men and concluded that the brain structure was different. Later he admitted to the press that he was gay and was absolutely committed to finding a biological explanation for his homosexuality. So he had a clear agenda. This does not nullify his findings, but it does cause me to take a second look at his claims. Unfortunately, in looking at his studies you find that the data does not support any firm conclusions on what LeVay set out to prove. More specifically, LeVay's autopsies of men who had died (1) could not show whether the alleged brain differences appeared before or after a pattern of homosexual activity, (2) had too small a sample to draw firm conclusions, and (3) used extremely imprecise criteria for classifying someone as "homosexual" or "heterosexual."[1]

Through our ministry we have also come across a lot of data that directly contradicts the "born gay" theory. But you never hear about these studies. The media ignores them. For example, there was a

British study published a few years ago that directly contradicted the idea that identical twins share a gay gene. Researchers found that in a low minority of cases when one identical twin was gay, the other was also gay. If genes were causative, why weren't identical twins always both gay or always both straight? But that's not what the study revealed. And so the mainstream media totally ignored this study published in a respectable British journal.[2]

I've seen this bias in lots of papers. Studies that appear to support inborn homosexuality get major headlines; those that appear to disprove it are ignored. We need to be aware that there is ongoing study on both sides of this question.

One final point: No matter what a study reveals, it has to be replicated. This is just good basic science. One study doesn't really prove anything. Its findings have to be duplicated by other researchers before it is considered valid. And none of the "gay gene" studies have been duplicated to date. (The Exodus website offers much more information on this subject. Go to www.exodusnorthamerica.org under "Library" and then "Homosexuality and Society.")

ROOTS AND CAUSES

If homosexuality isn't caused by a person's genes, how do we explain this condition? Although I can't prove that early-life experiences cause homosexuality, I can tell you from talking to hundreds of men and women that there are some background factors that are extremely common in gay men and women. Here are some patterns that we have observed over the past quarter-century of ministry at Exodus:

Sexual/emotional abuse: We have known for years that an overwhelming majority of women—and a significant number of men—struggling with lesbian/homosexual issues have suffered sexual abuse, usually at the hands of an older man. In the case of a young girl, this terrifying experience causes her to associate masculinity with pain, fear, and hurt. I believe these women grow up to reject men, and not just the man who abused them; their rejection is projected toward all men.

Many of these woman have told me that they began to dress in ways that deflected male attention. They wore baggy clothing to hide their developing figure; they avoided makeup and all other signs of femininity that would draw unwanted attention from men.

In the case of young boys who are molested, these experiences caused them to question their male sexual identity, which was often already shaky. These boys wonder, "What's wrong with me that a man finds me attractive in this way?"

Difficulty in same-sex peer relationships: Most of the men—and many of the women—coming through our counseling ministries report feeling "apart from" and "different than" others of their same gender when they were growing up. Often these kids adopted opposite-sex activities (boys played with dolls; girls played war games and climbed trees) and hung around opposite-sex friends. In my own case I remember clearly staying away from the boys' side of the playground at school. I couldn't play soccer very well; so I entered into all the girls' games like skip-rope. Most of my friends were girls. I felt accepted by them, but the boys only ridiculed me and called me names like "sissy." So I stayed away from same-sex peers most of the time.

Lack of bonding with same-sex elders: In a huge majority of cases, the men in Exodus tell us, "I never felt close to my dad." Even those of us whose father was physically present in the home felt somehow detached. "I never remember my father holding me or telling me that he loved me" is a frequent lament. Of course, the rise of single-parent homes has led to an epidemic of boys and girls growing up without a same-sex parent in the home. This does not cause homosexuality; however, unless appropriate role models are present in a young person's life, it can open the door for homosexual temptation to satisfy unmet same-sex emotional needs.

MAKING RIGHT CHOICES

So most of the men and women coming to your church for help will say, "I never chose these feelings." It's OK to acknowledge that by saying, "You know, I realize that." But then we need to confront them with the choices they do have: "Where are you going to head from today on?"

This is the choice that God gives all of us: "I have set before you life and death, blessing and curse. Therefore choose life, that you and your offspring may live" (Deut. 30:19, ESV). We *do* have a choice. We can decide what pathway we're going to head down from today on. The homosexually inclined single man has the same power and responsibility to remain sexually pure as the heterosexually inclined single man (this applies to married men too—sexual struggles don't stop when you put on a wedding ring!).

Am I going to resist my improper sexual desires or yield to them? This is the main area of challenge that we need to address in helping a counselee overcome a "victim" mentality. God doesn't focus on what brought these temptations into our lives; He wants to know how we are going to respond to them. Fight and flee? Or succumb and sin?

Through the power of Jesus Christ working in our lives, we *do* have a choice. In Him we are no longer victims of our past.

So *give hope for change.* This is the first thing that I tell anyone calling our office for advice. How should they handle the situation? The first principle is always, "Give hope." Life *can* be different. Through Jesus Christ we can take the first step away from homosexuality. It doesn't have to be a life sentence.

If you are a pastor, I encourage you to preach this good news. I've heard so many people tell me, "I grew up in the church. I've always known that homosexual behavior was sin. But I *never* once heard a pastor offer hope for me." They were sitting in the pew week after week, but they never had a word of hope and encouragement. Let's start offering a word of hope to those who struggle in silence alone.

There is another way that you can communicate hope: by talking about men and women who have changed. One of the most powerful things about Exodus is the men and women who offer their testimonies as proof that overcoming homosexuality is possible. There are literally thousands of Christians who have either overcome this problem successfully or are in the process of overcoming it.

At our annual national conference we have over a thousand delegates in attendance. I would guess that two-thirds of these people are former homosexuals and lesbians. There is such power when these people get together. The world doesn't even acknowledge they exist, but here is a huge auditorium full of them! It's very powerful and moving to witness this event.

WHAT DO THE SCRIPTURES SAY?

God is clear that homosexual activities are not part of His plan for humanity. Five passages of Scripture are commonly used to justify this position: Genesis 19, the story of Sodom and Gomorrah; Leviticus 18:22 and 20:13, the Moral Law; Romans 1, especially verses 26 and 27; 1 Corinthians 6:9-11; and a parallel passage in 1 Timothy 1:10.

I could spend this entire chapter reviewing these passages, and there are many excellent resources available through Exodus if you need more details. But there are a couple of issues that you might face in dealing with this among your parishioners. First, some people who are struggling with homosexuality may wonder if there is a loophole in the scriptural arguments. "Maybe God doesn't really condemn this activity. Maybe there is some way I can combine my Christian beliefs with a gay identity."

This is the position of the "pro-gay Christian" movement, which has become increasingly strong in the last twenty years. When I began working with Exodus in 1979, this movement was largely unknown; today its teachings are everywhere, even making inroads into evangelical congregations. For more information on this viewpoint, I highly recommend the book *A Strong Delusion* by Joe Dallas (Harvest House).

Joe was on the pastoral staff at an evangelical church in southern California. He used to scoff at the local gay church when he drove by it—until he got ensnared in homosexuality and found himself visiting the local gay congregation to see what they really believed. He became caught up in this false theology for several years and was actually training to become a minister in the Metropolitan Community Church (MCC), which is a pro-gay denomination.

But as Joe got more and more involved in this movement, he began to see that something was missing. He couldn't quite put his finger on the problem, but he knew there was an emptiness in his life.

One day he found himself watching a Christian television program, and he heard a sermon on the biblical perspective on homosexuality. Joe began to have doubts about the direction of his life. "What if I'm wrong?" he wondered. "What if the Bible really does condemn homosexuality?" Soon he was back in fellowship with his old church friends, and God pulled him out of the MCC. He left homosexual activities and eventually became the president of Exodus International. Today he speaks all over the world on the false theology of the pro-gay movement and how to counter its teachings.

There is one passage that I want to look at in more detail because it had such a powerful impact on my own life. If you are talking to a counselee and you're not sure which passage to share, I encourage you to consider reading these verses from 1 Corinthians 6:9-11:

> Or do you not know that the unrighteous will not inherit the kingdom of God? Do not be deceived; neither fornicators, nor idolaters, nor adulterers, nor effeminate, nor homosexuals, nor thieves, nor the covetous, nor drunkards, nor revilers, nor swindlers, will inherit the kingdom of God. Such were some of you; but you were washed, but you were sanctified, but you were justified in the name of the Lord Jesus Christ and in the Spirit of our God. (NASB)

This passage was a life-changing beacon of hope for me. In my late teens, I was beginning to read all the pro-gay theology books that were available back then. I knew that I was attracted to other men, but I didn't really know what to think about the Bible's stand on this issue. So I went to the library at my secular university and began checking out all the books on the Bible and homosexuality. Unfortunately, they were all pro-gay in their interpretation of the biblical passages. I really wanted to believe what these books were telling me, but I felt an inner resistance that I didn't fully understand. Today, of course, I believe that the Holy Spirit was gently resisting these erroneous interpretations of the Bible.

Somewhere in the midst of my struggling I came across this passage in 1 Corinthians. I read that the unrighteous will not inherit the kingdom of God and that I should not be deceived into believing otherwise. Then I read about a whole list of behaviors—including homosexuality—that the believers in the church of Corinth had been involved in.

Then I read, "Such were some of you." "Were"—that's past tense. I realized that the issue of overcoming homosexuality was not something new on the scene. The Gospel hadn't changed in two thousand years. People were being delivered from homosexual activities in Paul's day, and they still are today.

When I read this verse, I began to have hope. If God could change them, maybe He could change me too.

I love verse 11 of this passage: "You were washed." Despite what you hear today, homosexuality is not a clean or pure way of life. "You were sanctified" or set apart. You cannot be walking close to God and be involved in homosexual activities. It's impossible. "You were justified" or declared righteous. This shows me that homosexuality is not a right way to live. "Such were some of you." From the first century until now, people have been overcoming this sin. It is possible through the power of Jesus Christ.

THE BIGGER PERSPECTIVE

I also encourage you to keep in mind as you are counseling someone to look beyond these five passages that address homosexuality. We need to examine the bigger biblical picture of what God intended for men and women.

I know one man who was deeply involved in homosexuality. But after a few years John found himself dissatisfied. He also had a major drinking problem from hanging out in gay bars every night. Then he was befriended by a local pastor who was a regular customer at the copy shop where John worked. He didn't know why, but this pastor treated him with love and respect, even though John was obviously gay.

One day this pastor asked if he could visit John. "Can I come over to your house? There is something I want to share with you." John suspected that he was about to become this man's latest evangelistic project, but he agreed anyway. He was growing increasingly unhappy with his life and decided maybe this pastor had something he should look into.

So the pastor came to visit, and their conversation led right into a discussion of the Scriptures. But instead of talking about Romans 1 or 1 Corinthians 6, this pastor began talking about the first two chapters of Genesis and God's original plan for men and women. Then the pastor read Genesis 1:27, "And God made man in His own image, in the image of God He created him; male and female He created them" (NASB). Then they read Genesis 2:18 (NASB), "Then the LORD God said, 'It is not good for the man to be alone; I will make a helper suitable for him.'" God then created woman.

It was one of those divinely empowered moments, and the scales fell off John's eyes. He realized that homosexuality was not God's intent for him. Within weeks John became a Christian, and this pastor and his wife supported him in leaving homosexuality behind. Today John is happily married with two children. His life shows that the Scriptures can be very powerful. So don't stop at sharing that homosexuality is wrong; show a person what God's original intentions were. I think this can be very helpful.

HOW DOES CHANGE OCCUR?

As a Christian counselor, I believe that the process of changing out of homosexuality begins with salvation. I've seen that in my own life and in the lives of many other people. About 99 percent of the people contacting Exodus for help with this issue are born-again believers. Why do these people come to Exodus? Because they are experiencing a deep-seated conflict between their homosexual feelings and biblical beliefs. That's the crux of the dilemma that draws them to seek help from Exodus. And that's probably the crux of the struggle that will draw people to you for help.

Some Christians are surprised to hear this. They think that if you are a "real" Christian, you won't have problems like homosexuality. I disagree with that kind of thinking. I know all kinds of Christians who have all kinds of struggles, including this one. But being Christians with the Holy Spirit in our lives, we have the motivation to change and the power to change.

So make sure that this person has made a genuine commitment to

Christ. Don't take it for granted. Explore his or her faith with him or her. Is it real or theoretical? Is it head knowledge or heart experience?

Don't be surprised, however, if the person struggling with homosexuality has made a commitment to Christ at some point in his or her life. This is very often true. Such persons may be wandering far from God when they come for help, but often they have become Christians in the past. So they need a renewal of their faith, a recommitment and a fresh beginning with Him.

In my early twenties, I ended up in a small church where I was warmly embraced back into the faith. I renewed my commitment to Christ and ended up going to Bible college for three years. I had grown up in the church, but I must have been sleeping in Sunday school classes. I was really ignorant of the Bible! But in Bible college we were immersed in the Scriptures hour after hour. It was a great time! But after graduation I struggled for several years in knowing the next step for my life. I got involved in short-term missions with Youth With A Mission and began making preparations for long-term service overseas.

Then came an evening service that I'll never forget. A visiting speaker shared his experiences of witnessing in countries all around the world, with many hundreds of people coming to Christ. I longed for my life to count for God's kingdom just like this man's.

Then, as I shared earlier, I felt the challenge of the Holy Spirit: "You can't lead others into freedom until you have experienced it yourself." I felt nailed to the wall. I knew the Lord was pointing out the one area of my life that was still carefully hidden from my family and friends: my sexual identity struggles. And I was scared, really scared.

I remembered back several years when I had been at the end of my training with Youth With A Mission. One day I had been praying about my future, and God gave me a mental picture of myself handing out tracts in front of the largest gay bar in Vancouver, B.C. I thought, "No way! I'll do anything but that!"

Now I knew that the time had come to surrender this area of my life to Christ. I was facing the Lordship issue. I was a Christian and

222   Pastoral Leadership for Manhood and Womanhood

knew Jesus Christ in a personal way, but I was holding back part of my life from His control. Was I willing to give everything to Him, including my sexual struggles?

I wrestled with God for several days before, in sheer exhaustion, I said, "OK, Lord, my life is Yours. Totally Yours. Do with me whatever You want!"

Almost immediately I sensed that the Lord wanted me to move to California and become involved in an Exodus ministry near San Francisco. And that's how I ended up getting involved in Exodus International. That first step of obedience, yielding my sexuality to Christ, opened up a new door of healing and direction for me. That was twenty years ago, and I've been involved in Exodus ever since.

Going Deeper with God

Yielding to the Lordship of Christ opened the door for me to experience more of His healing in my life. Once I got to the San Francisco Bay Area my ongoing commitment to obedience continued, one day and one decision at a time. I discovered that I had lived most of my life behind walls, keeping everyone at arm's length to keep them from getting to know the "real" me. Now God began challenging me to "walk in the Light" (1 John 1:7, NASB) and become accountable to others. This was one of the hardest things I'd ever been asked.

You see, I had hidden my deep, dark secret from all my closest friends for years. Coming into a church fellowship where everyone knew from the first day the deepest struggle of my life was quite a change. It felt very strange. And yet people responded with genuine warmth and encouragement. For the first time in my life I felt accepted for who I really was, rather than the "good Christian boy" image that I projected. And that depth of fellowship was life-changing for me.

God began to dig out the underlying root issues that had fed my homosexual desires in the first place. Homosexuality is just a surface symptom; our job as counselors is to help someone discover the underlying roots and then begin to dig them up.

At the danger of being overly simplistic, I'm going to give my one-sentence summary of what male homosexuality is all about. This is a summary of everything I have learned in the past twenty years: *Male homosexuality is a search for same-sex affirmation and approval.* Gay men have usually grown up feeling very alienated from other boys. Often they feel alienated from their father also. This was true for me, and I don't know why. My father was home every night; he and my mother stayed married for fifty-four years until his death several years ago. But he did not know how to connect emotionally with me. He showed no affection toward me. I didn't sense a bonding with him.

One day my mother told me that I was my dad's favorite child. I was totally shocked; I had no idea. Even though I'm sure that Dad was extending love to me in his own way, I wasn't able to sense it or receive it. It was almost like we were living on different wavelengths. Radio waves are all around us, but unless you have a receiver, you'll never hear the sounds. That's how I was living, detached from Dad. So I grew up with a deep insecurity in my maleness. I felt vastly inferior to other boys. The other boys picked up on that; so I had difficulty with peer relationships.

In reaching puberty, I had a deep desire to connect with other men. But it became sexualized. This is where the enemy comes in with his deception. "Are you attracted to that man?" he whispers. "Then you must be homosexual." No, that's a lie. This boy is only looking for the fulfillment of his God-given need to bond with other males. But the emotional need gets twisted into a sexual desire, and the deception takes hold.

This is, ultimately, why God says no to homosexuality. It never meets the underlying need. I've known men who have had hundreds of sexual partners, and they are just as hungry for same-sex bonding as when they started. Tragically, many of them have become infected with HIV or other diseases in their frantic search for a sense of connection with other men. God wants to meet those needs, but not through promiscuous sex. Homosexuality will never meet the deeper need of the heart. Only godly and deep friendships with other men— and the love of the heavenly Father—can reach into those deep areas and bring fulfillment.

What about women? The overwhelming majority of women coming to our counseling centers have been sexually abused. We've known this for years. It is consistently over 80 percent. Now, I'm not saying this is true for all lesbians; I simply don't know. But I do know it's true for our female clients. So I believe that lesbianism represents a flight from masculinity. These woman are fleeing emotionally and physically from the source of their deepest wounds. Men represent hurt, pain, and fear, and these lesbian women want nothing to do with them.

These are just a couple of examples of the underlying root issues that are often present in the lives of these men and women struggling with inappropriate same-sex attractions. Family dynamics are also often present, such as ridicule or rejection of the child's sex ("I always wished you were a girl," one of my male friends heard constantly from his mother). Another thing I hear often from men is their feelings of acceptance and attachment with their mother and sisters. Maybe a father wasn't present in the home at all. So they patterned themselves after Mom; they became interested in the activities Mom did, like cooking, sewing, and cleaning. These are not female activities per se, but the boy became interested in them because he saw his mother's involvement. He may have even unconsciously copied the way Mom talked and walked. These boys grow up to be labeled as "effeminate," and it's really a tough battle to change these deeply ingrained habits that have been unconsciously adopted since early life.

So we need to spend time with these people and ask God to show us the underlying root issues that need to be overcome. This is where overcoming homosexuality becomes a tough, tough battle. There is no short, easy way out. It's a struggle that can take months and years of discipleship and Christian growth.

Don't look for a quick and easy answer. Ultimately, that can be more discouraging than simply admitting the battle is long and tough. Before I got involved in Exodus, I sought out counsel from a pastor who thought that "deliverance" was the key. (I'm not putting down demonic deliverance; it can be a helpful tool, but I don't believe it is the whole, instant answer.) This pastor gave me a book to read. At the end were sample prayers that you could speak out loud to perform deliverance on yourself. One of the prayers supposedly broke the power of homosexuality in a person's life. Now how is that for convenience? This guy didn't even have to pray for me himself—he could send me away with a book and have me do it myself! Needless to say, it did not work.

I've also talked to many other people who have experienced this kind of "instant" counseling. Sometimes it appears to work. But almost inevitably those homosexual feelings will return—whether it's a day, week, or even months afterward. The underlying root issues haven't been touched. And the person is devastated. Usually he or she is too embarrassed to go back to the counselor and admit he or she still has struggles. Such individuals are caught in a dilemma, and so they call Exodus for help.

Sometimes these people are in worse shape than before they were "delivered." They are confused and discouraged. They've been robbed of hope; sometimes they have been robbed of support and accountability in their home church. So this is a real problem we need to avoid. I'm uncomfortable with deliverance being presented as "the" solution to overcoming homosexuality. It's one key of many, so treat it appropriately.

TRIGGERS TO TEMPTATION

We've discussed early-life traumas and circumstances that can set a person up for homosexual temptations later in life. But once you begin counseling someone, you will find there are current issues that can be a struggle too. I call these "triggers to temptation." These people may have a period of success; they feel like they are doing well. Then they stumble and fall backwards. The root issues are triggered in some way. Here are a couple of examples:

Loneliness: This is a huge issue for many gays and lesbians, because they have struggled with feeling alienated from other people. Despite the growing acceptance of the gay movement, there is still a stigma attached to this issue in our society, especially in the conservative church. Even "ex"-gays can feel that stigma, the glance or stare that says, "I don't feel comfortable around you."

Insecurity: I remember returning to my home church in Vancouver, B.C., after I'd been involved in Exodus for a couple of years. God had done a lot of healing in my life, and I was going to share my story with all my friends back home. On the way to church that night, I was battling an inner struggle with fear and insecurity. These people had known me for years, but now I was going to reveal another part of my life. How would they react? What would they say? Would they reject me? Would it be awkward and embarrassing to face them afterward?

So I was driving to church, and I noticed that I was really struggling with visual temptation. I was noticing men on the street that usually I would ignore. What was happening? The Lord showed me later that my insecurity was triggering temptation. This is an example of how underlying emotions can prompt homosexual desires. So in the midst of a temptation it's helpful to ask, "What am I feeling right now?" and then figure out how to get that emotional need met in a healthy way.

There are also spiritual factors that can be at work. Spiritual warfare is a daily reality in the life of a former homosexual or lesbian. The mind is the greatest battlefield of all. There are a couple of specific areas where people are going to need help:

Memories: The ex-gay man or woman can battle a dozen distractions every day, sights or sounds or smells that trigger an association with past sin. People tell me, "I saw this guy in the post office that reminded me of my first lover twenty years ago. Suddenly all the feelings came rushing back." This can be extremely discouraging. We have to learn how to put off the flesh with its associations and memories of the past.

Lies: This is where the enemy has a field day. There are so many unbiblical patterns of thinking that can ensnare us. Here are some examples: "I'll never be normal." "No one would like me if they knew my past." "I'll always be lesbian or gay." These are thoughts that the enemy can plant in our minds, especially when we are in the midst of a struggle with temptation. We have to counteract the lies with biblical truth. What does God say? Who does He declare that I am?

God says that we are created in His image. Once we come to Christ, we have a new identity in Him. Unless we get ahold of these truths, we will continue to identify with our past. We will continue to define ourselves by our feelings, our temptations. And change will be prevented.

This is where internalizing Scripture can be so helpful—reading the Bible, memorizing relevant verses, worshiping God through the Psalms. We don't have any magic formulas for overcoming homosexuality at Exodus. We are simply promoting good old-fashioned Christian discipleship—with a specific application to this struggle. And it works!

When you really understand that, you'll realize as a pastor that you have a lot more tools at your disposal than you might have imagined. Let's give another example. A majority of Christian men dealing with homosexuality also struggle with pornography. It's everywhere—only a click away on the Internet. How should we help people? By giving them the same principles that we would give a straight guy struggling with the same issue. They are looking at different kinds of pornography, but the advice would be the same.

This carries over into all kinds of other problems that ex-gays might be struggling with: masturbation, impure thoughts, lust, inferiority, fear, insecurity, isolation, loneliness, laziness, immaturity. Take away the homosexual symptom and ask yourself, "What would I tell a straight man dealing with these issues?" That's the exact same advice to tell a former homosexual.

I got a strong dose of basic Christian discipleship during my first years at Exodus. I remember the first year going through the entire Bible and writing down every single verse that applied to my struggles. I collected verses on "thought life," "lust," "fear," "temptation." Then I applied each verse to my specific struggle with homosexuality, and I found the Bible was incredibly relevant to my deepest struggles. It was eye-opening, to say the least. I had never learned to apply the Bible so directly to *this* struggle before. So I encourage you to try this with your counselees. Get them into the Word, and ask them to come back with ten Scriptures the next week that they have found speak directly to some current issue in their lives. They will probably be amazed at what they find. They will be applying truths of God's Word to the deepest struggles of their life.

In Exodus I learned how to "walk in the Light" with others. Finally I found a safe place to confess my ongoing struggles with pornography, lust, masturbation, whatever—all those secret things that far too many Christian men face alone. I never found victory while struggling alone. God says to "confess your sins [faults, short-comings] to one another, and pray for one other so that you may be healed" (Jas. 5:16, NASB). Healing comes from walking in openness with other Christian brothers.

By the way, I am not implying that what I found in that small church in California will automatically fit your church as well. Maybe your church simply isn't ready to have former homosexuals publicly admit their struggles. But at the same time, these people will never make it alone. At least they can confide in you as pastor. But ideally they should have additional accountability with other close friends. Perhaps there is a Bible study or men's small group that could handle this type of openness.

If there is nowhere these people can find accountability, they are not going to make it in the long run. Many, many men have confessed to me, "I didn't go into gay bars looking for sex. I went looking for unconditional acceptance." If they can't find it in the church, they'll go looking elsewhere. This is one of the greater challenges we face today: making our churches safe places where people can come out from behind their walls and be real with each other, where all the deepest struggles of their lives can be shared and prayed about. When that happens, lives are changed in deep and profound ways.

As a pastor or leader or counselor, you have an awesome respon-sibility. Your reaction to someone's confession will have a profound influence on his or her life. If you react with understanding and com-passion, he or she will likely take a step forward toward wholeness and freedom. It's a real privilege in my office when I answer the phone and hear someone's confession: "You're the first person I have ever told. I have never, ever confessed this struggle before." When that happens, I feel like I am on holy ground. We do not know all the answers, but we can assure them, "God loves you. He has an answer for your life. There is hope for you." Don't get intimidated by the circumstances. Trust God to fill you with His wisdom. Then be available for Him to use you to bring hope and healing to those struggling with homosexuality.

1. See the response to LeVay by a medical doctor with a specialty in psychiatry: Jeffrey Satinover, *Homosexuality and the Politics of Truth* (Grand Rapids, MI: Baker, 1996), 78-81.

2. See M. King and E. McDonald, "Homosexuals Who Are Twins: A Study of 46 Probands," *British Journal of Psychiatry* 160 (1992), 407-409; the article is summarized in Satinover, *Homosexuality and the Politics of Truth*, 87-88.

12

"Someone I Love Is Gay": Church Ministry to Family and Friends

Bob Davies

———◦◦◦———

The issue of homosexuality is becoming increasingly prominent in our society today. It's a big shock, however, when the issue hits home and we realize that a close friend, relative, or family member is involved. We are faced with a myriad of questions: What do we say? How do we act? Should we continue relating to this person? Should we attempt to share our faith? What if they are not interested? And how do we act around their gay friends? The questions are endless.

Over the past twenty years that I've worked with Exodus International, I've talked to hundreds of friends and family members. So I have learned a lot from them. And I hear the same kinds of issues and questions surfacing over and over again.

THE CONCERNS OF PARENTS

The largest group that we get coming to us among family members is parents, particularly mothers (in fact, it is rare to be contacted by a father). So parents are probably the biggest group you will have to deal with as well. These parents are usually totally devastated, especially if the discovery that their child is gay has been made just recently.

I think of Anita Worthen, a good friend of mine and coauthor with me of the book *Someone I Love Is Gay* (InterVarsity Press). In the book, Anita tells the story of finding out about her sixteen-year-old son, Tony. Anita had come to Christ after Tony was born, and she'd had him out of wedlock. So she was raising him as a single mom, thinking she was doing a great job. She lived in a Christian community at that time, surrounded by other Christians who gave support to her and her son.

When Tony was about sixteen, Anita remembers him going off track a bit. She didn't know what was happening, but his actions began to cause concern. For one thing, he was staying out half the night, and he seemed to have become friends with a whole new group of guys she didn't know. So she was worried and concerned.

One afternoon she snuck into Tony's bedroom and found his wallet. Inside was a piece of paper with a list of names and phone numbers. Anita grabbed a pen and began copying down the information, when in walked Tony. Of course, he was terribly upset.

"Mom, what are you doing?" he yelled.

Anita tried to remain calm. "Tony, I'm concerned about you. It seems like you're beginning to hang around with a lot of friends I don't know. If you're ever out late at night, I need to know who to call."

Then came the bombshell. "Well, you know I'm gay, right?"

Anita remembers sitting there with her mouth open, in total shock. In that one instant her whole life changed. And she was devastated. For the next few months she floundered on what to do and where to find help.

I remember another father who said, "When this hit us, it felt like a freight train smashing into our nice, normal Christian family." So this discovery can cause huge shock waves in a family.

One mother even told me, "Finding out about a gay child is agony. It's almost like having a death in the family." This mother had lost two sons in death before discovering that another son was involved in homosexuality. "When someone dies," she said, "you can bury that person and move on with your life. But with homosexuality, the pain seems never-ending."

So I think the biggest challenge you will have to deal with as a pastor or counselor is helping these families go through their own emotional reactions. The big one, of course, is grief.

Some families who have never gone through this may wonder why the grief is so profound and prolonged for many parents. Let me give some insights here, especially for parents. Discovering a loved one is gay represents a huge loss. You may not have thought of it this way because the person is still alive. But there is a huge shift in perspective. The person they have known and loved for years now seems to have changed into a totally different person, with a very alien problem. So these parents are grieving the loss of the person they thought they knew.

There is a loss of security for these families. All of a sudden this person seems like a stranger. There is a whole hidden side to them that they have never known before. Of course, gay persons have a totally different perspective. Usually they have been aware of these feelings for years. In my own case, I told my parents about this struggle when I was in my late twenties. But I had known since age fourteen that I was attracted to other men and that this condition was called homosexuality. So I had struggled in silence for over a decade before taking the step of sharing my situation with my parents. It was a total shock to them, but it was an old issue with me by that time.

There is a loss of security when this hits a Christian marriage. One Exodus leader told me years ago that about one-third of his male clients were married men struggling with homosexuality. So it's not terribly unusual for spouses to be hit with this. In fact, there seems to be a new phenomenon happening these days that I hadn't heard much about before, and that is the increasing number of middle-aged men and women who are "coming out of the closet" and declaring their homosexuality. For some of them, there has probably been a struggle for years. In fact, they may have originally married in the hopes that their same-sex attractions would disappear—which rarely happens. If anything, the stresses of marriage can trigger even more temptations in this area.

What I suspect is happening here is that these middle-aged men and women have deep unresolved issues from their past, such as child-hood sexual abuse, that they have never dealt with. These hidden problems eventually surface, and then they manifest as inappropriate same-sex longings. The person doesn't know where on earth these feelings are coming from and, in today's "gay-affirmative" culture, wrongly assumes that the solution is to go out and have sex with a person of their own gender. After several experiences these people are deceived into thinking they have finally found the answer to their inner struggles, and they also conclude that they were gay all along but just didn't realize it. So they take on a false solution to a very genuine problem. It's a total deception, and they lose their marriage in the process.

One friend of mine was married for ten years before she "discovered" that she was a lesbian. Jane had been sexually abused as a girl, and she grew up with a deep bitterness toward men. Somehow she managed to function in her marriage in spite of this hatred, until she fell into a lesbian relationship. Then she was faced with the excruciating decision: continue to live as a lesbian in relationships that felt safe and wonderful or give that up and return to a marriage that felt barren and lonely.

Of course, with the proper counseling and support, Jane was able to discover that marriage to a man could be fulfilling, but she had a lot of emotional baggage to deal with first. Her motivation was given a huge boost when her husband gave her an ultimatum: "I'm leaving the marriage if you won't give up your lesbian friendships." Jane realized that she would lose the most important things in her life—her husband and children—if she persisted in same-sex intimacies with other women; so she turned away from those friends and recommitted her life to Christ. Today she finds wonderful fulfillment in her marriage and speaks all over the country on how God has done such a powerful work in her life.

Another loss is the shattering of future dreams. We all have ideas about our future. For parents, maybe it's the hope of having grand-children, or a big church wedding for an only daughter. We all have these fantasies. They are normal, healthy. Now they seem impossible. We mourn the future that may never happen.

There is also a loss of reputation. This continues to be a very difficult issue in the church today. There is still a stigma attached to homosexuality, and it affects the church at different levels. We even have senior pastors calling us for help with their own struggles. How can they tell anyone? They might lose their job!

I remember twenty years ago when I was new at the Exodus office. One night I was working overtime, and the phone rang. It was a Lutheran pastor from the Midwest, and he told me that he struggled with homosexuality. He also told me that he had never, ever told anyone about this secret. It had become a huge burden that was crushing his life. Over the next couple of hours, out came the whole story. It was a huge relief to him. All the time I was wondering, "Who am I to be counseling this pastor?" I was just new to the whole ministry myself! But I'll never forget the relief that pastor felt just in telling another human being about the deepest struggle in his life.

We also hear from pastors' wives, youth pastors, church musicians, and other Christian leaders. They are terrified that others will find out.

I think the key loss, however, is the loss of relationship with this individual. Whether or not they move away from us, there is something that has been lost in this relationship. It has been irrevocably changed. There is a loss of innocence that can be very heartbreaking. I've heard of mothers who have sobbed for days, then stayed indoors for months after finding out about a gay son. They have gained weight, lost sleep, had their hair fall out, experienced itchy teeth and a "golf ball in the stomach"—all kinds of strange physical and emotional symptoms due to great stress and loss.

So this huge sense of loss triggers the grief cycle, which goes through predictable stages, just like a death in the family. There is shock, emotional release, bargaining with God, resignation, finally moving on—all the same things that happen with other major traumas. So encourage the family members who come to you, "What you are feeling is normal. This is healthy. And this is temporary." Life won't always be this burdensome. That can be a tremendous relief in the midst of the situation.

Some family members—especially fathers—may cope in a whole different way: denial. They minimize the situation with comments like, "Ah, it's just a phase. He'll grow out of it." Then they tell their wives, "Stop being so upset," which, of course, makes the wife even more mad and emotional!

Some husbands may even throw out a few spiritual platitudes like, "Why can't you just give it to the Lord?" and similar thoughts. The idea that this is a temporary phase is usually a form of denial. What these fathers don't realize is that their child has probably had this struggle for years already, and the problem is not going to disappear in a few days.

"RAW" EMOTIONS

It seems like people are finding out about Exodus earlier in the process than they used to. Years ago it wasn't unusual for people to call us after weeks or months of searching for answers. Today, with the Internet and fabulous search tools, people can find out about Exodus the same day. So we get phone calls from people who have learned of a family member's homosexuality less than twenty-four hours prior to calling us. They are very raw. Sometimes all they can do is sob out their hurt and confusion.

As time goes on, there may be other emotions, like anger. "How could this 'perfect' son do this to me?" They take it very personally. There can also be anger at other people, such as a spouse who is not supportive or friends who withdraw. There may even be anger at God. As one mother said, "I thought God spared Christian families from the really 'big' sins like this one!" Or a wife may wonder, "How could God lead me into this marriage when He knew all along that my husband was gay?" So be prepared for some deep emotions to come up, and be ready to patiently listen. Sometimes there are no satisfying answers, but we can be a safe shoulder to cry on.

Sometimes there is also anger at the child's gay partner. "He's the problem. If it weren't for him, my son wouldn't be caught up in this." This is what Anita Worthen went through. When her sixteen-year-old son got caught up in homosexuality, she found out that he had been seduced sexually by his high school guidance counselor. She was livid! Tony had grown up without a dad; so he was searching for same-sex affirmation and bonding, and this older man took advantage of him.

Anita thought the problem would be solved if she could get him away from this older man. So she shipped him a thousand miles away to a small town in Oregon where her brother lived. But that didn't solve the problem. Soon Tony had linked up with the gay community in that town; he even visited the local gay church! Anita realized that the problem was inside Tony, not just who his friends were.

Parents and loved ones can also go on a massive search for "the" solution. We hear from them all the time. They are desperate to "fix" their gay son. Then they can get on with their lives—and no one else needs to find out! They want an answer. They hear that people have been through counseling at Exodus and eventually moved into marriage. So they want to give their son's phone number to us, so we can call him and get everything straightened out fast. We never go into these types of "forced" counseling, because we have discovered that the motivation to change has to come from within the individual with the problem. Going to a counselor to keep Mom happy isn't going to work. The motivation has to go much deeper than pleasing someone else. It has to be the deepest desire of one's heart, usually as a result of conviction from God that it's His will to pursue such counseling and change.

Typically life gets worse for these parents before it gets better. They go through a phase of grief where they are almost immobilized with emotional pain. They have trouble coping with the responsibilities of daily life. They may even lose a job over this. One mother said, "I don't know how I held onto my office career. Every day I would sit at my desk, and the tears would slip down my face. I felt like if I ever started really crying, I'd never be able to stop." Marriages can suffer; other children in the home can feel neglected. This can be quite a debilitating phase for these parents to go through.

Finally, with the passage of time and the help of the Lord, these families will usually move into the final phase of grief where life picks up and carries on. The problem is not solved, but normal functioning returns in spite of the problem. In real life, of course, people can slip back into the grief at a moment's notice, although usually it is not as deep and prolonged as initially.

There can be triggers for renewed grief. Perhaps a son breaks up with his homosexual partner, and the parents are filled with great hope. He may even move home again. Then, after a few months, he moves in with some other guy, and the parents are devastated again.

Or—and this is a huge issue—the son confesses that he is infected with HIV. In the 1980s this was virtually a death sentence. Thankfully, with the new drugs available today, it has moved into a "chronic illness" type of situation for many men. I know men who have been suffering minimal health symptoms for over fifteen years. So a lot has changed with AIDS in the past twenty years. But it is still a terrifying thing for a parent or spouse to hear.

This is the situation that Anita went through. She and her husband (she married later in life) were missionaries in the Philippines when her son called her to announce that he had the HIV virus. That triggered a whole huge cycle of grief for her. Here she was on the other side of the world serving God—and now this! It was hard for her to figure it all out, but she soon had people all over the world praying for her, and she found comfort in knowing that God was in control of the whole situation.

You don't have to be an expert on homosexuality to help these family members and friends. We are not trained counselors or therapists at the Exodus office; we are actually the referral headquarters for about 115 ministries around the country. But people call us all the time who think we are the "experts" on this issue. As soon as we answer, they launch into their story.

I think of one mother I talked to recently who was devastated over her gay son. We talked for a while, and I gave her encouraging phrases like "This must be so hard for you" and "I'm really sorry to hear about this in your family." When I was able to draw the conversation to a close and make the appropriate referral to a ministry in her area, she told me, "Oh, you were so wonderful. This has been the most helpful conversation I've ever had with anyone about my son."

I hadn't really shared any new and startling information with her; I'd simply listened carefully and with genuine sympathy. And she got tremendous relief and comfort. Sometimes it's really quite simple. We can be a physical representation of the love of Christ to these hurting people.

Homosexuality can be a very intimidating issue for us to face; there is so much that we still don't understand about it. After being in Exodus for twenty years, I still don't know all the answers. But I do know that as I keep close to Christ and try to pray constantly that I will be a reflection of His love and grace, I have the power to help these people. I have answers that will help them.

So don't be intimidated by these surface issues and problems. Step back and take a look at the bigger picture. Through Christ we have the answers to life's biggest issues. He is with us and in us to help us walk through these tough counseling situations.

THE RIGHT FOCUS

One other thing: When talking to family members, remember to focus on their needs. As we talk about the gay loved ones and what they are doing, what they are saying, what they are needing, the conversation can distract us from the person we should really be focusing on—the family member in front of us. What is this mother needing? What is this wife struggling with?

I think back on another story from Anita Worthen. After she found out about Tony, she went looking for help. First she went to a local church that had a major counseling department. She was handed a little card where she had to write down the problem, so she could give it to the counselor when her name was called. "I didn't even know how to spell homosexuality," she says today with a laugh.

When the next available counselor came out to the waiting room and read the card, Anita says all the blood drained from his face. He knew that he was really in over his head! He was obviously feeling really inadequate and unprepared to meet with this distraught mother. Unfortunately, he started his counseling session with a little Bible study about the sinfulness of homosexuality.

"That approach was so far from what I needed," Anita says. "I was in shock. I was in grief. I needed somebody to walk alongside me in the midst of my turmoil." Sometimes we can get so distracted from the issue at hand. We think, "Homosexuality? OK, let's go to Romans chapter 1" without thinking about it a bit further. Maybe we'll cover that chapter—but not right away. What does this person need right now? Maybe we can't promise such individuals that everything will turn out fine, but we can promise them that God is always going to be with them, that God is a loving God, that He doesn't condemn them for this situation, that God will give them the strength and grace each day as they reach out to Him. These are basic principles that apply to a multitude of situations, including this one.

OUR OWN EMOTIONS

There are emotions in ourselves that we'll have to deal with, especially *fear*, the fear of inadequacy. This can seem like such a complicated issue. I encourage you to put aside your fears and remember that most of what you'll say—at least in the first session or two—are similar to dealing with parents or other loved ones of *anyone* in spiritual rebellion. Let's say, for example, that this woman's son is living with a woman but is not married to her. She would probably be distraught, confused, guilty about "where did I go wrong?"—very similar emotions to dealing with a gay son. What would you tell a mother in that situation? The same principles apply. Focus on her needs, her questions, her fears, her guilt. You'll have lots of time later to deal with the more specific questions about homosexuality (in the meantime, you can go to our website to find out more—www.exodusnorthamerica.org). We need to focus on the basics and walk alongside this grieving family member.

We can also face a fear of the unknown. What if sexual abuse is involved? AIDS? Is it safe to shake this person's hand? To invite him or her into our home for a meal? There are a lot of questions that come up about homosexuality, and sometimes, quite frankly, it seems easiest to simply avoid the whole issue in the first place. However, it is now so prevalent in our society and among our church members that it cannot be ignored. It simply is not going to go away.

There are also a lot of fears among other church members. For example, parents may fear that this man struggling with homosexuality will molest their kids. Or they may fear that other gays will come in if the word gets around that the church offers a compassionate helping hand for gays and lesbians.

The answer to dealing with others' questions is education. Talk about the issues, whether it's in the context of a sermon on morality or a small-group Bible study on Romans. These things need to be addressed, and most church members have never had an opportunity to ask their questions.

I look at the biblical model of Jesus Christ. He didn't avoid the hard social issues of His day. He talked to prostitutes and religious hypocrites alike. Christ went out into His culture, and He really engaged people. He touched the lepers. He reached out to the untouchables. These are issues we need to wrestle with in our private prayer times. What fears are keeping us from reaching out beyond the church walls—or into the lives of church members who have deep-seated sexual identity struggles?

PARENTS' GUILT

Guilt is also a huge issue, especially for parents. It's common for them to ask, "Where did we go wrong?" They feel like total failures in one of their most important God-given roles.

I've talked to many gay men over the years who never felt affirmed by their fathers. Many of them also experienced great difficulty in other areas of their lives, however. It's unfair to say a person *causes* another person's homosexuality. At the very most, our parental sins may open the door for homosexual temptation. Other times, the key situation is not the parent's behavior as much as it is the child's response. Parents may be giving firm, loving boundaries, but the child perceives them as harsh, condemning, unloving.

Sexual abuse is common, especially among the gay women we minister to. Sometimes it's within the family; other times it had nothing to do with the family, and the parents had absolutely no knowledge of it. One woman I know was raped by a family friend after she had baby-sat his children for the evening. She was terrified to tell her dad, who used to bellow, "If anyone hurts my little girl, I'll kill him!" So she stuffed her fear and growing hatred for men and ended up pursuing lesbianism in college. Her parents had absolutely no way of knowing what was troubling her.

So parents feel a lot of guilt. But we all live in a fallen world. We have all made mistakes as parents. None of us is perfect. That's why Jesus came to die for our sins! We need forgiveness just as much as our gay loved ones do. Quite frankly, a lot of parents facing this situation were no better or worse than any other parents on their block. But the enemy turned whatever imperfect childhood situations occurred to his advantage and brought along a homosexual temptation. The child succumbed and began to move in the direction of a homosexual identity.

So we parents cannot undo the past. But we can find forgiveness. And we can seek to make amends with the person, if needed. My friend Anita was a single mom. She realized that her sins as a teen had led into a less-than-ideal situation for her son. So she went to him and asked his forgiveness. She did what she could to make the situation right. As she saw her son pursuing other men who were twenty years older, she knew that he was searching for a father's love. She felt awful, but she couldn't undo the past. She had to renounce the condemnation and accept the Lord's forgiveness for her own past.

Parents can be plagued with the "what ifs." What if I'd become a Christian earlier in life? What if I'd been a better parent? What if I'd been more aware of my son's struggles? What if . . . what if . . . what if? These types of thoughts can be tough to overcome. Obsessing over the past is not going to change anything. We must move forward, with God's help.

It's also helpful to remember that God was the perfect heavenly Father, and his first "children" still disobeyed! They were raised in a perfect environment, but they still sinned. Throughout the Scriptures we can find examples of very godly parents whose children went astray in major ways. We also have current examples, such as Billy Graham's son Franklin, who was a "prodigal son" as a youth. What an embarrassment! But there is no direct cause-and-effect correlation here. As our children mature, they begin to make moral choices as adults over which we have no control. And we have to realize that we are not responsible for what we cannot control.

As our children move into adulthood, we lose control. We have done our best. We have sown into their lives, but ultimately it is *their* choice what direction they are going to take. None of us have been raised in perfect families.

TEMPTATION VS. SIN

We also have to keep in mind that homosexuality *does* involve choices. We don't believe that most gay men and women choose to have same-sex attractions, but they do choose what to do with them. Do they act upon them or resist them?

I use my own life as an example. Even though I struggled with same-sex attractions, I never fell into the behavior with another man, not even one time. So it *is* possible to resist sin, no matter what our feelings, no matter how strong the flesh pulls us in a certain direction. Through the overcoming power of Jesus Christ, we can resist.

There are still endless arguments about what causes homosexuality. The studies are inconclusive. We don't believe it is primarily genetic or inborn. But some evangelical parents have gone astray in their own ideas over their guilt. They have embraced the "born gay" theory to justify their own kid's situation. This is a tragedy. Embracing a lie won't free us—only facing the truth, no matter where it leads us.

MINISTERING TO GAY FRIENDS

A lot of Christians may come to you for advice who have gay friends— or friends whom they suspect are gay. What should they do? In contrast to what may be instinctive, I encourage these Christians not to pull away and withdraw, but actually to move into the relationship. Seek to deepen the friendship. These people need to know that you are safe, that they are comfortable around you, before they will bare this intimate part of their lives.

I remember the very first time in my own life that I shared this problem with someone else. This man was my best friend in Bible college, and I really trusted him. I remember it was a big risk in telling him, because there was a possibility that he would run to the authorities and I would be kicked out of school. But that never happened. He kept my secret, and I've always been thankful for that.

Several years later I told another friend, a woman in my youth group whom I totally trusted. She gave me some good advice when she encouraged me to seek help from my pastor. Then I told him too, and he responded with love and compassion (although he did not really know how to help me). So we have to realize that this person feels very, very vulnerable when he confesses this struggle to you. It can be a terrifying risk for him (or her). He has to know that you are safe, that you can keep a confidence, that you will not betray him by talking to others about his struggle. You must earn the right for him to tell you such a private matter.

So ask God to make you a better friend. Ask God to bring to light what is hidden in the darkness. And begin being more open about your own struggles. If you're a guy and your friend is also male, maybe you can share your own struggle with lust. Ask for his prayers. Work on deepening the friendship, so he will feel safe in opening up to you.

Ultimately, you may even want to bring up the subject of homosexuality, but be general, and be very neutral in your attitude. Don't make a disparaging remark about "those queers." I've heard many stories of Christians who overheard these kinds of comments in the church lobby. They took note of who was saying them and promised themselves that they would *never* confess their struggle to that insensitive individual.

It's also insensitive to ask, "Are you gay?" If they aren't, it can give rise to a deep offense. "Why did you ask that? What in my voice or actions made you think such a thing?" This type of questioning can actually lead to temptation or questioning or confusion, especially in a teenager. So be careful.

What about friends who are actively and openly homosexual? I would take the homosexual part out of the question and ask, how would you treat them if they had a live-in lover of the opposite sex? This situation is similar. We stigmatize homosexuality in our culture, but I think God sees it as just another form of immorality, no worse than any other form of fornication or adultery. So ask yourself what you would say to a Christian friend who was justifying an affair or a single friend having sex without being married. Then use your answer to provide some guidelines on how to treat a friend who is actively engaging in homosexuality.

SOME CAUTIONS

There is a need for awareness and even some caution, however, in reaching out to those who are seeking to overcome homosexuality. Sometimes we don't realize our own vulnerabilities in the relationship. This is especially true in the case of a woman reaching out to an ex-gay woman.

Over the years we've seen some Christian women with the very best of intentions get involved in a discipleship relationship with another woman struggling with lesbianism. Somewhere along the line the relationship goes awry, and they get sexually involved. How does this occur?

Sometimes the straight woman is emotionally needy and vulnerable in ways that she is not aware of. Perhaps she and her family have just moved to a new city, and she hasn't yet established a network of new friends. Her husband is diving into a new job, and he's away from home for twelve hours every day. She can be set up by her circumstances to be needy, lonely, and vulnerable. It may seem far-fetched, but this type of thing has happened many times.

A woman can also be set up by unresolved issues from her past, particularly sexual abuse or other emotional wounding by men. She instinctively is drawn to other wounded women, and they can form a close-knit friendship that becomes enmeshed, exclusive, and very unhealthy. Eventually it becomes affectionate and sexual. Before this woman knows what is happening, she has fallen into a full-fledged lesbian affair.

So it's important that we stay balanced in our relationships and not disciple others out of our own emotional neediness. This type of situation is rare for men; the average heterosexual male has such a deep distaste for anything remotely connected to gay sex that there is no danger of him being pulled into immorality. More common is the feeling that the ex-gay man he's discipling is overly dependent emotionally on him.

Men who struggle with homosexuality have usually felt disconnected from other men. They seek emotional attachment through sexual escapades. So when a friendly straight man begins discipling them, they can feel connected in a way they never have before. A problem arises if the ex-gay man begins centering all his relational needs around this one straight friend. The friend can feel trapped and drained by this emotionally needy friend. So the ex-gay man should be drawn into group activities such as Bible studies, men's breakfasts, or ball games where he can find friendship with a group of accepting men.

Typically an ex-gay man is starving for acceptance and friendship with other healthy men. I've seen many churches where this type of support exists, and it can bring a deep healing into the lives of men who are striving to overcome homosexuality. So although there are risks and challenges involved, this type of outreach can make a radical difference in many people's lives.

Above all, we can remember that we have "Christ in [us], the hope of glory" (Col. 1:7, NASB). Christianity becomes real and potent when we give it away, when we reach out to hurting people and see the power of Jesus Christ transforming their lives through us. The gay and lesbian community is a huge and virtually untapped mission field. And for every gay or lesbian activist, often there are parents and other family members who are hiding in the background—many of them sitting in church pews each Sunday totally mystified on how to respond to their gay loved one. Let's face this challenge head-on and make a radical difference in the future of our society.

13

HELPING SINGLE ADULTS HANDLE MORAL FAILURES

Dick Purnell

———∞∞∞———

Out of the corner of my eye I noticed her. She sat quietly in about the twentieth row of the auditorium where I had just finished addressing the large audience of university students on the topic "Why Relationships Fail." Many people lined up to ask me questions, but she remained seated.

After the last person had left, she walked up to me and asked, "Can I speak to you?"

"Well, sure."

Making certain no one could hear, she spoke softly. "I am one of the leaders of the group that invited you to come and speak. No one knows this, but four months ago I got involved with a man, and now I have a venereal disease." As she lowered her head, she added, "I guess I will never deserve a decent man for the rest of my life."

The deep pain in this woman's soul showed in her anguished eyes. All of the dreams that she'd probably had of remaining chaste for her future husband were decimated. Her longings had been shattered. What man would want a soiled woman with a sexually transmitted disease? She was shocked, dismayed, depressed, filled with hopelessness.

Many singles can relate to her plight because they are in similar situations. They feel as if they will enter a relationship with excess baggage. Some may not realize how much they have been seared by sexual immorality. The media and society in general promote sex without commitment. They glamorize premarital sexual intercourse—"all the popular people are doing it."

Solomon predicted the end result of a man who commits adultery. "All at once he followed her like an ox going to the slaughter, like a deer stepping into a noose till an arrow pierces his liver, like a bird darting into a snare, little knowing it will cost him his life" (Prov. 7:22-23, NIV).

George Barna states in *Single Adults*, "Three out of four never-been-married adults contend that co-habitation is morally acceptable. A majority of couples live together before getting married these days, a substantial increase from the 10% who did so in 1965."[1]

I am on the national speakers team for FamilyLife Marriage Conferences. Even though the material is directed toward married couples, many engaged couples attend. We conduct a special session exclusively for these couples, where a male speaker addresses the men and his wife addresses the single women. When I address the men, I often ask, "How many of you are having sex with your fiancées?" Usually 60 to 70 percent admit their involvement.

If they are typical of engaged couples, it means many of the unmarried couples sitting in church on Sunday are living together. Thus a large number of singles are no longer virgins.

Barna's research shows that cohabiters have a 48 percent greater chance of experiencing a divorce than do individuals who did not live together prior to marriage. Cohabiters who eventually marry are also more likely to be victims of domestic violence, depression, dissatisfaction with life, shorter life spans, and sexual anxiety.[2]

Moral failure is deeply ingrained in a person's life. To discuss the pain and memories of wrong sexual decisions is difficult. Often people try to mask the scars with defense mechanisms, but the consequences keep reminding them of their wrongdoing.

Sexual intercourse is more than a physical act. It involves the emotions, self-image, mind, and spirit. A person gives away knowledge of himself in a way that is unlike any other means. In a committed, loving marriage sex is beautiful and fulfilling. But when sexual immorality occurs, a negative dagger is plunged deep into a person's psyche. Research has shown that if individuals don't discipline themselves to handle their sexual drives when they are single, they have a greater likelihood of being unfaithful to their spouses once they are married.

The quagmire of immorality is extremely difficult to escape. Since it affects the totality of a person, the path to healing and freedom is complicated. Just saying, "Have faith in Jesus. He will give you strength" is not enough.

Many pastors never talk about single adult issues from the pulpit. Sexual issues may be presented, but often from a totally negative perspective. "Don't do it" is the bottom line that singles hear. The things they struggle with are somehow taboo to discuss. Therefore singles are left to figure out the answers for themselves.

Here are some of the questions I hear: So what does the Bible say about finding someone to marry? How should a twenty-eight-year-old, never-married man handle his God-given desire for sex? What can a thirty-three-year-old divorced mother of two children do with her sexual feelings? What are practical steps to get out of an illicit affair with the mother of your child? How does a woman burdened with regret find real peace? Is it possible to regain one's virginity after it has been stolen through sexual abuse?

These and thousands of other painful questions have been addressed to me. At the end of each of my conferences, I conduct an open forum when people can ask me any question they have about the opposite sex. I instruct them to write their questions on a card, indicating only whether they are male or female. As I read each question out loud and answer it, a hush envelops the audience. "Finally someone is addressing my problems" is the most frequent response I get. By the way, single women ask just as many questions about sex as men do. There are definite social changes going on.

One more issue before we talk about solutions. When the word *sex* is used, in many pastors' minds they are thinking "sexual intercourse." But for many people (especially young people) intercourse may not be involved. Today the phrase could be called "sexual outercourse." Sexual outercourse includes oral sex and everything else except penetration of the male into the female. Outercourse is not considered sex because it doesn't end with intercourse. Therefore, a person involved in this still considers himself or herself a virgin.

Teens and other singles "hook up" rather than date. Hooking up means you get together with someone to do whatever you want sexually just for one night. One guy said to me, "I can lie naked in bed with a girl and not even think about it." There are no emotional expectations afterward, no commitment for anything beyond that night. "Sex without commitment" has now become "sex without attachment."

But the truth is, whether one commits premarital sexual outercourse or intercourse, there are inevitable consequences. These fall into four categories:

#1: Psychological: There is tremendous guilt deep down inside—guilt for breaking God's moral law—guilt for violating the Ten Commandments—guilt for exposing their total beings to someone who is not committed to them. Sure, the world blunts the conscience and ridicules the truth. The media flaunt sex outside marriage, and millions are anesthetized by evil clothed in beauty. "Though they know God's decree that those who practice such things deserve to die, they not only do them but give approval to those who practice them" (Rom. 1:32, ESV). The conclusive fact remains that God judges people according to His righteous law—whether they believe in Him or not. The clear message of Romans 1 is that they are "without excuse" (Rom. 1:20, NIV).

Along with guilt comes a tremendous loss of self-esteem, a sense of shame. They feel dirty. They feel somehow they are a used product. Many, many people feel like they are caught in a trap. They have given in to lust and decadence in order to find thrills, intimacy, and acceptance. But they have ended up with a terrible control-freak monster. Lust is never satisfied, and it robs its victims of joy, true fun, satisfaction, and genuine intimacy. The lie of the world is that sex without attachment has no consequences. "Live for today—don't worry about tomorrow." But those who get involved are reaping the whirlwind.

Immorality brings devastating emptiness. When you have been intimate with someone and it doesn't satisfy, there is significant disillusionment. Then comes the haunting question, "What do I do now?"

#2: Relational: Jealousy, arguments, breakups, and even violence occur when two people violate each other. I believe one of the major reasons why couples break up is because they have gotten too close too soon. The old saying is true: "Women give sex to get love, and men give love to get sex." They use each other to get what they want. Even though selfishness is covered with romance for a while, the real battles begin when both want to be in control. Sexual immorality does not produce self-centeredness; rather it is fueled by the get-what-you-want drive.

One of the surprising consequences of immorality is burnout. God has designed love to be built on giving, but lust focuses on getting. The more one delves into promiscuity and corruption, the less relationships satisfy. The result is a downward spiral into kinkier sex—lewd pictures, mechanical devices, multiple partners, pornography, sadism, and all sorts of evils.

#3: Physical: Millions of people are infected with sexually transmitted diseases (STDs,) including AIDS, brought on by promiscuous sexual activities. An estimated twelve million new sexually transmitted cases occur each year. Sixty-seven percent are among men and women under the age of twenty-five. At current rates, at least one person in four will contract a sexually transmitted disease (STD) at some point in his or her life.

Medical experts are now discovering that STDs have a variety of effects on the body. Dr. Michael Heller, director of the House Staff Teaching Program, Emergency Medicine Department of Franklin Square Hospital, Baltimore, writes, "It is now known that STDs can affect every organ system. Diseases caused by sexual practices can affect virtually any body function, while the genital region may be clinically uninvolved. The known manifestations of STDs are increasing."[3] The list of resultant problems includes tendonitis, arthritis, urethritis, hepatitis, abdominal pain, gastrointestinal infections, AIDS, aseptic meningitis, eye infections, and cervical cancer.

Guilt and misery plague people who are affected. I can't tell you the number of people who have asked me, "How do I tell the person I am dating that I have a venereal disease?" Can you image the shock and dismay when the truth is learned? It is a heart stopper—and a passion stopper.

Also, an unwanted pregnancy certainly throws complications into a relationship. Often the couple splits up, or if they do get married under duress, the marriage many times doesn't last long. Over 25 percent of births are to unwed mothers. There is a lot of heartache and pain in that statistic. Millions of other pregnancies are terminated by abortions. A developing fetus is treated as merely tissue to be discarded, and a future life is trashed.

This is the dark side of a night of "fun."

#4: Spiritual: Of all the devastating consequences of premarital sexual immorality, the spiritual effects are the most severe—and the least realized. The spiritual repercussions are felt in this life and in the one to come (1 Cor. 3:12-15). There is a little saying I learned as a child that explains this area well: "Sin will keep you from the Bible, and the Bible will keep you from sin." Sexual sins will yank a person away from God very quickly. Who wants God around when he or she is planning to have sex with someone who is not his or her spouse? An individual tells God to stay far away, to not come near when he or she is descending into immorality. In the process of shoving God away, a person hides from the only One who can give him or her satisfaction in this life and assurance of eternal life to come.

When we walk in the darkness, we have fellowship with those who walk in the darkness. Our companions pull us down to their level of behavior and attitudes. We don't want to be around faithful Christians because it is too convicting. Who wants to join others in worshiping a holy God when one's life and attitudes are in the gutter? All interest in knowing God and serving Him vanishes. A hostile attitude sets a person against the Lord and His followers. As Jesus says, "Enter through the narrow gate. For wide is the gate and broad is the road that leads to destruction, and many enter through it. But small is the gate and narrow the road that leads to life, and only a few find it" (Matt. 7:13-14, NIV).

People often do not value the spiritual dimension of life, especially Someone who threatens to take away their "toys" of sexual immorality, addictions, and lust. Yet Christ is the only one who has the words of life, and He promises true life to all who follow Him. What a pity to miss that.

The beauty of God is that He doesn't give up on us. He constantly seeks the lost, the downtrodden, the gutter-dwellers, the scarred, the diseased, the scum, the spiritually dead. He repeats in a trillion ways, "Come to me, all you who are weary and burdened, and I will give you rest" (Matt. 11:28, NIV).

When soiled single adults respond to the Lord's invitation and want to return to Him, how do they do it? Yes, their journey starts with true repentance, understanding the Gospel of Christ, and placing their faith in Him for forgiveness and eternal life. But how can a person get out of the gutter of immorality and sin? How can you help a single adult transform his attitudes and behavior into holy living?

The road to restoration is not easy, nor is it impossible. It will take internal motivation, faith in God, and time. From my interaction with single adults and counseling them, I have concluded that the following "Steps to Freedom" are the key issues in counseling singles to overcome their past and/or their present moral failures. Also, these points could be an outline for a presentation to a single adult group. My assumption is that the person(s) you share these with is already a Christian and wants to become a more faithful follower of Christ.

WHAT TO TELL SINGLES WHO HAVE EXPERIENCED MORAL FAILURE

Part of the material that follows is addressed directly to those you are trying to help, part to you as the one engaged in this ministry.

Step 1: Accept God's Forgiveness

In order to find personal healing and emancipation from wrong moral choices, it is important to grasp the significance of two things: your responsibility for your choices and the depth of God's forgiveness. We are what I call "Teflon people." The responsibility for our failures is easily sloughed off and put on others. Adam started it all. In the Garden of Eden, he chose to disobey God's direct command. After he sinned, he hid in the bushes when he heard God approaching (Gen. 3:8-12).

God called out to him, "Where are you?" Now God did not ask that because He could not find him. He wanted Adam to realize that his disobedience had put a barrier between himself and God. When the Lord asked him what happened, Adam replied, "Well, the woman You gave to be with me, she gave me from the tree, and I ate." Notice he said, "the woman You gave me." He blamed God for his wrong choice, and then he blamed Eve. Of course, Eve blamed the serpent. From Adam's point of view, he was the only one who was right. He was saying that God was wrong to give him Eve, and Eve was wrong for giving him the forbidden fruit. Adam felt justified in his own mind.

I meet people all the time who give Teflon excuses for their immorality. This is like trying to nail Jell-O to a wall. "God hasn't brought the right person into my life yet. So how could I help myself when I have all these unmet desires?" "Well, all the Christians I know are very unattractive. What's wrong with a little excitement while I wait for God?" "I have been waiting a long time. I just couldn't wait any longer." "Who cares what God thinks? He doesn't like anything that is fun." God is their whipping boy. God and everyone else is the problem. "They are the real culprits—not me."

The beginning of forgiveness and healing is to take responsibility for your actions and choices, to admit they are sinful. You violated the Ten Commandments. Adultery is a violation of God's will (1 Cor. 6). People need to read the verses in the Bible, and not just hear them quoted. In the postmodern mind-set, truth is what a person decides. Holding an actual Bible and reading the verses conveys God's supreme authority. "Look for yourself. This is what God says." Give the Spirit of God time to work in their hearts. When the Holy Spirit convicts people, He does a very good job.

Confessions of sins is not just, "Lord, forgive me of my sins." It is easy to say that flippantly. First John 1:9, "If we confess our sins," means to name the sins. "This is what I have done, Lord: I have cavorted around. I have gone to bed with these three different guys. I have been living with this girl." Name your transgressions so God can specifically forgive those sins. True confession of sins is accepting responsibility and admitting that God is right.

The extent of God's forgiveness is that He pays the penalty for our sins and frees us from the condemnation our sins have brought on us. The Old Testament concept of removal is significant for a person to grasp. "As far as the east is from the west, so far has he removed our transgressions from us" (Ps. 103:12, NIV). I always wondered why God used the phrase "as far as the east is from the west." Why didn't He choose "as far as the north is from the south"? One day I was thinking about that, and I realized that if I start at the North Pole and go toward the South Pole, as soon as I hit the equator I am in the south. Thus it is a measurable distance. But if I start on the equator and go east, I never get to the west. I just keep going east. The east is an infinite distance from the west. In Hebrews 10:17 the Lord states that He wills to forget the sin that He has forgiven. That concept is critical for people to internalize, as we will see in the next section. Once we take responsibility for our sins and admit that God is right, the shed blood of Christ washes us clean. Accept God's forgiveness as your personal possession.

Step 2: Forgive Yourself

So many sermons end with confession and forgiveness. But that is only the beginning. How can people pick up the pieces of their broken lives? Where do they learn how to get out of the chains that have kept them in the dungeon of despair and guilt? The first step is to thank God that you are a forgiven person. Then take the next step and forgive yourself. When the immoral woman cried at Jesus' feet and poured out her expensive ointment, He said, "Your sins are forgiven. . . . Your faith has saved you; go in peace" (Luke 7:36-50, NIV). On another occasion He turned to another immoral woman after those who were clamoring for her death had left and asked her,

"'Woman, where are they? Has no one condemned you?' 'No one, sir,'
she said. 'Then neither do I condemn you,' Jesus declared. 'Go now
and leave your life of sin'" (John 8:1-11, NIV). In effect, Christ was
telling each of these women (and lots of other people), "I forgive you;
so forgive yourself and make changes in your life."

When I say, "Forgive yourself," I mean there is no need for continuing in self-punishment and wallowing in guilt. People beat themselves down all the time. They have done something wrong, or a
whole series of things wrong. They say, "I am a bad sinner. I can never
live the Christian life." Christ didn't tell the women, "Go, and ago-
nize about how terrible you are. Keep worrying about what you did.
Maybe one of these days you will deserve My forgiveness."

His message was rather, "Now that I have gotten you out of the
mud, live in such a way that you don't get back into it. Get on the rock
of God, and move forward with your life." Forgiven people have to
understand that Christ releases them from self-punishment (putting
yourself down, depreciating yourself, thinking you are the world's
worst sinner that ever came along). All that does is drill your self-
image into the floor and immobilize you.

If you have experienced God's forgiveness but refuse to forgive
yourself, you are telling Christ that His forgiveness is not enough.
Forgiving yourself is saying, "Yes, I am a sinner, but I have been saved
by God's grace and liberated. I am free to leave my old life behind."
The classic example is the apostle Paul. From a prison cell near the end
of his life, Paul recalled his former evil life (1 Tim. 1:12-17): "Christ
came into the world to save sinners—of whom I am the worst" (NIV).
He said he was the world's worst sinner. But God had delivered him
and had given him a great ministry by His grace. Even to the day Paul
died, he remembered what Christ had done for him. Paul thanked
God for forgiving him. He forgave himself, took up the cross, and followed Christ the rest of his life.

Forgiving yourself as God forgave you takes the stinger out of the
memories. The sting in bad memories is the resentment felt toward
other people, but the stinger is the self-destructive attitudes about
yourself. It is OK to remember the old life; in fact it is very good to

remember. Peter cautions, "For if you possess these qualities in increasing measure, they will keep you from being ineffective and unproductive in your knowledge of our Lord Jesus Christ. But if anyone does not have them, he is nearsighted and blind, and has forgotten that he has been cleansed from his past sins" (2 Pet. 1:8-9, NIV). Remember the depths of degradation from which God has set you free. Why? Because then you will remember how great God's grace has been to you. Without His constant sustaining strength, you would go right back there. Don't forget that!

All along the wilderness journey, God kept telling the Israelites, "Remember what I have done for you." After He brought them into the land, He commanded them to set up twelve stones on the bank of the Jordan River to remind them (and the generations to come) that God had miraculously fulfilled His promises. "In the future, when your children ask you, 'What do these stones mean?' tell them that the flow of the Jordan was cut off before the ark of the covenant of the LORD. When it crossed the Jordan, the waters of the Jordan were cut off. These stones are to be a memorial to the people of Israel forever" (Josh. 4:6-7, NIV).

You can tell your friends and family, "Yes, I was an evil person. I will never forget that. But God rescued me, and He has changed my life. He gets the glory, and look at all He has done for me." God has taken out all the resentment, the recrimination, and the self-deprecation and has replaced them with the fruit of the Holy Spirit. Allow the memories to be a lesson for the future.

Step 3: Expect Powerful Changes

A victim mentality pervades our society. Maybe that should be a headline in a magazine. I can't tell you the number of people I come across that feel powerless. Single adults say the biggest disadvantage of being single is loneliness. Many have told me their problems and then added at the end, "I have never told anyone else what I have told you." When I encourage them to talk with someone about their significant problems, they will retort, "I have no one I can confide in." When people consider themselves to be all alone to face the trials of the world, they feel weak and vulnerable. It is tiring to depend on no one except yourself.

First, concentrate on the resurrection of Christ. That is the central tenet of the Christian faith. If Christ is still dead in an unmarked grave somewhere, we are powerless to face the onslaughts of evil. But since He arose in great power, He can pour strength into us through the Holy Spirit so we can overwhelmingly conquer all kinds of obstacles (Rom. 8:37). By faith we have the resurrection power of Christ available to empower us (Eph. 1:19-20).

God broke the bonds of death surrounding Christ like a toothpick. If He could break that mighty grip, He can break whatever binds you. He can break the chains of an illicit affair. His power can liberate you from addiction to sexual lust, whether that takes you to Internet porn or whatever. The Holy Spirit can give you courage to stand for righteousness when all your friends frequent sleazy bars. His guidance is available to establish healthy, moral, and satisfying relationships. His love is far more attractive than the superficial "love" offered by selfish vultures. When you feel trashed by the world, He will assure you of His love for you and His good, acceptable, and perfect will for your life. You can rise up out of the ashes. Why? Because Christ arose too. His powerful resurrection guarantees you eternal life.

Second, build a support group, an accountability group of several same-sex friends with whom you can entrust your thoughts and heart. Center your discussions on the Bible, and encourage each other to walk strongly with the Lord.

Because I was single until forty-two years old, there were many nights I struggled with my loneliness. In my middle thirties I was assistant pastor in a church. I was an assistant pastor, but I had just as many problems as everybody else. I was an open book. I prayed, *Lord, how do I change? How can I handle all of this?* I wanted to be a godly man, but I sure was having problems in my mind with wanting a wife. I felt so defeated. Almost every day I would pray, *Lord, take away this desire for a woman—I can't handle it.* Then one day as I was praying about this, I suddenly realized that I was asking God to take away my manhood and make me abnormal. I am so thankful to God for unanswered prayer! If He had answered my prayers, I would not be married today. When you become a Christian, God doesn't neuter you.

Well then, how do you handle this urge? Build good friendships with the opposite sex, and rely on the Lord to do His will in your life. Develop a support group of friends who will pray with you and for you. Be honest toward one another, and hold each other accountable. Ask for specific prayer: "This weekend I don't have a date, and I am lonely. Please pray for me, especially between the hours of 9 P.M. and midnight. That is the hardest time for me, when I am tempted the most." Next time you talk with your support group, share how you handled the weekend. Praise the Lord for victories, and continue to pray for power to overcome temptations. We need to expect powerful changes and to "spur one another on toward love and good deeds" (Heb. 10:24, NIV).

Step 4: Guard Your Mind

I look at the human mind as a wild bull. It can never be fully tamed. However, you can put a ring in its nose and lead it where you want to go much of the time. Before you became a Christian, your mind roamed freely, thinking about what it wanted to. You may have provoked your mind with impure thoughts by filling it with lewd material and immoral living. Your lifestyle fed the raging bull of your mind with worldly values and experiences.

When you became a Christian, you discovered that the wild bull of your mind was not instantly transformed. The old thought patterns, ideas, habits, activities, and temptations were still raging. The wild bull charged recklessly through your nice Christian expectations and challenged your attempts at moral reforms. You have fallen many times, and you are weary with the battle. "I'm just going to give up and go back to the old way. It was easier."

Yes, it was easier—because you were dominated by your corrupt nature, our godless culture, and Satan himself. However, the consequences of that life are destruction and eternal death. When you gave your life to Christ, you changed sides in the battle. You chose peace with God and eternal life. Your former allies became your enemies and are at war against you. But you have on your side Someone greater than all the combined forces of wickedness—the resurrected Christ. Now you are in a battle between the old life and the new one.

You are the only guardian of your mind. You choose what goes into it. There is an acronym in the computer world—GIGO. It stands for "Garbage In, Garbage Out." If you put into your computer wrong facts, it will output wrong facts. Your mind is the same way. Whatever you put into it will eventually come out. When it comes to your mind, change GIGO to stand for "God In, God Out." If you want the truth, beauty, and purity of God's Word to show up in your behavior, you need to fill your mind with the Bible.

The apostle Paul urges you, "Whatever is true, whatever is noble, whatever is right, whatever is pure, whatever is lovely, whatever is admirable—if anything is excellent or praiseworthy—think about such things" (Phil. 4:8, NIV). Take up the full armor of God to fight and be victorious (Eph. 6:10-20). Change your victim mentality to a victory mentality. You can do this by fervently praying to the One inside you, who is greater than he that is in the world (1 John 4:4). Fill your mind with God's truth.

The Bible never says that the Word of God cleanses your mind from all evil memories. It cleanses your heart. Whatever you think and whatever you have experienced has been in your brain since you were a little kid—it just takes time to bubble up into your consciousness. The more truth you take in through your reading, thinking, talking, and experiencing godly things, the more you will smother the bad with God's good. Your life will reflect godly living. Remember to always mix truth with faith (Heb. 4:12; 11:6).

Here is a godly thing to feed your mind: Learn to become good friends with the opposite sex. Many singles look at a member of the opposite sex as a potential conquest—"someone to meet my needs and rescue me out of singleness." Put your emphasis on developing a friendship by building common interests, encouraging godly behavior, and appreciating the differences. Whether or not it turns into a love relationship, it is enjoyable to develop a healthy, top-quality friendship with the opposite sex. If God does bring you together, you will have built a firm foundation for a Christ-centered marriage.

Step 5: Dissolve Negative Relationships

There are two primary kinds of people in this world: those who build you up and those who tear you down. Associate with the people who encourage you and demonstrate by their lives how to walk with God.

If you are sexually active with someone who is not your husband or wife, my appeal to you is to stop immediately. Whether you like to think about it or not, you are hurting each other emotionally, mentally, spiritually, and even physically. If you truly love the person, you will want to do what is best for him or her under the direction of the Lord Jesus Christ. The Bible is very clear as to God's will—that you abstain from sexual immorality and control your sexual urges so you will honor God (1 Thess. 4:1-8).

If you care for the person and want to maintain the relationship, the best thing is to decide to go cold turkey—no sexually stimulating actions from this moment until you are married. That is hard to do, but you have the Lord on your side. He will give you the courage to honor each other's sexual sanctity. By the way, if you do this, you will find out in less than a month whether your dating partner really loves you or just loves your body.

I hear weak rationalizations all the time from people who want to hang onto the wrong kind of people. It saddens me how blind they can be. If Christ is not the center of a relationship, then the self of the man and the self of the woman are in control. That is a formula for pain and misery.

One of the greatest gifts you can give to a future marriage partner is a mind disciplined to seek the Lord in all things. The fruit of the Spirit (Gal. 5:22-23) and a humble spirit (Phil. 2:3-4) are so attractive. They make for a satisfying, fun-filled relationship.

Step 6: Purify Your Passions

You know there is nothing wrong with passions, unless they lead you the wrong way. Your passions are the intense driving emotions that often are ungovernable. Your longings are the significant desires deep inside you that will bring you a sense of satisfaction when they are fulfilled.

Let me give you an example of how longings and passions interact. Suppose one of your strongest longings is to develop an intimate, close love relationship that will lead to a lifelong, committed marriage that is centered around the Lord. Is that your longing? Okay, now Friday night comes along and you are a little bit lonely with no one to date. Your buddies come over to your place and say, "Let's have some fun and go to the clubs. We'll get some drinks and enjoy ourselves."

It sounds like fun, but you realize that you will be tempted to get involved in activities that you know are not what God wants for you. You begin to struggle inside with the choice. You decide to go along with your friends. What's wrong with that? You don't plan to do anything bad. But soon you are involved in the activities, and the temptations to lower your standards are very enticing. Your passions quickly become inflamed with fleshly desires.

If you follow these passions, you will likely destroy the fulfillment of your deepest longings. I know someone who chose to have "fun" one night and contracted a sexually transmitted disease he will live with for the rest of his life. I know a woman who followed her passions, got drunk, and had an accident on the way home. She died in the hospital the next day.

If you long for a satisfying, Christ-centered marriage, spend time with people who exhibit the qualities that go into that kind of a relationship. Say no to any temptation that would pull you away from fulfilling that dream, even if it means spending some Friday nights reading or working out at a gym.

The Bible is filled with stories of passions that people displayed. Some led to destructive events, and some led to godly adventures. Jesus proclaimed that the greatest of all commandments is to "'love the Lord your God with all your heart and with all your soul and with all your mind.' This is the first and greatest commandment. And the second is like it: 'Love your neighbor as yourself'" (Matt. 22:34-40, NIV). If you spend your life passionately loving God and people, you are right in the jet stream of the Spirit of God. That is purified passion.

God encourages us to refine many passions. "Pursue" is one of the words used in the Scriptures to indicate this. This word is used for a hunter who has wounded an animal; he relentlessly pursues the creature through the woods and fields until he captures his prize. He is energetic, persistent, and determined. The apostle Paul tells Timothy, "Flee the evil desires of youth, and pursue righteousness, faith, love and peace, along with those who call on the Lord out of a pure heart" (2 Tim. 2:22, NIV).

Pursue the kinds of activities that will develop godly characteristics. Pursue the kind of relationships that will lead to the kind of marriage you want. Pursue the kind of career that will utilize your God-given talents and interests. Pursue moral purity.

Live for your longings, and purify your passions.

These "Steps to Freedom" are applicable for married people, not only singles. Emphasize learning lessons from the past, but don't stay there. Paul gives the goal for his life: "I do not consider myself yet to have taken hold of it. But one thing I do: Forgetting what is behind and straining toward what is ahead, I press on toward the goal to win the prize for which God has called me heavenward in Christ Jesus" (Phil. 3:13-14, NIV).

Here is a story of encouragement you can share with the people you counsel. I know a woman named Julie. Julie struggled to get her life together. She had received Christ when she was seventeen years old, but she continued to live on the wild side. During high school and college she was deeply involved in drugs, alcohol, and partying. But she felt a deep void in her heart. She tried to fill it with boyfriends and parties, but the despair grew worse. She was tired of living but afraid to die.

Allison, one of Julie's neighbors, was a Christian. She witnessed to her several times, but it did not seem to do any good. As they talked one day, Allison said, "Julie, why don't you get your life together? Come to Christ and let Him be the Lord of your life."

"Oh, I've tried many times to do that, but I always fail," she responded. "I can't do it."

"Yes, you can," Allison urged.

"No, I can't."

"Yes, you can."

"No, I can't."

"Yes, you can."

"Do you really believe I can?" Julie asked with a puzzled look.

"Yes," Allison said confidently. "Jesus Christ wants you to come to Him, accept His forgiveness, and trust Him to change your life."

Julie's faith was so weak that she didn't think God could fix her broken life. But she knew Allison loved Christ and that she believed He could change her life. So Julie stepped out on Allison's faith. "I will try it because you believe God will help me. Someday I hope to grow in my own faith."

Julie took the steps to freedom. That was more than twenty years ago. She has had many ups and downs, but Christ has directed her paths and motivated her to grow strong in Him. She is now happily married to a godly man, and they have two lively children.

How about you? Do you believe Christ can restore your purity and joy? Do you believe He will set you free from moral failure to live a life of godliness and purpose?

If you have a hard time believing it, go on my faith. You can do it with His help!

1.   George Barna, *Single Adults* (Ventura, CA: Issachar Resources, 2002), p. 69.
2.   Ibid.
3.   "Generally Unrecognized Effects of Sexually Transmitted Diseases," *Medical Aspects of Human Sexuality*, January 1985, pp. 179.

14

Pastoral Responses to Domestic Violence[1]

David Powlison, Paul David Tripp, and Edward T. Welch

—∞—

Couples who publicly sit at peace in church pews can nevertheless be at war. They attack each other, defend ground, attempt manipulative guerrilla tactics, and declare occasional truces. When war has been declared, there is sin on both sides; but when violence is involved, typically a strong male oppresses a female. With God's grace, these afflicted women will begin to look to the church for help. When they do, what are some basic biblical guidelines for your ministry to such women—and to their husbands?

PART ONE: HELPING THE VICTIM
BY EDWARD T. WELCH

> *The LORD is a refuge for the oppressed, a stronghold in times of trouble.*
>
> —PS. 9:9, NIV

Begin by Listening to the Cries of the Oppressed

As an imitator of Christ, you begin by listening to the cry of the sufferer: "You hear, O LORD, the desire of the afflicted; you encourage them, and you listen to their cry" (Ps. 10:17, NIV). Granted, this may seem self-evident; what other starting point could there be? The victim must be heard. But in a situation like this, it's especially important that your listening be something more than simple information gathering or a perfunctory first step.

Why? Because our Lord encourages the cries of the oppressed. The sheer number of psalms that call out for God's protection indicate that we serve a loving Lord who never gets tired of listening to—and acting on—the cries of the needy. God is the righteous judge who takes note of injustice and hates oppression, but He is more than a judge. He is the One who, in unfailing love, comes close to His suffering people. His listening occurs in a relationship between the weak one and the compassionate Hearer-Shepherd.

Listening is also important because many victims of violence are reluctant to speak openly. They may fear that openness will lead to retaliation by the abuser. They may feel ashamed that they contributed to the war, *although they are not responsible for the violence done to them*. They may consider their problems unworthy of a pastor's or a friend's attention, or they may feel ashamed that their husbands could dislike them to the point of violence.

Unfortunately, some are also reluctant to speak because of how quickly some pastors and friends turn to the refrain, "Forgive and forget." Some women are told that as soon as the abuser asks for forgiveness, it is the victim's responsibility to forgive—and to never bring up the subject again. Not only is the idea of immediately forgetting sin questionable teaching, but to make "forgive and forget" the primary biblical emphasis in situations like this leaves women feeling as if *they* are now the guilty ones because they can't drop the issue.

For these reasons, you cannot overestimate the importance of really listening to a suffering woman. Listen to her not as a detective who wants to quickly solve a case, but as a brother or a sister mourning with those who mourn.

Since real biblical listening is linked to action, you may find that what you hear (especially if the violence has been personal and dangerous) means taking the victim for a medical examination, calling the police, or providing a temporary safe place for her to stay. If the home is potentially unsafe, it is wise to inform the perpetrator that his wife has revealed the violence and is staying at an undisclosed safe place. It may be appropriate to encourage a battered woman to press legal charges, so that her God-ordained civil authority can be used to help bring an end to this evil (see Rom. 13:1-5).

It will also be important for you to point out that submission to God-ordained authority does not mean that she simply stay in the home and continue to suffer. David was submissive to King Saul's authority (see 1 Sam. 26:23), but he fled when Saul began to physically threaten him (see 1 Sam. 19:10-18, etc.). And the apostle Paul fled from Damascus when King Aretas was trying to capture him (2 Cor. 11:32-33). Love for one's husband will mean preventing him from continuing to do evil.

If the woman is confident that returning home will not lead to her physical harm (and you share that confidence), then your listening should include a more systematic review of the violent, controlling patterns in the marriage. It's best when this information is specific and written down. It can then be used to confront the abuser according to Matthew 18. The husband must be made to understand that the church's leadership takes domestic violence very seriously and will act to protect his wife even as they also seek to minister to him and hold him accountable.

Teach the Oppressed to Put Their Hope in God

The victim must be encouraged in her faith. As in all suffering, she may think that God is indifferent and aloof, or that the perpetrator is all-powerful. Either way, suffering is always a time for God's people to know and rely on the God who truly hears. Furthermore, if a victim is ever to move toward a repentant perpetrator in love and to open herself to love and trust, she will need the strength that comes from a robust faith. She especially needs to know the following:

God does not forget (Psalm 10; 56:4). Personal trouble does not mean that God has forsaken His people. On the contrary, God is on the move in response to our prayers for deliverance. We cannot always see this deliverance immediately, but God will without doubt deliver

His people. The story of God's work in the lives of those who suffer is not over. Remind suffering women to keep their eyes open, watching for God's strong hand at work in their lives.

Jesus knows our sufferings. Jesus experienced violence at the hands of His own people. In fact, His suffering led to His death. Seeing this can begin to lighten or outweigh a woman's grief.

For the woman who feels forsaken by God, the sufferings of Christ can be a great comfort, one that even exceeds the sympathy and comfort offered by women who have had the same experience. At a women's shelter, a victim of violence is surrounded by people who understand; but in the throne room of God, she will be embraced by One who understands perfectly, grieves deeply, and loves completely.

The cross is the timeless evidence of God's love for His people and His toughness with sin. Sin and suffering will always remain a mystery. Neither make sense in a world God created as good. Yet God's love, demonstrated to us in Jesus, also exceeds the limits of our imagination, and His justice leaves observers silenced. In a world where a woman cannot trust the one closest to her, the greatest blessing you can offer is the assurance of God's loving and watchful presence.

Teach the Oppressed to Disarm the Abuser

The victim must know how to preempt and respond to ungodly anger. Whether or not the woman returns immediately to the home, she must learn "a spirit of power, of love and of self-discipline" (2 Tim. 1:7, NIV). Too often responses to violence swing between timidity and revenge. Both reveal the abuser's ongoing control and dominance in the victim's life. Instead of these two extremes, wives need to be led in a biblical course that is humble *and* powerful.

A key text is Romans 12:21: "Do not be overcome by evil, but overcome evil with good" (NIV). In the context of Romans 12, radical freedom from an abuser consists of loving the enemy more, not less—but on *God's* terms, not the abuser's. This moves us beyond the question, "What do I need from him?" to "How do I overcome with the love of Christ?"

When in doubt, confess your sin to the abuser. Everyone knows how difficult it is to confess sin to another person. To confess it to a violent abuser seems utterly impossible (and unwise). But there might be no more powerful response to the sin of others. A woman who is strong in the Lord does not stand on her own righteousness. She stands on the righteousness of Christ and can therefore confess her own sin, beyond the reach of the abuser's condemnation. *Of course, this does not imply that her actions caused the violence or abuse.* The confession is simply for sin that God has exposed in her life. "Then you will see clearly to remove the speck from your brother's eye" (Matt. 7:5, NIV).

For some women, *confrontation might be harder than confession.* It might be easier to assume they deserved sinful treatment than to make a stand against sin. Or they might be afraid that confrontation will lead to divorce. But one way to love the abuser is to clearly portray his sin and its consequences. Minimizing or ignoring sin can be spiritually deadly for both parties. However, such confrontation should always be done in the presence of a third party.

Forgive quickly, but don't allow the abuser's request for forgiveness to be the end of the discussion. Reconciliation *begins* when the perpetrator asks for forgiveness. An outbreak of violence uncovers a larger pattern of control, arrogance, and unreasonable, unending demands. Such patterns should never be swept away with the words, "Will you forgive me?" The flesh and the devil thrive when hurts and sins are kept in the dark. For this reason, a wife can love her husband by letting him know the consequences of his sin in her life. This is not done to hurt; it is done to heal.

Speak with gentleness and love. We often overlook the power of words, but words can disarm angry people. It can be a great encouragement for a woman to know that "a gentle answer turns away wrath" (Prov. 15:1, NIV). Although the woman is *not* the cause of the violence, she nevertheless has some power to subdue it with humility, gentleness, and love.

Domestic violence is in many ways as damaging to a marriage relationship as adultery. We should never minimize its impact on the victim. But, as with all suffering, we should also never minimize the grace of God to these victims. God reserves unique glimpses of

Himself to those who have been oppressed, and He gives them power to shake off the twin enemies of timidity and rage.

PART TWO: HELPING THE ABUSER
BY PAUL TRIPP AND DAVID POWLISON

> The grace of God has appeared . . . teaching us to say "No" to ungodliness and worldly passions, and to live self-controlled, upright, and godly lives.
>
> —TITUS 2:11-12, AUTHOR'S PARAPHRASE

People who publicly sit together in church pews on Sunday morning are not thereby prevented from doing violence to each other once they get home. Ministry to the violent—like ministry to any with immediately destructive sins—demands wide-awake, bold, knowledgeable intervention, full of grace and truth. The physically abusive are criminal as well as wicked, just like sexual predators. They are also highly deceptive. The perpetrators of domestic violence need grace—effectual, real, life-changing grace. As they become willing to look at themselves in the mirror of truth and embrace the Messiah, they can and will genuinely change. Scripture says a great deal about the sins of anger and violence—and about the ways of the Redeemer of sinners. What considerations should control your efforts to help such men (and sometimes women)?

The Common Need for Grace

Violent people have much in common with other people—both with those who want to help them and with those they hurt. We are all basically alike: "No temptation has seized you except what is common to man" (1 Cor. 10:13, NIV). Interpersonal hostility comes in many forms—attitudinal, verbal, financial, physical, sexual. It comes with many degrees of intensity, from grumpiness and bickering to assault and murder. Every argument is, in principle, on a continuum with outbreaks of actual violence. So domestic violence is not different in kind from other typical sins. This fact produces both confidence and humility in those who seek to help others. If you know how to deal with your own sins of anger, you will have good things to offer others who struggle. I [David Powlison] once counseled a couple who had had a gunfight in their home! Personal repentance from irritability and a critical attitude helped me both to understand them and to proceed surefootedly. Would-be helpers of the violent are not the sinless coming to the sinful. We are finders of grace coming to those who need grace.

Similarly, you should typically expect to find two sinners embroiled with each other, not one irredeemable monster oppressing one innocent victim who needs no redemption. God will be at work in the lives of both people. So explore incidents of violence in detail. You will usually find places where both parties need God's grace to change. Perhaps one spouse draws most of the attention because he acts with his fists; but on closer inspection the other spouse may skillfully wield her tongue in ways that seek to bring hurt through use of words. Outbursts of violence are usually extreme instances in more widespread, low-grade patterns of conflict. Look for the common sins that both parties share, as well as for the unique outbreaks of sin in one party. You want to help both people become more loving, wise, and peaceable.

Those who want to help a troubled couple must handle with great care the truths in the last two paragraphs. Abusers distort these truths regularly. Are all of us tempted to anger? Abusers will turn that into an excuse: They are just "one of the boys," and violence is not that serious. Are the victims of violence also sinners, whose sins play into and play off the abusers' sins? Batterers will turn that into an excuse and an accusation: The fault really lies in their victims. If you want to help, don't allow the abuser to twist truth into gross lies.

The Fog of Evasion

You need to know what violent people are like because they easily create a fog of confusion and evasion. Sin is deceitful; that is the lesson of Jeremiah 17:9: "The heart is deceitful above all things and beyond cure. Who can understand it?" (NIV). Violent people neither know themselves, nor let others know them. They are habitual liars and hiders who often create elaborate patterns of deceit. They tend to conceal what they do; if that fails, they downplay its seriousness. If that fails, they blame-shift, portraying themselves as somehow unjustly accused, innocent, and victimized. If that fails, they tend to wallow in despair and "repentance" to make people feel sorry for them. Bear in mind the following characteristics of sin that typically characterize the violent:

Underneath the violent act is a pervasive selfishness. His pleasure, his agenda, his desires, his demands, his cravings dominate much of life. Counseling must not let the more conspicuous sin of violence distract attention from the foundational evil of a lifestyle characterized by "ungodliness and worldly passions." Often the awareness of sin is superficial: The abuser may regret his occasional violence but rarely recognizes his selfish lifestyle or the specific passions that drive him.

Expect to encounter intricate, subtle patterns of self-deception. Abusers often feel sorry for themselves: "I'm really the victim, and my anger is just a reaction." They often express the self-righteous opinion that "I'm not really like that" or "I know I shouldn't do that, but . . ." Often they demonstrate a marked ability to live with a divided heart, living two lives in two worlds. A man might hit his wife and then, an hour later, shift gears and calmly lead a Bible study.

Expect to encounter intricate patterns of winsome deceit toward others. Violent people (like sexual predators) are often gifted seducers. They win people, creating trust again in the very people they've mistreated and betrayed. They skillfully manipulate other people—the victim, the would-be helpers—into feeling guilty and responsible for what happened and for now making it better.

Expect to encounter self-deceived versions of "confession and repentance." It is almost as if they could deceive God—though, of course, they really only deceive themselves and others. They may seem to say the right Christian words or feel the right feelings, but their "repentance" is often Godless. It expresses remorse for damaging their self-image or their reputation in the eyes of neighbors. Such "repentance" actually serves the very same pride and fear of man that create the sins of secret violence. Violent people typically misuse grace or misunderstand it.

Grace becomes "cheap," and repentance becomes "jumping through hoops" to assuage the conscience and get back into the good graces of other people. It can even become a tool of sin, a quick fix—sometimes calculating—that sweeps problems under the rug. They may weep, pray, and pledge it will never happen again, without any of the fundamental changes involved in repentance and faith in Christ, that "change of mind" and "turning" that lead to a change of life.

They often intimidate and manipulate their victims. Violence is frightening. It is a tool of control. You will sometimes find it hard to get the facts even from the violated. Perhaps she wants to preserve the present moments of peace, or fears that her honesty will lead to more abuse later. She may even have been threatened: "If you tell, then . . ." The victim may be deeply ashamed that the family has these problems and may not want to make the depth of evil known. All this adds up to the fact that you may have to overcome a conspiracy of silence in the family that serves to protect the evildoer. In all these ways and more, domestic abuse is a "secret" sin. You must be prepared to drag it into the light.

THE WORD OF GRACE IN JESUS CHRIST

Violent people need Christ; we see this in Hebrews 3:12-14 (NIV):

> *See to it, brothers, that none of you has a sinful, unbelieving heart that turns away from the living God. But encourage one another daily, as long as it is called Today, so that none of you may be hardened by sin's deceitfulness. We have come to share in Christ if we hold firmly till the end the confidence we had at first.*

The drift of sin is always away from the living Christ. That is a heart problem that needs daily attention. Jesus, who died for sinners, is gracious; and grace is effective.

Aim for a fundamental restructuring of heart and lifestyle. Cosmetic adjustments that make the person's behavior more socially acceptable are not enough. You must expose the heart issues that motivate violence: cravings for power, love, control, comfort, money, respect, pleasure. About what things is this person willful? The batterer's violence is not about his wife; it is about himself and the flagrant idolatries he brought into the marriage. Violent people play god and so act like the devil rather than serve God. They must repent of the "vertical" sins that fuel the "horizontal" sins. Both the motives and behaviors of hostility must be laid bare (Jas. 3:5-12; 3:14-16; 4:1-4; 4:6; 4:11-12).

Aim to solve the minor versions of the major sins as well as the major outbreaks. A judgmental attitude, grumbling, irritability, bickering, and arguing usually precede violence and express identical themes of the heart. People who learn to repent of grumbling—and thus learn both gratitude and contentment in Christ—will rarely need to repent of assault and battery.

Give people the living Christ Himself. Jesus is abundant in loving-kindness and terrible in wrath. Violent people need to know the love of Christ. They deserve the violence of God, but He gave them the Lamb of God. Jesus loved sinners, the ungodly, the wicked, the weak, enemies of God. He died so those who live might no longer live for themselves. God freely gives grace and wisdom from above (Jas. 1:5; 1:17; 3:17; 4:6; 4:10). Effectual, life-rearranging grace is available for all who need it. Violent people need to learn to fear the Lord of wrath. He is jealous and holy (Jas. 4:5; 4:12). A person committing an act of violence lives without the fear of the Lord; he acts and reacts as if there were no God. But in fact, "everything is uncovered and laid bare before the eyes of him to whom we must give account" (Heb. 4:13, NIV). To begin to live radically in public is to live without the secrecy that violence depends on.

Bring violent people to God-centered repentance (Jas. 4:6-10). Internal changes come first. Compare their "repentance" to real repentance (Ps. 50; 51), godly versus worldly sorrow. To know the Christ of the Gospel is to rearrange heart and soul so that sin can no longer thrive. Settle for nothing less. Those who seek find. Those who believe receive the Holy Spirit. How do you know someone has truly repented? You'll know. Time always tells genuineness from pretense. You will see fundamental changes in relationships, first with God and then with others.

One area of needed repentance may be a horrible distortion of male headship in marriage, a distortion that justifies violence rather than love and self-sacrifice in imitation of Christ (Eph. 5:25-33) and that wrongly believes in male superiority and female inferiority rather than equality in value and dignity before God (Gen. 1:27).

Help repentant believers learn the practical, peaceable, loving alternatives to manipulation, blame-shifting, intimidation, and violence (Jas. 3:13; 3:17-18). People can learn to listen, to ask questions, to ask forgiveness, to take a time-out, to ask for help, to postpone decision-making, to give in tangible ways—the actions of the wisdom from above. Love can and will replace not only moments of violence, but the pervasive lifestyle of selfishness and willfulness. This is not perfection, but progress. A person who has more and more give is a person with less and less room for hating and hitting.

Many violent domestic abusers witnessed or experienced domestic violence in their own homes growing up. If this is the case, there will be learned patterns of behavior that need to be discussed and replaced with new patterns. In addition, there will be a need to come to genuine forgiveness of those who have harmed them (Matt. 6:15), committing to God's justice the wrong that was done to them (1 Pet. 2:23) and receiving comfort and healing from God for the evil they saw or suffered (2 Cor. 1:3-5).

Employ the resources of the community of Christ (Jas. 5:19-20; Heb. 3:12-14). People who are repenting of violence need more than weekly, "formal" counseling. They need radical honesty, accountability, reminders, encouragements, models, daily exposure to the light of day, prayers of intercession. I have never known an incident of domestic violence to occur during a public church service or a phone call to a person's pastor or small group leader! Help the perpetrators of such sins to come out of hiding and live in the open. Sin thrives in dark corners; righteousness thrives in the daylight. A person who has changed internally toward Christ will willingly desire the humbling structures of accountability to Christ's people in order to save him from himself.

How will you help the privately violent? Their souls must be rearranged to seek and know the Christ of the Gospel. Without that fundamental, living relationship with Christ, you can't teach enough truth, you can't shine the light of insight brightly enough, you can't put up enough fences, you can't make enough plans, you can't invite enough commitment, you can't bring in enough people, you can't be enough like Christ. But when violent sinners embrace the love of Jesus Christ, these things—doctrine, heart insight, structure, plans, commitment, community, counsel—become channels and expressions of effectual grace. That is real help and hope.

1.   This chapter is available in booklet form from Presbyterian and Reformed Publishing Company under the title *Domestic Abuse: How to Help* and is reprinted here by permission.

15

Standing Courageously in Your Home, Church, and Community

Paige Patterson

On May 16, 1569, after Dirk Willems preached the Gospel in Asperen, Holland, he went home with a family in the church. During the night there was a commotion at the front door. The master of the house came to Willems and said, "It is the sheriff. He is looking for you and is going to take your life. You must flee." So Dirk Willems fled out the back window as quickly as he could. Although he scarcely had time to put on his boots, he made his way south in order to cross the border into Germany.

The sheriff realized what had happened and had the benefit of being on horseback; so he followed rapidly after Willems. But Willems got to the frozen river first. He was able to cross on the ice to the other side safely because he was so light. The sheriff, realizing that he could not risk taking his horse onto the river (since he did not know how thick the ice was), dismounted and attempted to pursue on foot. But the chain with which the sheriff intended to bind Dirk Willems and other paraphernalia made him too heavy for the ice. When he got almost to the other side, the ice gave way, and the sheriff plunged into the water. He attempted to extricate himself, but the weight of the chain and the rest of his gear made it impossible for him to escape from the icy water.

Willems heard the crack of the ice and turned to see what was happening. The sheriff made eye contact with him and began to cry, "Help! Help! Save me! I am going to drown." Dirk Willems watched him for a moment and then slowly turned to the south to save his own life. He knew he was safe now; the sheriff would never be able to get out of the water. However, he walked only a few yards when he heard the sheriff shout, "For God's sake, help me!" Willems hesitated in his southerly march. He knew that if he came back, it would cost him his life. However, the prospect of walking away from a drowning man who might not know the Lord was more than Willems could do. He turned, came back, and put a hand on the sheriff's arm to pull him out of the water. As he lifted him, he felt the chain slip onto his own arm. A few days later he was burned at the stake for his testimony for Jesus.

Do twenty-first-century followers of Christ possess the moral and spiritual courage of a Dirk Willems? Is there sufficient conviction in the evangelical community to stand for the Bible's teachings on manhood and womanhood in the face of the almost universal disparagement from the politically correct establishment? Or has spiritual anemia so scuttled the strength of the saints as to render them spiritually impotent in an arrogant day?

You will recall that the era represented in the period from approximately 1375-1050 B.C. was described as one in which every man did what was right in his own sight. The saga about Gideon is found in Judges 6, beginning with verse 11:

> Now the Angel of the Lord came and sat under the terebinth tree which was in Ophrah, which belonged to Joash the Abiezrite, while his son Gideon threshed wheat in the winepress, in order to hide it from the Midianites. And the Angel of the Lord appeared to him, and said to him, "The LORD is with you, you mighty man of valor!" Gideon said to Him, "O my lord, if the LORD is with us, why then has all this happened to us? And where are His miracles which our fathers told us about, saying, 'Did not the LORD bring

> *us up from Egypt?' But now the LORD has forsaken us and deliv-
> ered us into the hands of the Midianites." Then the LORD turned
> to him and said, "Go in this might of yours, and you shall save
> Israel from the hand of the Midianites. Have I not sent you?" So
> he said to Him, "O my Lord, how can I save Israel? Indeed my
> clan is the weakest in Manasseh, and I am the least in my father's
> house."*
>
> —VV. 11-15, NKJV

In the rise and fall of the fortunes of Israel, as depicted in the
story of the judges, the people would sin, and God would bring a people to chastise them and bring judgment upon them. After a time
Israel would cry out to God, and God would raise up a judge to
deliver them. In this case, the Bible states that there came against
Israel not only the Midianites but also the Amalekites and the people
of the East (v. 3).

So the Midianites and the Amalekites and all the enemies of the
East swooped down upon Israel, and the hearts of the people were
filled with fear. Gideon himself was found in a winepress threshing
wheat. You might as well try to hang the wash out to dry in a hurri-
cane as to thresh wheat in a winepress. All over the ancient Near East
you will find the threshing floors upon the mountaintops where they
could take advantage of the prevailing breeze. Threshing in a winepress was certainly an exercise in futility. Why was Gideon there?
Because he was terrified!

The Bible says that suddenly the Angel of the Lord appeared to
him and said, "The LORD is with you, you mighty man of valor!"
Gideon said, "Who in the earth are you talking to?" He knew no man
of valor. Could the angel possibly mean *him*? Gideon asked, "If God
is really with us, then why do we never see any of His miracles?
What has happened to the Lord that He does not intervene on our
behalf?" Have you ever noticed that God does not answer Gideon's
question? Rather, God says in verse 14, "Go in this might of yours,
and you shall save Israel from the hand of the Midianites. Have I not
sent you?"

You know the rest of the story. Gideon said that if the one appearing before him was really from the Lord, he should wait a moment, and then Gideon brought out a meal for the Angel of the Lord. The Angel of the Lord stepped back and touched the end of it with his staff. When he did, fire came out of the rock and consumed that meal. Gideon was then transformed from a cowering renegade into a faithful patriot.

What do you need to learn from this, evangelical pastors and leaders? First, *courage has its fountainhead in a meeting with God.* You can never produce courage based on a program. You can never produce courage by preaching to people about it. *Ultimately courage arises only when you have been with the Lord.* How on earth did Daniel face the den of lions? He faced it because three times every day he went to God in prayer with the shutters open. It did not deter Daniel that everybody knew he prayed or that there was danger involved because he had been with the Lord! With each of the great heroes of the faith, you will find it is in the time spent with God that courage is born.

If you have the courage to stand up to a society that insists on political correctness and says that what evangelicals believe is no longer politically correct, you must wait on God until such time as you fear Him more profoundly than you fear the world. Occasionally somebody has said to me, "Well, Paige, you really had a lot of courage to do what you did in turning the Southern Baptist Convention back from liberalism." I sometimes say, "Well, thank you. I appreciate it." But deep down in my Texas heart I want you to know the truth about the matter. I was not overrun with courage! I just feared God more than I feared the Southern Baptist Convention. As long as I feared God more than Southern Baptists, the Southern Baptists who happened to be in charge at that time were not the ultimate issue for me. The real issue was: Where is God on this matter? The only way you will ever have the courage that you need is if you have been with God.

On May 30, 1416, Jerome of Prague was burned at the stake. He had been incarcerated in a vermin-filled dungeon for 130 days. He had endured every conceivable indignity. Prior to this experience he had even fallen into a recantation of his faith. But when the moment came for him to be taken from the dungeon to the stake, Jerome knelt and prayed as they piled wood and straw around him. In the midst of his prayer, the executioner went behind him where he thought Jerome could not see and was about to light the fire. Jerome of Prague sensed what was transpiring. He interrupted his prayer, turned around, looked right into the eyes of his executioner, and said, "Light the fire in front of me and not behind me. For if I feared it, I would not have come here."

What transformed him from one who had recanted his faith only 150 days earlier to a man who was willing to give his life at the stake? Jerome tells us himself that during 130 days of solitary confinement, when the only person to whom he really had access was God, he found the strength he needed to pay the ultimate price. Courage has its fountainhead in a meeting with God.

Second, *courage is only a virtue in the presence of fear.* Look at Judges 6, beginning in verse 25:

> *Now it came to pass the same night that the LORD said to him, "Take your father's young bull, the second bull of seven years old, and tear down the altar of Baal that your father has, and cut down the wooden image that is beside it; and build an altar to the LORD your God on top of this rock in the proper arrangement, and take the second bull and offer a burnt sacrifice with the wood of the image which you shall cut down." So Gideon took ten men from among his servants and did as the LORD had said to him. But because he feared his father's household and the men of the city too much to do it by day, he did it by night.* (NKJV)

Gideon was instructed by God to destroy the altar to Baal. But he was afraid, and that is both normal and understandable. There is a big difference between courage and swaggering bravado. I remember once as a college freshman when I didn't know this difference. I am a graduate of Hardin-Simmons University. This West Texas university is rather unique in its particular athletic emphasis because the sport *du jour* is not football or basketball or baseball—it is rodeo. When I arrived there as a freshman, the first day in the dormitory I met my roommates and suite mates. They were from ranches in West Texas and explained to me that real men participate in rodeo. I had been on a ranch many times and had ridden horses with some regularity, but I had never participated in rodeo. However, since my masculinity was subject to adjudication by a group of ruffians, what choice did I have? So I said, "Well, fine. I will do it." They said, "We will meet you down at the arena."

And so I swaggered down to the arena. A group of cowboys were sitting there on a bench, and as I approached, I noticed they were wearing wicked smiles. They said to me, "What event do you want to try?" I replied, "Well, what's hardest?" They said, "Bull riding." I said, "Bring 'em on." I did not realize that you drew lots to determine which animal you would ride. They brought the hat, and I drew. My lot fell upon a finely honed killing machine named Cream Puff. I will never forget him. When I looked at Cream Puff, I was not certain how much he weighed, but my rough estimate was somewhere around twelve thousand pounds. For horns, he had two scimitars that seemed to be aimed at me. And when I looked at him, he looked back as if to say, "Thank You, God, for this chump."

"What do you do? How do you ride him? What is the safest way to do it?" I asked my new cowboy companions. They said, "What you want to do is to stay away from the business end." I looked back at Cream Puff and could not discern any part of him that was not designed for business. Later I recognized that they were deliberately misleading me because they knew I would fix my attention upon the horns and sit as far back away from those as I could. A simple understanding of physics, in which I had not yet indulged, would have taught me that the part of the bull that moves the least is right in the sway of his back close to his shoulders. You do not want to be too far to the back or too close to the front. You want to be right there at the shoulders, but I did not know that then. So I stayed "as far away from the business end" as I could and sat as far back on the bull as I could.

Well, the gate opened, and out we came. The first buck sent me well up into the air. But I had a strong hold on that rope. So at one point it arrested me, and I began a descent. Now, the difficulty with my descent was that after I had ascended, the bull had gotten back low to the ground and recharged all of his posterior anatomy, which was now rapidly ascending to meet my descending posterior. What happened next I relive every time I go to a football game and watch a punt. I was the first astronaut; and I can tell you that after I reached the apex of my orbit and started down, Cream Puff was long since at the other end of the arena. I plunged back to the earth and hit so hard that I knew every bone in my body must have been broken. I glanced toward my friends, who were also on the ground—in peals of laughter. Then I glanced the other way, and Cream Puff had arrived at the end of the arena and turned around and found me. Broken bones or not, a remarkable motivation sweeps over you in a moment like that. Well, some people would say that my effort was real courage. Most would say it was sheer idiocy! It was, in point of fact, swaggering bravado.

Compare such foolishness to the courage exhibited by Winston Churchill, writing in *The Gathering Storm* in 1948 when he said to the British people:

> Still if you will not fight for the right when you can easily win without bloodshed; if you will not fight when your victory will be sure and not too costly, you may come to the moment when you will have to fight with all the odds against you and only a precarious chance of survival. There may even be a worse case. You may have to fight when there is no hope of victory because it is better to perish than to live as slaves.

Now there is a man who knew fear. But in the midst of his fear he also understood that truth, justice, and freedom were causes for which one must sometimes fight. Evangelicals are right in having discerned the biblical message about manhood and womanhood for the family today. The question is, in your fear of a frowning society, even in your mortification at being labeled Neanderthal and old-fashioned and narrow, will you meet with God and determine to walk tall and share your faith with a desperately confused world?

Finally, *the display of one man's courage may produce revival in others.* Read what happened to Gideon:

> *And when the men of the city arose early in the morning, there was the altar of Baal, torn down; and the wooden image that was beside it was cut down, and the second bull was being offered on the altar which had been built. So they said to one another, "Who has done this thing?" And when they had inquired and asked, they said, "Gideon the son of Joash has done this thing." Then the men of the city said to Joash, "Bring out your son, that he may die, because he has torn down the altar of Baal, and because he has cut down the wooden image that was beside it." But Joash said to all who stood against him, "Would you plead for Baal? Would you save him? Let the one who would plead for him be put to death by morning! If he is a god, let him plead for himself, because his altar has been torn down!"*
>
> —JUDG. 6:28-31, NKJV

Joash had been afraid of his fellow Israelites. Only the night before he had succumbed to the hardness of his own heart and had allowed that image of Baal to remain in his backyard. But thanks to the courage of his son, he suddenly was revived. He reasoned, "If my son can stand for God, then I can stand for God's truth also." Therefore he stood before his detractors knowing that to defy a mob intent on vengeance might indeed cost him his own life. "Let Baal contend for Baal," shouted this encouraged saint.

The great news is that if evangelicals were to stand up for what is true, in love and compassion, but without compromise, and say, "Look, we cannot rewrite holy Scripture. God has spoken, and whatever God says is what we are going to say. Whatever the consequences, we will stand with confidence," revival would follow. Like Shadrach, Meshach, and Abed-Nego, you must say:

> *"O Nebuchadnezzar, we have no need to answer you in this matter. If that is the case, our God whom we serve is able to deliver us from the burning fiery furnace, and He will deliver us from your hand, O king. But if not, let it be known to you, O king,*

that we do not serve your gods, nor will we worship the gold image
which you have set up."

—DAN. 3:16B-18, NKJV

If you would stand with courage for the truths of God's Word, you would be amazed to see the revival that would take place across this land and beyond.

The other day I was asked to visit a church on the border of North Carolina and Virginia. I was told that I would be meeting with some hostility because the church was dealing with issues of family and biblical manhood and womanhood because one of the associate pastors in the church was female. The church had heard the egalitarian position. They were now interested in hearing the complementarian side, but not everybody in the church was interested. I was told that those opposed would be there with war paint and that I would be the target. I replied, "Sounds like fun to me."

Well, it was an interesting evening. I took along one of my students. On the way home he said to me, "Dr. Patterson, I never knew old people could be so mean." I said, "Son, if they are mean when they are younger and the Lord does not get ahold of them, they only get meaner as time goes on." But overall the results were good, and God gave us favor. The meeting began, and three hours later I was still answering questions. As the meeting progressed, a remarkable transition occurred. A whole group of those dear, sweet people who had begun the meeting with a certain reticence had moved to tacit approval and even ended up coming to the microphone and defending the complementarian position. I just stood there and watched it all take place. I was reminded once again that when people whose hearts have been redeemed hear the Word of the Lord, they are inexorably drawn to it, and they will stand for the truth.

You, too, must take heart and stand for the truth. You might start out alone, but before long look around, you will have a troop following behind. Let it be known throughout this land that God has spoken and that we are simply attempting to be obedient. The watching world has abandoned the nobility of the home and the sanctity of motherhood and grandmotherhood. We must never forget to challenge women to choose to go God's way and so to know the richest blessings of God.

In Fort Worth, Texas, there stands one of the great seminaries of all time—Southwestern Baptist Theological Seminary. The founder of that seminary was Benjamin Harvey Carroll. No more remarkable figure ever towered over the Texas plains than B. H. Carroll. In his senior years his 6'6" frame sported a long white beard that came down below his belt. But he had not always been a fervent believer. As a matter of fact, B. H. Carroll (a strong man, accurate with a pistol or any other firearm) had been a Texas Ranger. B. H. Carroll was at that time a tough, hard-drinking, hard-riding atheist. He did not believe in God at all. He had been shot, and for the rest of his life he would limp, but even this had no effect on his unbelief. As a young man in the prime of his life, he had really only one thing going for him.

At home he had a diminutive mother who did not look large enough to have given birth to a man like Benjamin Harvey, but she was larger than you knew. For though her frame was small, not a day would go by without her spending hours in prayer for her wayward son. "God, save him. God, protect him long enough for him to come to You." She never had a career of her own. She would have been despised by most of today's society because she spent her primary energies at home, cooking meals and mending and washing the clothes and keeping the house in order. She would have been denigrated as a person of very little worth.

But she knew God, and she knew how to pray. She knew that her first assignment was somehow to get Benjamin Harvey to Christ. An evangelist came to have a camp meeting. She began to ask Benjamin if he would go. He loved his mother, although he had no sympathy with her faith. Finally, to humor her, he said, "All right, Mother, I will go to the camp meeting." He went one night, and he was unaffected. He went back the next night because he saw how happy it made his mother. He was unmoved by all that happened. In fact, he laughed at the preacher, who was a man of little erudition. But because it made his mother so happy and he did not have anything else to do, he went back the third night. After the service was over and most folks had gone, he stayed around.

What happened? In what is possibly the most remarkable sermon ever preached west of the Mississippi River, entitled "My Infidelity and What Became of It," Benjamin Harvey Carroll wrote about his own experience in the fall of 1865 in these words.

> The meeting closed without any change of heart upon my part. The last sermon had been preached, the benediction pronounced, and the congregation was dispersing. A few ladies only remained seated near the pulpit and they engaged in singing. Feeling that the experiment was ended and that the solution was not found, I remained to hear them sing. As their last song they sang "O land of rest for thee I sigh, when will the moment come when I shall lay my armor by and dwell in peace at home." The singing made a wonderful impression upon me. Its tones were soft as the rustling of angels' wings. Suddenly there flashed upon my mind like a light from heaven the Scripture that said, "Come unto me all you that labor and are heavy-laden and I will give you rest." I did not see Jesus with my eye, but I seemed to see Him standing before me looking reproachfully and tenderly and pleadingly, seeming to rebuke me for having gone to all other sources for rest but the right one and now inviting me to go to Him.
>
> In a moment I went, once and forever casting myself unreservedly and for all time at Christ's feet and in a moment the rest came, undescribable and unspeakable, and has always remained with me from that day until now. I gave no public expression of the change that had passed over me, but I spent the night in the enjoyment of it wondering if it would be with me when the morning came.
>
> When the morning came, it was still with me brighter than the sunlight, sweeter than the songs of birds. And now for the first time I understood the Scripture which I had so often heard my mother repeat, "You shall go out with joy and be led forth with peace and the mountains and the hills shall break forth before you into singing and all the trees of the field shall clap their hands." When I reached home I said nothing about the

experience through which I had passed, hiding the righteousness of God in my own heart.

But it could not be hidden. As I was walking across the floor on my crutches, an orphan boy whom my mother had reared noticed and called attention to the fact that I was whistling and crying at the same time. I knew my mother heard him. So to avoid observation I went at once to my room and lay down on my bed and covered my face with my hands, but I heard her coming. She pulled my hands away from my face and gazed long and steadfastly upon me without a word. Then a light came over her face that made it seem to me as the shining on the face of Stephen. And there with trembling lips she said, "My son, you have found the Lord." Her happiness was indescribable. I don't think she slept that night. She seemed to fear that with sleep she might dream and wake to find the glorious fact was but a vision in the night.

I spent the night at her bedside reading Bunyan's *Pilgrim's Progress*. I read it all night and when we came with the pilgrims to Beulah Land from which Doubting Castle could be seen no more forever and when that sight of the heavenly city was within the sound of the heavenly music, my soul was filled with the rapture and such an ecstasy of joy that I have never ever before experienced. Then I knew as well as I know now that I would preach. It was to be my life work. I would have no other work.

I am happy that Benjamin Harvey Carroll's mother was not pursuing her own career. I am grateful to God that she was not caught up in lesser assignments but understood that she could shake a world through Benjamin Harvey Carroll. I declare to you without fear of anyone proving otherwise that there are five thousand Baptist churches in Texas this very night because, as far as any human agency goes, Benjamin Harvey Carroll, that converted Texas Ranger, breathed into the life of Texas Baptists the fire of truth and the courage of conviction. Every student who has ever studied at Southwestern Seminary looks back to that tall figure and says, "He is the founder of my school." Then look behind him and you will find a little woman praying, "Oh, God, save my son" because she understood that her most important assignment was to be wife and mother and to pray her children into the kingdom of God. And through that son she has shaken nations for the cause of Christ.

The time has come for wimpy, conservative, Bible-believing, evangelical Christians to get over their cowardice and to parley with God until they decide to be courageous enough to tell the truth to a watching world, then to get ready because God will give them an army to follow after. God bless us all.

SCRIPTURE INDEX

GENERAL INDEX